ONE WEEK LOAN

THE REVERIES

OF THE SOLITARY WALKER

ISBN 0-87220-162-7 (paper)
ISBN 0-87220-163-5 (cloth)
Originally published in 1979 by New York University Press
Original ISBN 0-8147-1019-0 (cloth)
Original Library of Congress Catalog Card Number 78-24806

The publication of this work has been aided in part by a grant
from the University of Maryland.

Jean-Jacques Rousseau

THE REVERIES

OF THE

SOLITARY WALKER

Translated, with Preface, Notes,
and an Interpretative Essay
by
Charles E. Butterworth

HACKETT PUBLISHING COMPANY
Indianapolis/Cambridge

To BILLY, who prized valor most
March 30, 1946—January 11, 1967

99   3 4 5 6 7 8 9 10

Jean-Jacques Rousseau: 1712–1778

The Reveries of the Solitary Walker was first published posthumously in 1782 from an unfinished manuscript.

Copyright © 1992 by Hackett Publishing Company, Inc.

Printed in the United States of America

Cover design by Listenberger Design & Associates

For further information, please address

Hackett Publishing Company, Inc.
P.O. Box 44937
Indianapolis, Indiana 46244-0937

Library of Congress Cataloging-in-Publication Data

Rousseau, Jean-Jacques, 1712–1778.
    [Rêveries du promeneur solitaire. English]
    The reveries of the solitary walker/Jean-Jacques Rousseau; translated with preface, notes, and an interpretative essay by Charles E. Butterworth.
        p.   cm.
    Includes bibliographical references and index.
    ISBN 0-87220-163-5.   ISBN 0-87220-162-7 (pbk.)
    I. Butterworth, Charles E.   II. Title.
PQ2040.R5E5   1992
848'.509—dc20   92-28212
                                            CIP

The paper used in this publication meets the minimum requirements of American National Standard for Information Sciences—Permanence of Paper for Printed Library Materials, ANSI Z39.48-1984.

CONTENTS

PREFACE

Shortly after Jean-Jacques Rousseau died on July 2, 1778, two notebooks filled with his handwriting were found among his personal effects. Unlike most of the other notebooks and papers he left behind, these had been partially edited. What is more, the material in these two notebooks had been organized in the form of a book of essays and assigned a title by Rousseau: *The Reveries of the Solitary Walker*. This work, consisting of nine finished essays or "Walks" and a long paragraph introducing a Tenth Walk, is Rousseau's last: according to the chronology outlined in the Second Walk, it was only shortly before October 1776 that he decided to compose these essays; the Tenth Walk opens with the declaration that it is being written on Palm Sunday in 1778, that is, a few weeks before his death.

However, the significance of the *Reveries* derives from the intrinsic quality of the essays, not from its status as Rousseau's last work. It is important to identify the *Reveries* as his last work only to place the uniqueness of his arguments into proper perspective and to alert the reader to the difficulties connected with presenting an accurate version of the text.

Because *The Reveries of the Solitary Walker* seems at first to be so similar to all of Rousseau's other works, the suggestion that it is unique may meet with disbelief. Yet, despite a superficial similarity with his other writings, it is ultimately quite different from them. Although it is autobiographical, as are many of his other writings, it is not apologetic. In the First Walk, for example, Rousseau characterizes these essays as a sort of sequel to the *Confessions* and then speaks about himself throughout the rest of the book with the candor that is so characteristic of the *Confessions* and the *Dialogues*, but he never seeks to plead his uniqueness or to establish his ultimate worth as he did in those other works. The portrait he sketches of himself in the *Reveries* allows us to understand Rousseau the thinker far more thoroughly than do the self-portraits of the *Confessions* and *Dialogues*. Similarly, while the *Reveries* is written in rich and gentle prose, while it is captivating and positively lyrical at times, it is never as sentimental or as passionate as his other works. Finally, even though questions about politics, human nature, God, ultimate happiness, and the nobility of lying are raised in this work as in his other writings, they are answered differently here. For example, in the course of the inquiry into the grounds for his religious beliefs in the Third Walk, a very obscure reference is made to the relationship between his own beliefs and those set forth in the *Émile* as the "Profession of Faith of the Savoyard Vicar." Despite the tendency students of Rousseau have to cite this reference as proof that the Savoyard vicar's profession of faith is the same as Rousseau's, the reference is really not all that conclusive. Apart from the problem that the argument of the larger context in which the "Profession of Faith of the Savoyard Vicar" occurs—that is, the *Émile*—runs completely counter to the vicar's statement, there is the additional problem that in the *Reveries* Rousseau never states what his own beliefs are. Moreover, in the immediately preceding Walk, Rousseau makes a declaration about the nature of God which cannot be reconciled with the vicar's statements about God's nature. It seems, then, that the real point of the reference is to draw a sharper distinction between his own position and the one he set forth for others in his earlier writings.

Examples such as these could be multiplied, and they will be considered extensively in the Interpretative Essay. The reason for alluding to them here is to buttress the claim for the uniqueness of the *Reveries* and to suggest that this uniqueness is related to the status of the *Reveries* as Rousseau's last work. Because the discussions in this work frequently return to problems serious critics had already observed in his thinking and present his views in a new light, it is hard to escape the impression that Rousseau intended this work as a final statement of his thought. By presenting *The Reveries of the Solitary Walker* as something he wrote to read over to himself in his old age, Rousseau endowed it with a special veneer of spontaneity and frankness indicative of a final accounting. Yet, by describing these essays as the pastime of a lonely old man and by exposing his thought more through allusions and elliptical suggestions than through direct arguments, he was able to remain as discreet as ever in his last statement.

The other consideration calling for the recognition of the *Reveries* as Rousseau's last work is that it is unfinished and consequently never benefited from his meticulous attention to the details of publishing. *The Reveries of the Solitary Walker* was first published in 1782 through the joint efforts of three of Rousseau's friends: the Marquis de Girardin, Paul Moultou, and Pierre-Alexandre Du Peyrou. Unfortunately, that edition is marred by careless errors as well as by numerous false readings. Many of the latter can be traced to incorrect readings of the manuscript, to attempts to improve Rousseau's style, and to a clearly erroneous understanding of the sense of certain passages.

In spite of these defects, the text of the 1782 edition was reprinted a number of times in France and in Switzerland from the last years of the eighteenth century through the first half of the twentieth. Until 1948, when two critical editions based on new examinations of Rousseau's manuscript appeared, it was the only text available. That year, John S. Spink's edition was published by Didier in Paris, while Marcel Raymond's was published by Droz in Geneva. Apparently neither scholar was aware of the work pursued by the other. With two notable exceptions, Raymond's edition subsequently served as the basis for more than a dozen other publications of the *Reveries:* Henri Roddier went back to the manuscript to establish the text of his edition, which was published by Garnier in 1960; and Sylvestre de Sacy's attempt to establish a critical edition by utilizing the different

editions of Spink, Raymond, and Roddier, as well as Raymond's
second edition of the text for the Pléiade series in 1959, was
published by Gallimard in the Livre de Poche series in 1965. All
of this publishing activity notwithstanding, there is to date no
edition of the *Reveries* which is completely faithful to Rousseau's
manuscript.

Although the *Reveries* has been translated into English, as well
as into Danish, Swedish, Romanian, Italian, and even into Korean,
Chinese, and Turkish, none of these translations has called forth a
more accurate text. The English translation of the *Reveries*, based
on the 1782 edition, was published in New York by Brentano's
about fifty years ago. In addition to carrying over into English the
errors contained in the 1782 edition, this translation is flawed by
the translator's persistent efforts to rewrite Rousseau's prose: the
order of words used in apposition is inverted; some of the words
used in an enumeration are dropped; and Rousseau's paragraphs
are restructured. Moreover, any attempt to acquire a clear com-
prehension of Rousseau's argument is hampered by the translator's inconsistent handling of key terms, strange rendering of
idiomatic expressions, and confusing annotations.

The present translation was undertaken to present in English a
text that would be faithful to the letter and spirit of Rousseau's
manuscript, a text that would render the meaning of the *Reveries*
accurately without sacrificing too much of the beauty of Rousseau's prose. To arrive at the best possible version of Rousseau's
original text, the unique manuscript of the *Reveries* was carefully
examined and compared with the existing critical editions. In
Appendix A, the manuscript has been described quite extensively,
and some of the notes to the translation identify manuscript
readings missed in the existing editions.

As is only proper for a faithful rendering of Rousseau's thought,
his paragraphing has been scrupulously respected throughout the
text. However, while no question arose about how to handle
Rousseau's paragraphs, there were many questions about how to
handle his punctuation within paragraphs. In addition to differences between French and English conventions for punctuation,
there are differences between Rousseau's own style of punctua-

tion and that normally adhered to in French. The punctuation of the manuscript has nevertheless been followed in the translation as much as good sense would allow. When it appeared that Rousseau's style and thought could be better communicated by breaking his long sentences into shorter ones or by transforming his dependent clauses into independent clauses, that was done.

With respect to the actual task of translating, the goal has been to transmit the sense of Rousseau's prose and of his exceptional style. Still, that goal is more easily stated than attained. In the inevitable conflicts between accuracy and felicity of expression, the former always prevailed. Every effort has been made, for example, to translate key words in a consistent manner even when such lexical fidelity resulted in less than lyrical English.

Notes have been added to help the reader understand the text. Some explain the way certain words have been translated or the way the text has been altered to approximate better English usage. Others identify places, plants, persons, and literary allusions. In addition, occasional references in the text to events in Rousseau's life have been amplified in the notes by indicating how the event was explained in the *Confessions*. Moreover, Appendix B contains a translation of the way Rousseau discussed his stay on St. Peter's Island in the *Confessions*.

Allusions in the *Reveries* to events and periods of time in Rousseau's life are so numerous that a brief account of his life might be helpful. Generally speaking, his activities and accomplishments can be divided into seven different epochs. Such a division does not accord with Rousseau's division of the *Confessions* into twelve books, because his account of his life in the *Confessions* was intended as an explanation of how his sentiments developed rather than as a sequential enumeration of the various events in that full and tumultuous life, and because he finished writing the *Confessions* almost a decade before his death.

Rousseau's childhood and early adolescence in Geneva correspond to the first epoch (1712–28), while the period of his growth into manhood and close relationship with Mme de Warens (1728–

42) corresponds to the second. The early years of his Parisian
sojourn (1742–49) appear to belong to a third epoch of his life,
and the period of his growing discontent with Parisian society
along with the period of his moral reform (1750–56) to a fourth.
Those years of solitary existence on the outskirts of Paris until the
events following the publication of the *Émile* forced him to flee
from France (1756–62) seem to form another clear division in his
life. Book XII of the *Confessions* covers the troubled years in
Switzerland and ends in 1765 with Rousseau being forced to leave
St. Peter's Island; those years, together with the time of his
sojourn in England and his wanderings in France until his return
to Paris in 1770, seem to constitute a sixth epoch. The final
division covers the period of his life from his return to Paris until
he began to write the *Reveries*.

Geneva was the center of Rousseau's life from the time of his
birth on June 28, 1712, to his precipitate departure shortly before
his sixteenth birthday. The death of his mother within a few days
of his birth and his father's forced exit from Geneva under unfavorable conditions about ten years later deprived Rousseau of a
normal family life. For about two years after his father left Geneva, Rousseau and a cousin of his age were sent as boarding pupils
to the Lambercier family just outside Geneva (see Third Walk).
When the two boys were brought back to Geneva, Rousseau was
apprenticed to the city clerk. The unsatisfactory character of this
arrangement quickly became apparent to all parties, and shortly
before Rousseau's thirteenth birthday he was apprenticed to an
engraver. According to the poignant accounts of the *Confessions,*
the next three years were among the unhappiest of his life. Several months of dejection and his life in Geneva ended in 1728 with
the closing of the city gates as he was returning from a walk: since
he had been locked out of the city on previous occasions and had
been threatened with severe punishment by his master should he
be locked out again, Rousseau decided to strike out on his own.

During the next fourteen years, Rousseau grew to manhood and
began the difficult task of self-instruction. Ribald episodes and
youthful adventures filled the first seven years, while the latter
seven were given over to general withdrawal, quiet meditation,

and extensive study. But whatever his activities or projects during these years, they centered around Mme de Warens, the lady to whom he had been directed immediately after leaving Geneva (see Tenth Walk). His attachment to her grew during this period from something resembling filial affection to deeper feelings of tenderness and love. According to Rousseau, it was for her sake that he went to Turin and converted to the Roman Catholic faith. And after having been chased from the household staff of one noble family in Turin (see Fourth Walk) only to be taken into the household of another noble Turinese family and assured of a promising career as its diplomatic emissary, the desire to see Mme de Warens prompted him to abandon present security and future glory and to return to her in Annecy. A peaceful year with Mme de Warens was then followed by about a year and a half of carefree wanderings and extravagant escapades. Rousseau's foot voyages took him to Lyon, and even to Paris, while his escapades included a brief stint as interpreter to a fake archimandrite (who claimed to have been sent to Switzerland for the purpose of raising money to rebuild the Holy Sepulcher) and a painfully funny attempt to pass himself off in Lausanne as a music teacher from Paris. Growing more serious as the age of twenty approached, Rousseau returned to Mme de Warens, who was then living in Chambéry. For the next few years he worked assiduously at learning music and gradually broadened his interests to include the study of history, literature, philosophy, mathematics, and natural science. On at least two occasions, Rousseau referred to the five or six years from about 1735 until 1740, spent mainly in Chambéry and at a country house in the nearby valley of Les Charmettes, as among the happiest of his life. They were years of relative calm and of deep study, little else. But the joy of this period was doomed to be short-lived. Two brief periods of separation persuaded Rousseau that the only way for him to maintain his deep affection for Mme de Warens was to live far away from her.

That conclusion was followed by the decision to go to Paris, where for about seven years he sought in vain to make a place for himself. His first efforts at gaining recognition centered around the novel method he had devised for writing musical scores with numbers. Although the project was sound, Rousseau was unable to persuade the Academy of Sciences or the general public that it should be adopted and thus turned his attention to other activities. Among these was a post as secretary to the French ambassador to Venice, which he was forced to resign after serving less than a year because of violent arguments with the ambassador. When he returned to Paris following this diplomatic interlude, he felt more confident about his talent for musical composition and devoted all his efforts to finishing an opera he had been working on for some time. Completed in 1745, *The Gallant Muses* was considered for the Paris Opera, but Rousseau anticipated its rejection and withdrew it to make revisions. Whatever the problems in this work, his knowledge of music was sufficiently recognized that he was invited to write the articles on music for the *Encyclopédie* by its coeditor, Diderot, with whom he had formed a cordial friendship. At about this time he entered into the lasting relationship with Thérèse Levasseur which was formalized by marriage almost twenty-five years later. For the most part, however, this was a period of frustration and thwarted ambition. It ended with the sudden inspiration that prompted the fervent prose and unconventional pronouncements of the *Discourse on the Sciences and the Arts*, otherwise known as the *First Discourse*.

Awarded a prize in 1750 and published the following year, the *First Discourse* won Rousseau immediate recognition. Either because of his engaging style or because he had dared to criticize the arts and sciences in the citadel of the Enlightenment, Rousseau was so besieged by refutations that it took him two years to respond to the best of them. All the while he continued to compose music, and his efforts resulted in *The Village Soothsayer*. Performed before the king at Fontainebleau in October 1752 and then at the Paris Opera about six months later, it was received with overwhelming acclaim. The famous *Preface* to his play *Narcissus*, in which he attempted to show that his criticism of the arts was consistent with his own participation in the arts, was also published at this time. It was followed by the *Letter about French Music*, a pamphlet which praised Italian over French music and caused a great stir in Paris. Thus, within three years, Rousseau passed from relative obscurity to the summit of fame and controversy. During all this activity, his reflections on human nature and politics were being shaped into the argument of the *Discourse on the Origin and Foundations of Inequality among Men,* or *Second Discourse.* The program of personal reform he had adopted shortly after the publication of the *First Discourse* and the new insights he acquired while writing the *Second Discourse* now seemed to demand his withdrawal from Parisian society. During a visit to Geneva, he decided to return to the Protestant faith and take up his Genevan citizenship again. That visit to Geneva had been so pleasant and his discontent with the affectations of Parisian society was so intense that he almost decided to move to Geneva. However, the unfavorable reception of his *Second Discourse* in Geneva made him reconsider, and he joyfully moved into the little house in the forest of Montmorency renovated for him during his absence by his good friend Mme d'Épinay.

Rousseau's decision to move to this house, the Hermitage, and thereby to remove himself from Parisian society was generally disapproved by his friends. They refused to believe that anyone would voluntarily choose such solitude and accused him of seeking only to enhance his reputation. But Rousseau was convinced that this was precisely the change he needed, and in later years he referred to the date on which he moved to the Hermitage as the period in his life when he truly began to live. Although lonely, these six years of voluntary withdrawal were productive. The long *Letter to M. Voltaire* (1756) criticizing his two poems about natural law and about the earthquake in Lisbon, the brilliant *Letter to M. d'Alembert about the Theater* (1758), the *Julie* or *New Héloïse* (1760), the *Social Contract* (1762), and the *Émile* (1762) were finished during this time. In addition, Rousseau made an extract of the works of the Abbé de St. Pierre and composed two long essays about the abbé's political ideas (1756) and also wrote his first autobiography in the form of *Four Letters to M. le Président de Malesherbes.* The *Letter to M. d'Alembert* and the *New Héloïse* had tremendous success and sealed his reputation as a writer. However, while Rousseau was so busily engaged in his writing, his friends were occupied with gossip and rumors about him. He was accused of being neglectful and generally haughty, of hypocrisy, and deceit. One series of misunderstandings led to a rupture with Mme d'Épinay and Rousseau's move from the Hermitage to a cottage belonging to the Prince de Condé at Mont-Louis near Montmorency. Another series of misunderstandings led to a break with his old friend Diderot, which he announced by means of a clever footnote in the *Letter to M. d'Alembert* and for which he was generally blamed. Still, all of this was minor compared with the storm that followed the publication of the *Émile*, the book Rousseau considered to be his best and most useful work. Alerted during the night of June 8–9, 1762, that the Parliament of Paris was about to condemn the *Émile* and issue a warrant of arrest against him, he hurriedly put his affairs in order and had barely taken flight toward Switzerland when the bailiffs of the court arrived to arrest him.

The journey to Switzerland was uneventful. Rousseau was allowed to cross the border without any difficulties, and he went to the home of an old friend in Yverdon. But the easy crossing of the border was no harbinger of peaceful days in Switzerland. Two days after his departure from Montmorency, the *Émile* was burned in Paris; a week afterward, both the *Émile* and the *Social Contract* were burned in Geneva. On July 1, the government of Bern decreed that Rousseau must leave its territory. Fortunately he was able to find a place of refuge in Môtiers. In November, Rousseau finished his *Letter to Christophe de Beaumont*, a spirited and eloquent defense of the *Émile* against the condemnation the archbishop of Paris had issued against that work. He then tried to defend Genevan republicanism and its Protestant basis, as well as himself, by replying to the *Lettres Écrites de la Campagne (Letters Written from the Countryside)* with his own *Letters Written from the Mountain*. Its appearance toward the end of 1764 occasioned new outbursts. The book was burned in the Hague as well as in Paris; the pastor of Môtiers attacked Rousseau from the pulpit, thereby inciting the populace against him; and in September 1765 Rousseau's house was stoned during the middle of the night. Forced to seek refuge elsewhere, he went to St. Peter's Island in the middle of Lake Bienne (see Fifth Walk). But the island was under the jurisdiction of the government of Bern, and after a stay of about five weeks he was ordered to leave the island immediately. Rousseau first considered going to Berlin, then changed his mind and accepted David Hume's invitation to go to England. Arriving in London early in 1766, he settled in the town of Wootton, which is not far from Birmingham. His stay in England was quite short and was punctuated by a bitter quarrel with Hume and an inexplicably angry exchange of letters with his host in Wootton, Richard Davenport. After about a year and a half in England, Rousseau suddenly returned to France. The following years were frenetic. After staying at Trye near Gisors in Normandy for a year, Rousseau moved to Grenoble, on to Bourgoin midway between Lyon and Grenoble, and finally settled in the village of Monquin just outside Bourgoin. During these years of frenzy, Rousseau feared being recognized by the public and tried to disguise himself or to hide behind a false name. Thérèse had accompanied him through all these troubled times since the flight from Montmorency. In 1768, they were married in Bourgoin. Somehow, despite the upset and turmoil, Rousseau was able to continue to write; the *Confessions,* begun in 1764 or 1765, was finished toward the end of 1769 or 1770. He returned to Paris in June 1770.

Rousseau's real difficulties began with the period of voluntary withdrawal in the forest of Montmorency. Acclaimed as a great writer on the one hand, he was denounced as a scoundrel and unsociable wretch on the other. He thought honesty and virtue demanded that he act according to his principles and shun the false conventions he scorned, but his friends and acquaintances accused him of hypocrisy and wickedness. Then, the book he considered to be his best, and certainly to be no different in substance from any of his other writings, was proclaimed to be destructive of the Christian religion and of all government everywhere. That judgment forced Rousseau to flee France and to be for a number of years at the mercy of the republican governments he had tried to defend. These governments banished him from one refuge after another. No sooner would he settle down than he would be forced to flee. These were trying experiences, and Rousseau did not always respond well to them. Sometimes he overreacted; at other times he seemed completely oblivious to the danger signals. But it was the apparent injustice of these tribulations that especially angered him: here he was, accused of precisely those things of which he considered himself most innocent and others most guilty; here he was, not only accused but actually punished, while the truly guilty went untouched. He could not attribute such injustice to pure coincidence and thus came to the conclusion that he was the victim of a plot, that some of his friends and many of his enemies had decided to bring him to an ignominious end. Two things might have moved them to such nefarious deeds: simple jealousy or recognition that his passionate defense of unsophisticated virtue and republicanism undermined their own attempts to favor enlightened despotism. These conjectures, whose validity has recently been corroborated by scholars, haunted him for some time and prompted most of his strange actions during the difficult years of exile.

They also dominated his mind in the years following his return to Paris. He spent a number of months writing the *Considerations about the Government of Poland* and then turned to the sequel to the *Confessions*—the *Dialogues.* Started in 1772, this long work of self-explanation and justification was not finished until 1776. The *Dialogues* is a painful work to read, and Rousseau admitted that it had been quite painful for him to write. Occasional botanical forays and some music copying were the only activities that lightened this gloomy task. Otherwise Rousseau kept to himself and suspiciously regarded every visitor as a spy for the leaders of the plot, as someone trying to keep him from finishing this important work. Somehow with the termination of the *Dialogues,* the spell was broken. For a number of reasons, he was seized by a new spirit when he decided to begin the *Reveries.* Since the First and Second Walks are intended as an explanation of that new spirit, it seems fitting to turn to the *Reveries* at this point.

The joys of finishing a book are many, but chief among them is that of acknowledging the assistance rendered by different people and institutions. I am very grateful for the discerning suggestions Ann Charney and Mary Pollingue made about the translation; their criticism and advice were invaluable. I owe much to the judicious remarks Philip Lyons made about the Interpretative Essay, to Alan Seltzer's very thorough critique of the entire manuscript, and to Terence Marshall's criticisms, as well as to the various comments and probing questions put forth by the friends who read and discussed this work with me during the winter of 1976. And I greatly appreciate the effort expended by Jean Sproul, Martà Tvardek, and Lillian Foster in typing the various versions of the work. To enumerate the many ways in which my wife, Deborah, contributed to this project would be an almost endless undertaking; suffice to say that she deserves to share the joys of seeing this finally come to an end.

I would also like to acknowledge the generous assistance of the Department of Government and Politics as well as of the Graduate School of the University of Maryland and of the Earhart Foundation for the financial aid which enabled me to pursue this project and facilitated the publication of this volume.

While none of these persons or institutions can be held responsible for any shortcomings in the work, I hope that none will have reason to regret having helped bring it to the light of day.

FIRST WALK

I am now alone on earth, no longer having any brother, neighbor, friend, or society other than myself. The most sociable and the most loving of humans has been proscribed from society by a unanimous agreement. In the refinements of their hatred, they have sought the torment which would be cruelest to my sensitive soul and have violently broken all the ties which attached me to them. I would have loved men in spite of themselves. Only by ceasing to be humane, have they been able to slip away from my affection. They are now strangers, unknowns, in short, nonentities to me—because that is what they wanted. But I, detached from them and from everything, what am I? That is what remains for me to seek. Unfortunately, that inquiry must be preceded by a glance at my position. This is an idea I must necessarily follow out in order to get from them to me.

Although I have been in this curious position for fifteen years and more,[1] it still seems like a dream to me. I still imagine that I am being tormented by indigestion, that I am sleeping badly, and that I am going to wake up fully relieved of my pain and find myself once again with my friends. No doubt about it, I must have unwittingly made a jump from wakefulness to sleep or rather from life to death. Dragged, I know not how, out of the order of things, I have seen myself cast into an incomprehensible chaos

1

where I distinguish nothing at all; and the more I think about my present situation the less I can understand where I am.

And how could I have foreseen the destiny which awaited me? How can I conceive of it even today when I am given up to it? Could I in my good sense have supposed that one day I, the same man that I was, the same that I still am, would—without the slightest doubt—pass for and be taken as a monster, a poisoner, an assassin; that I would become the horror of the human race, the plaything of the rabble; that the only greeting passersby would give me would be to spit on me; that an entire generation would, by a unanimous agreement, find delight in burying me alive? When this strange revolution occurred, taken unprepared, I was at first overwhelmed by it. My agitation, my indignation, plunged me into a delirium which has taken no less than ten years to be calmed; [2] and having stumbled in the interval from one error to another, from one mistake to another, from one foolish act to another, my imprudent actions furnished the masters of my fate all the tools they have skillfully utilized to make it irreversible.

I struggled for a long time as violently as I did in vain. Without cleverness, without craft, without dissimulation, without prudence, candid, open, impatient, carried away, I only entangled myself more by struggling and incessantly gave them new holds they have been careful not to neglect. Finally, feeling that all my efforts were useless and that I was tormenting myself to no avail, I took the only course which remained—that of submitting to my fate without railing against necessity any longer. I have found compensation for all my hurts in this resignation through the tranquility it provides me, tranquility which could not be united with the continual toil of a resistance as painful as it was fruitless.

Another thing has contributed to this tranquility. Among all the refinements of their hatred, my persecutors omitted one which their animosity made them forget: that was to increase its effects so gradually that they could incessantly sustain and renew my sufferings by forever hurting me in a new way. If they had been clever enough to leave me some glimmer of hope, they would still have that hold on me. They would still be able to make me their plaything by means of some false lure and then break my heart by a continually new torment that would frustrate my expectations. But they exhausted all their resources in advance; in leaving me nothing, they deprived themselves of everything. The defamation, depression, derision, and disgrace with which they have covered me are no more susceptible of being increased than mollified; they are as incapable of aggravating them as I am of escaping them. They were in such a hurry to bring the toll of my misery to its peak that all human power aided by all the tricks of Hell could add nothing more to it. Physical suffering itself, instead of increasing my torments, would bring diversion from them. By forcing screams from me, it would perhaps spare me groans; and the rending of my body would stay the rending of my heart.

What do I still have to fear from them, since everything is over? No longer able to make my condition worse, they can no longer alarm me. Worry and fright are evils they have delivered me from forever: that's always a comfort. Real evils have little hold on me; I resign myself easily to those I experience, but not to those I dread. My alarmed imagination brings them together, turns them over and over, draws them out, and increases them. Anticipating them torments me a hundred times more than being in their presence, and the threat of them terrifies me more than their actual arrival. As soon as they occur, the event—removing whatever imaginary power they had—reduces them to their correct value. Then I find them greatly inferior to what I had imagined; and even in the midst of my suffering I do not fail to feel relieved. In this state, freed from any new fear and delivered from the turmoil induced by hope, habit alone will suffice to make more bearable for me day by day a situation which nothing can make worse; and to the extent that feeling becomes blunted with the lapse of time, they have no other way to stir it up again. That is the good my persecutors have done me by prodigally using up all the shafts of their animosity. They have deprived themselves of all mastery over me, and henceforth I can laugh at them.

Not quite two months ago, complete calm was reestablished in my heart.[3] For a long time I no longer feared anything, but I still hoped; and this hope, deluded one moment and frustrated another, was a hold by which a thousand diverse passions incessantly perturbed me. An event as sad as it was unforeseen has finally just erased this weak ray of hope from my heart and has made me see my fate forever and irreversibly fastened here-below. Since then I have become unreservedly resigned, and I have found peace again.

As soon as I began to catch a glimpse of the whole extent of the plot, I gave up forever the idea of winning the public back over to my side during my lifetime; and, for that matter, now that this winning them back can no longer be reciprocal, it would henceforth be quite useless to me. In vain would men return to me; they would no longer find me. Because of the disdain they have inspired in me, dealing with them would be insipid to me and even burdensome; and I am a hundred times happier in my solitude than I could ever be living among them. They have torn all the charms of society from my heart. At my age, those charms cannot sprout anew; it is too late. Henceforth, whether men do good or evil to me, nothing concerning them makes any difference to me; and no matter what they do, my contemporaries will never mean anything to me.

But I still counted on the future; and I hoped that a better generation, examining more fairly both the judgments made about me by this one and its conduct toward me, would easily unravel the cunning of those who direct it and would finally see me as I am. This is the hope which made me write my *Dialogues* [4] and prompted me to a thousand foolish attempts to pass them on to posterity. This hope, though remote, held my soul in the same agitation as when I was still looking for a just heart in this century; and the hope that I cast in vain into the future also rendered me the plaything of the men of today. I stated in my *Dialogues* what I founded this expectation on.[5] I was mistaken. Fortunately, I sensed it early enough to find an interlude of complete calm and absolute rest before my last hour. This interlude began in the period of which I am speaking, and I have reason to believe it will not be interrupted again.

Very few days pass without new reflections confirming how greatly mistaken I was to count on winning back the public even in another age, since with respect to me it is led by guides who are continually renewed in the groups [6] that have taken a dislike to me. Individuals die, but not collective groups. The same passions are perpetuated in them, and their ardent hatred—as immortal as the Demon which inspires it—is as active as always. When all of my individual enemies are dead, doctors and Oratorians [7] will still live; and even if I had only those two groups as persecutors, I could be sure that they would not leave my memory in greater peace after my death than they leave me in during my lifetime. In time, perhaps, the doctors—whom I really offended—can be appeased. But the Oratorians—whom I loved, whom I esteemed, in whom I had complete trust, and whom I never offended—the Oratorians, church people and half monks, will be forever implacable. Their own iniquity constitutes the crime for which their self-love [8] will never forgive me. And the public, whose animosity they will take care to nourish and stir up continually, will be no more appeased than they.

Everything is finished for me on earth. People can no longer do good or evil to me here. I have nothing more to hope for or to fear in this world; and here I am, tranquil at the bottom of the abyss, a poor unfortunate mortal, but unperturbed, like God Himself.

Everything external is henceforth foreign to me. I no longer have neighbors,[9] fellow creatures, or brothers in this world. I am on earth as though on a foreign planet onto which I have fallen from the one I inhabited. If I recognize anything around me, it is only objects which distress me and tear my heart asunder; and I cannot cast my eyes on what touches and surrounds me without forever finding some disdainful object which makes me indignant or a painful one which distresses me. So let me remove from my mind all the troublesome objects I would bother myself with as painfully as I would uselessly. Alone for the rest of my life—since I find consolation, hope, and peace only in myself—I no longer ought nor want to concern myself with anything but me. It is in this state that I again take up the sequel to the severe and sincere examination I formerly called my *Confessions*. I consecrate my last days to studying myself and to preparing in advance the account I will give of myself before long. Let me give myself up entirely to the sweetness of conversing with my soul, since that is

the only thing men cannot take away from me. If by dint of
reflecting upon my inner dispositions I succeed in putting them in
better order and in correcting the evil which may remain in them,
my meditations will not be entirely useless; and even though I am
no longer good for anything on earth, I will not have completely
wasted my last days. The leisurely moments of my daily walks
have often been filled with charming periods of contemplation
which I regret having forgotten. I will set down in writing those
which still come to me and each time I reread them I will enjoy
them anew. I will forget my misfortunes, my persecutors, my
disgrace, while dreaming of the prize my heart deserved.

These pages will, properly speaking, be only a shapeless diary
of my reveries. There will be much concerning me in them,
because a solitary person who reflects is necessarily greatly preoccupied with himself. Moreover, all the foreign ideas which pass
through my head while I am walking will also find their place in
them. I will say what I have thought just as it came to me and
with as little connection as the ideas of the day before ordinarily
have with those of the following day. But a new understanding of
my natural temperament [10] and disposition will come from that
all the same by means of a new understanding of the feelings and
thoughts which constitute the daily fodder of my mind in the
strange state I am in. These pages can be considered, then, as an
appendix to my *Confessions;* but I no longer give them that title,
no longer feeling anything to say which merits it. My heart has
been purified in the forge of adversity and, in carefully sounding
it, I hardly find any reprehensible inclinations remaining. What
would I still have to confess now that all earthly affections have
been torn from it? I have no more reason to praise than to blame
myself: I am henceforth nothing among men, and that is all I can
be, no longer having any real relations or true society with them.
No longer able to do any good which does not turn to evil, no
longer able to act without harming another or myself, to abstain
has become my sole duty and I fulfill it as much as it is in me to do
so. But despite this desuetude of my body, my soul is still active; it
still produces feelings and thoughts; and its internal and moral life
seems to have grown even more with the death of every earthly

and temporal interest. My body is no longer anything to me but an encumbrance, an obstacle, and I disengage myself from it beforehand as much as I can.

Such a unique situation surely deserves to be examined and described, and to this examination I consecrate my last moments of leisure. To do so successfully, it would be necessary to proceed with order and method; but I am incapable of such work, and it would even take me away from my goal, which is to make myself aware of the modifications of my soul and of their sequence. I will perform on myself, to a certain extent, the measurements natural scientists perform on the air in order to know its daily condition. I will apply the barometer to my soul, and these measurements, carefully executed and repeated over a long period of time, may furnish me results as certain as theirs. But I do not extend my enterprise that far. I will be content to keep a record of the measurements without seeking to reduce them to a system. My enterprise is the same as Montaigne's, but my goal is the complete opposite of his: he wrote his *Essays* only for others, and I write my reveries only for myself.[11] If in my later days as the moment of departure approaches, I continue—as I hope—to have the same disposition as I now have, reading them will recall the delight I enjoy in writing them and causing the past to be born again for me will, so to speak, double my existence. In spite of mankind, I will still be able to enjoy the charm of society; and decrepit, I will live with myself in another age as if I were living with a younger friend.

I wrote my first *Confessions* and my *Dialogues* in constant anxiety about ways to keep them from the rapacious hands of my persecutors in order to transmit them, if it were possible, to other generations. With this work, the same worry no longer torments me; I know it would be useless. And now that the desire to be better understood by men has been extinguished in my heart, only profound indifference remains about the fate of my true writings and of the testimonies to my innocence—which have perhaps already all been forever reduced to nothing. Let them spy out what I am doing, let them worry about these pages, let them seize them, suppress them, falsify them; henceforth none of that both-

ers me. I neither hide nor show them. If they take them away
from me while I am living, they will not take away from me the
pleasure of having written them, nor the memory of their content,
nor the solitary meditations whose fruit they are and whose
source can be extinguished only when my soul is. If from the time
of my first calamities I had known not to rail against my fate and
to take the course I take today, all the efforts of men, all of their
dreadful contrivances, would have had no effect on me, and they
would no more have disturbed my rest by all their plots than they
can henceforth disturb it by all the successful results of those
plots.[12] Let them enjoy my disgrace at will; they will not prevent
me from enjoying my innocence and from finishing my days in
peace in spite of them.

NOTES

1. About fifteen years before this was written, that is, on June 9, 1762,
the Parliament of Paris condemned Rousseau's *Émile* and issued a writ of
arrest for him. He had been alerted the night before and was therefore
able to flee toward Switzerland before the police came to arrest him.
During the next twelve years or so, he was forced to flee one place after
another and frequently subjected to unkindness. By suggesting that this
position of enforced solitude has endured longer than fifteen years, Rousseau may be tracing it to the events surrounding his bitter quarrel with
Mme d'Épinay in December 1757 and his subsequent departure from the
Hermitage, the little house near the forest of Montmorency that she had
renovated for him and offered to him in 1756. In the *Confessions*, Books
IX and X, he explained how the quarrel arose and declared that all of his
troubles began at about this time. See *Confessions* in *Oeuvres Complètes
de Jean-Jacques Rousseau* ("Bibliothèque de la Pléiade"; Paris: Gallimard, 1959-70, vol. 1, pp. 472-501, esp. pp. 492-93; see also pp. 579-84.
(This edition of Rousseau's works will hereafter be cited as *OC*.)
2. This probably refers to the period beginning with the forced exile
from St. Peter's Island in October 1765 until the unsuccessful attempt to
deposit a copy of his *Dialogues* (see n. 4) on the altar at Notre Dame in
Paris in February 1776 and would include his very strange conduct just
prior to leaving England in May 1767. For an indication of Rousseau's
thought about the way he was treated in England, see *Dialogues, OC* 1,
pp. 740-59 and 779-85.
3. In May 1776 Rousseau made a last, futile attempt to interest others
in his plight. He composed a leaflet, entitled *To Any Frenchman Who*

Still Loves Justice and Truth, and tried to distribute it to people passing by on the streets. To his utter amazement, most people handed the leaflet back, declaring that it was not addressed to them. This seems to be the "event as sad as it was unforeseen" to which he refers a few lines below. When he recounted this experience, Rousseau bore witness to the resignation he speaks about here and vowed that he would henceforth be calm: "I have, then, made up my mind completely. Removed from everything pertaining to the earth and to the senseless judgments of men, I am resigned to being forever disfigured among them without counting any the less on recompense for my innocence and suffering. My happiness will have to be of another order; I ought no longer to seek it among them, and they are no more able to prevent it than to understand it. Destined to be prey to error and falsehood in this life, I await the hour of my deliverance and the triumph of truth without any longer seeking them among mortals. Removed from every earthly affection and even delivered from the worry of hope here-below, I see no other hold by which they might still trouble my heart's repose. I shall never repress the first movement of indignation, impulsive emotion, or anger and do not even try to do so any longer; but the calm which follows this fleeting agitation is a permanent state that nothing can ever again pull me out of." See *Dialogues, Histoire du Précédent Écrit, OC* 1, pp. 986-87.

Because a correct identification of the event Rousseau is referring to is closely linked to the identification of the time at which he began to write the *Reveries,* this reference has been extensively discussed. Cf. *Les Rêveries du Promeneur Solitaire,* ed. H. Roddier (Paris: Garnier Frères, 1960), pp. xlii-xlvii; and Robert Ricatte, "Un Nouvel Examen des Cartes à Jouer," *Annales de la Société Jean-Jacques Rousseau,* 35 (1962), pp. 239-56.

4. The *Dialogues* carries the full title of *Rousseau, Juge de Jean-Jacques, Dialogues.* There are three dialogues, preceded by an introduction which explains the purpose of the dialogues as well as why the dialogue form was chosen and followed by an epilogue which describes how Rousseau tried to insure that the writing would be safeguarded for future generations. The only two characters in these dialogues are "Rousseau" and "a Frenchman." At first, the Frenchman expresses great hostility toward the terrible author who was responsible for evil books like the *Émile,* but Rousseau, who is presented as someone sympathetic to that terrible author (designated only as "Jean-Jacques"), slowly brings the Frenchman to the point of acknowledging the tender soul and true feelings of humanity characteristic of the real Rousseau. This is done by urging the Frenchman to use his own critical faculties and to read the books he has been led to believe are so evil.

Although the *Dialogues* was finished in 1776, it was not published until after Rousseau's death.

5. Cf. *Dialogues, OC* 1, pp. 661-64 and 987-89. Rousseau argued that the public treated him the way it did because it had been led to believe that he deserved to be treated in such a manner. Because he still believed that people desire to act decently and according to principle, Rousseau tried to structure the argument of the *Dialogues* in such a way as to convince them of the foolishness of their conduct toward him. The conversion of the Frenchman which takes place during the course of the *Dialogues* is an illustration of how Rousseau thought people's opinion might be changed.

6. Literally, "bodies" *(corps)*.

7. The Oratorians are a society of secular priests who take no monastic vows. St. Philippe de Néri founded the society in Rome in 1564, and Pope Paul V approved the order in 1612. In France the society was organized by Pierre de Bérulle.

In the *Confessions*, Book X and Book XI, Rousseau spoke harshly of one Oratorian, Father Bertier, and of two of Bertier's acquaintances, even going so far as to accuse these acquaintances of having stolen some of his papers shortly before the *Émile* was condemned. However, he also spoke with pleasure of a little picnic he had with two Oratorians at Montmorency the day before the *Émile* was condemned. *OC* 1, pp. 504-6, 570-71, and 579.

Later, in the *Dialogues,* Rousseau specifically accused Father Bertier's two acquaintances of being in the service of d'Alembert and the Oratorians, in general, of having become "dangerous enemies." *OC* 1, pp. 905-6 and notes.

8. In all of his writings Rousseau made a very clear distinction between self-love *(amour-propre)* and love of self *(amour de soi)*. The latter is a natural affection of the soul and tends to our self-preservation. As long as it remains within its natural limits, it has nothing reprehensible in it. Self-love arises from an erroneous development of love of self and pertains largely to comparison with others; it is a bad kind of pride. It leads to no human good and often prompts the vicious acts which make human society bad. (Cf. Eighth Walk and *Émile*, Book IV, *OC* 4, pp. 491-93). *Amour-propre* will always be translated as self-love and *amour de soi* as love of self.

9. Reading *prochains* with the manuscript. (Unless otherwise indicated, the readings of Raymond's 1959 edition in the Pléiade series, *OC* 1, pp. 993-1099, have been adopted.)

10. The French term *mon naturel* has been translated as "my natural temperament" to distinguish it from references to "my nature" *(ma nature)*.

11. In his *Essays*, Montaigne claimed to write only for his own sake. See *Essays*, vol. 1, "To the Reader: 'Reader, this is a book of good faith From the outset, it warns you that I have sought no goal in it other than a

domestic and private one. I have given no thought to serving you or to my fame. My strength is not up to such a project. I have dedicated this work to the private benefit of my relatives and friends, so that when they have lost me (which they will soon do), they might again find some trace of my states and moods and that in this way they might sustain their acquaintance with me in a fuller and livelier fashion. If I had wanted to curry the favor of the world, I would have primped more and would have presented myself in a studied pose. I want to be seen in my simple, natural, and ordinary way without adornment or artificiality, for I am depicting myself. My defects and naive manner will be clearly visible in this work, at least to the extent that respect for public opinion permits. Had I been in one of those nations that are said to live even now in the sweet freedom of the first laws of nature, I assure you that I would quite willingly have painted myself completely, and completely naked.' "

Rousseau expressed a similar criticism of Montaigne in the *Confessions,* Book X: "I don't know what fantasy had for some time caused Rey to urge me to write my memoirs. Although from the point of view of events they were not very interesting until then, I felt they could become interesting because of the frankness with which I was capable of writing them and I resolved to make a work which would be unique in its unparalleled truthfulness so that a man might at least once be seen as he was within. I had always laughed at Montaigne's false naïveté in pretending to admit his defects while taking great care to give himself only likeable traits. Nonetheless, I felt—I who always did and still do believe myself to be, all things considered, the best of men—that there was no human inner self, however pure it might be, which did not hide some odious vice. I knew that I was publicly depicted with traits so dissimilar to my own and sometimes even so disfigured that in spite of the bad, none of which I wanted to be quiet about, I could only gain by showing myself as I was." *OC* 1, pp. 516-17.

12. Literally, "all their successes" *(tous leurs succès).*

SECOND WALK

Having, then, formed the project of describing the habitual state of my soul in the strangest position in which a mortal could ever find himself, I saw no simpler and surer way to carry out this enterprise than to keep a faithful record of my solitary walks and of the reveries which fill them when I leave my head entirely free and let my ideas follow their bent without resistance or constraint. These hours of solitude and meditation are the only ones in the day during which I am fully myself and for myself, without diversion, without obstacle, and during which I can truly claim to be what nature willed.

I soon felt I had too long delayed carrying out this project. Already less lively, my imagination no longer bursts into flame the way it used to in contemplating the object which stimulates it. I delight less in the delirium of reverie. Henceforth there is more reminiscence than creation in what it produces. A tepid languor enervates all my faculties. The spirit of life is gradually dying out in me. Only with difficulty does my soul any longer thrust itself out of its decrepit wrapping; and were it not that I am hopeful of reaching the state to which I aspire because I feel I have a right to it, I would no longer exist but by memories. Thus, in order to contemplate myself before my decline, I must go back at least a few years to the time when, losing all hope here-below and no longer finding any food here on earth for my heart, I gradually became accustomed to feeding it with its own substance and to looking within myself for all its nourishment.

This resource, which I thought of too late, became so fruitful that it soon sufficed to compensate for everything. The habit of turning within eventually made me stop feeling and almost stop remembering my ills. By my own experience, I thus learned that the source of true happiness is within us and that it is not within the power of men to make anyone who can will to be happy truly miserable. For four or five years, I habitually tasted those internal delights that loving and sweet souls find in contemplation.[1] Those moments of rapture, those ecstasies, which I sometimes experienced in walking around alone that way, were enjoyments I owed to my persecutors. Without them I would never have found or become cognizant of the treasures I carried within myself. In the midst of so many riches, how could a faithful record of them be kept? In wanting to recall so many sweet reveries, instead of describing them, I fell back into them. This is a state which is brought back by being remembered and of which we would soon cease to be aware, if we completely ceased feeling it.

I fully experienced this effect during the walks which followed my plans to write the sequel to my *Confessions,* especially during the one I am going to speak of and during which an unforeseen accident came to interrupt the thread of my ideas and give them another direction for some time.

After lunch on Thursday, the 24th of October, 1776, I followed the boulevards as far as the Rue du Chemin-Vert which I took up to the heights of Ménilmontant and from there, taking paths across the vineyards and meadows as far as Charonne, I crossed over the cheerful countryside which separates these two villages; then I made a detour in order to come back across the same meadows by taking a different route.[2] In wandering over them, I enjoyed that pleasure and interest which charming places have always given me and stopped from time to time to look at plants in the vegetation. I noticed two I quite rarely saw around Paris, but which I found to be very abundant in that area. One is the *Picris hieracioides,*[3] belonging to the family of composite plants; and the other is the *Buplevrum falcatum,*[4] belonging to the family of umbelliferous plants. This discovery delighted and amused me for a very long time and ended in the discovery of an even rarer plant, especially in high places, namely, the *Cerastium aquaticum* [5] which, in spite of the accident that befell me the same day, I have come across in a book I had with me and have now placed in my herbarium.

Finally, after having looked thoroughly at several other plants I saw still in bloom and which I was always pleased to see even though I was familiar with their aspect and name, I gradually turned away from these minute observations so as to give myself up to the no less charming, but more moving, impression which the whole scene made on me. A few days before, the grape-gathering had been completed; strollers from the city had already withdrawn; even the peasants were leaving the fields until the toils of winter. The countryside, still green and cheerful, but partly defoliated and already almost desolate, presented every-where an image of solitude and of winter's approach. Its appearance gave rise to a mixed impression, sweet and sad, too analogous to my age and lot for me not to make the connection. I saw myself at the decline of an innocent and unfortunate life, my soul still full of vivacious feelings and my mind still bedecked with a few flowers—but flowers already wilted by sadness and dried up by worries. Alone and forsaken, I felt the coming cold of the first frosts, and my flagging imagination no longer filled my solitude with beings formed according to my heart. Sighing, I said to myself: "What have I done here-below? I was made to live, and I am dying without having lived. At least it has not been my fault; and I will carry to the author of my being, if not an offering of good works which I have not been permitted to perform, at least a tribute of frustrated good intentions, of healthy feelings rendered ineffectual, and of a patience impervious to the scorn of men." I was moved by these reflections; I went back over the movements of my soul from the time of my youth, through my mature age, since having been sequestered from the society of men, and during the long seclusion in which I must finish my days. I mulled over all the affections of my heart with satisfaction,

over its so tender but blind attachements, over the less sad than
consoling ideas on which my mind had nourished itself for some
years; and with a pleasure almost equal to that I had in giving
myself up to this musing, I prepared to remember them well
enough to describe them. My afternoon was spent in these peaceful meditations, and I was coming back [6] very satisfied with my
day when, at the height of my reverie, I was dragged out of it by
the event which remains for me to relate.

I was on the road down from Ménilmontant almost opposite
the Galant Jardinier [7] at about six o'clock when some people
walking ahead of me suddenly swerved aside and I saw a huge
Great Dane rushing down upon me. Racing before a carriage, the
dog had no time to check its pace or to turn aside when it noticed
me. I judged that the only means I had to avoid being knocked to
the ground was to make a great leap, so well-timed that the dog
would pass under me while I was still in the air. This idea, quicker
than a flash and which I had the time neither to think through nor
carry out, was my last before my accident. I did not feel the blow,
nor the fall, nor anything of what followed until the moment I
came to.

It was almost night when I regained consciousness. I found
myself in the arms of three or four young people who told me
what had just happened to me. The Great Dane, unable to check
its bound, had collided against my legs and, bowling me over with
its mass and speed, had caused me to fall head first: my upper jaw
had struck against a very rough pavement with the whole weight
of my body behind it; and the shock of the fall was even greater
because I was walking downhill and my head had struck lower
than my feet.

The carriage the dog was with was following right behind it
and would have run me over had the coachman not reined in his
horses instantly. That is what I learned from the account of those
who had picked me up and who were still holding me up when I
came to. The state in which I found myself in that instant is too
unusual not to give a description of here.

Night was coming on. I perceived the sky, some stars, and a

little greenery. This first sensation was a delicious moment. I still had no feeling of myself except as being "over there." I was born into life at that instant, and it seemed to me that I filled all the objects I perceived with my frail existence. Entirely absorbed in the present moment, I remembered nothing; I had no distinct notion of my person nor the least idea of what had just happened to me; I knew neither who I was nor where I was; I felt neither injury, fear, nor worry. I watched my blood flow as I would have watched a brook flow, without even suspecting that this blood belonged to me in any way. I felt a rapturous calm in my whole being; and each time I remember it, I find nothing comparable to it in all the activity of known pleasures.

They asked me where I lived; it was impossible for me to say. I asked where I was; they told me: "at the Haute-Borne." [8] They might just as well have said: "on Mount Atlas." In succession, I had to ask what country I found myself in, what city, and what district. Even that was not enough for me to know where I was. It took me the whole distance from there to the boulevard to recall my address and my name. A gentleman I did not know, but who was charitable enough to accompany me a little way, learning that I lived so far away, counseled me to get a cab at the Temple [9] to take me home. I walked easily and sprightly, feeling neither pain nor hurt, although I kept spitting out a lot of blood. But I had an icy shiver which made my jarred teeth chatter in a very uncomfortable way. When I reached the Temple, I thought that since I was walking without trouble it was better to continue on foot than to risk perishing from cold in a cab. Thus I covered the half-league [10] from the Temple to the Rue Platrière, walking without trouble, avoiding obstacles and coaches, choosing and following my way just as well as I would have done in perfect health. I arrived, opened the lock [11] they had installed at the street door, climbed the staircase in darkness, and finally entered my home without incident, apart from my fall and its consequences, of which, even then, I was not yet fully aware.

My wife's cries upon seeing me made me understand that I was worse off than I thought. I passed the night without yet being

aware of, or feeling, my injuries. Here is what I felt and discovered the next day: my upper lip was split on the inside up to
my nose; outside, the skin had held firm and prevented the lip
from being split completely open; four teeth had been pushed
into my upper jaw; the whole part of the face which covers it was
extremely swollen and skinned; my right thumb was sprained and
very large; my left thumb hurt painfully; my left arm was
sprained; my left knee was also very swollen, and a severely
painful bruise totally prevented me from bending it. But with all
this upset, nothing broken, not even a tooth: now in a fall like this
one, that is good luck bordering on the marvelous.

That, very faithfully, is the story of my accident. In a few days
this story spread through Paris, so changed and distorted that it
was impossible to recognize it in any way. I should have counted
on this metamòrphosis in advance. But so many bizarre circumstances were joined to it, so many obscure remarks and reticences
accompanied it, they spoke to me about it in such a ridiculously
discreet manner, that all these mysteries worried me. I have
always hated the dark; it naturally fills me with a dread which the
darkness they have surrounded me with for so many years could
not have diminished. Of all the unusual events of this time period,
I will relate only one, but one sufficient to permit judgment about
the others.

M. Lenoir, lieutenant general of the police,[12] with whom I had
never had any dealings, sent his secretary to inquire about my
tidings and to tender me pressing offers of service which, given
the circumstances, appeared to me to be of no great use for my
relief. His secretary did not fail to urge me very insistently to
avail myself of these offers, even going so far as to tell me that if I
did not trust him, I could write directly to M. Lenoir. This great
eagerness and the confidential manner which accompanied it led
me to understand that beneath it all was some mystery which I
tried in vain to penetrate. Hardly that much was needed to alarm
me, especially given the state of agitation my head was in from
my accident and the resultant fever. I abandoned myself to a
thousand troubling and sad conjectures and made commentaries

on everything which went on around me, commentaries which were more a sign of the delirium of fever than of the composure of a man who no longer takes interest in anything.

Another event occurred which completely destroyed my serenity. Mme d'Ormoy [13] had sought me out for some years without my having been able to guess why. Pretentious little gifts and frequent visits without purpose or pleasure showed me well enough that she had a secret goal in all that, but not well enough what that goal was. She had spoken to me of a novel she wanted to write to present to the queen. I had told her what I thought of women authors. She had intimated that the goal of this project was to restore her fortunes, a goal for which she needed protection; I had nothing to reply to that. She later told me that, having been unable to gain access to the queen, she was determined to give her book to the public. It was no longer the moment to give her advice she had not asked me for and which she would not have followed. She had spoken of showing me the manuscript beforehand. I begged her to do nothing of the sort, and she did nothing of the sort.

One fine day during my convalescence I received this book from her completely printed and even bound. In the preface I saw such swollen praises of me, laid on so clumsily and with so much affectation, that I was disagreeably impressed by them.[14] The crude fawning which was so perceptible in it was never associated with benevolence; about that, my heart could never be deceived.

A few days later, Mme d'Ormoy and her daughter came to see me. She informed me that because of a note it contained, her book was causing the greatest fuss. I had hardly noticed this note while flipping rapidly through the novel. I reread the note after Mme d'Ormoy's departure. I examined the way it was constructed. I believed that in it I discovered the motive for her visits, her wheedlings, and the swollen praises of her preface; and I judged that there was no other goal in all of this than to dispose the public to attribute the note to me and consequently to burden me with the blame it would attract to its author in the circumstances under which it was published.[15]

I had no means of putting an end to this fuss and the impression it could make; the only thing I could do was not foster it by continuing to endure the vain and ostensive visits of Mme d'Ormoy and her daughter. Here is the note I wrote to the mother for this purpose:

Rousseau, not receiving any authors in his home, thanks Mme d'Ormoy for her kindness and begs her to honor him with her visits no more.

She replied to me by a letter, honest in appearance but contrived, like all those which people write to me in such cases. I had barbarously plunged a dagger into her sensitive heart and I must believe by the tone of her letter that because of her intense and true feelings for me, she would never endure this break without dying. So it is that straightforwardness and frankness in everything are horrid crimes in the world, and I appear nasty and ferocious to my contemporaries when I am guilty of no other crime in their eyes than that of not being false and perfidious as they.

I had already gone outside several times and had even strolled in the Tuileries quite a few times when I saw, by the astonishment of several of those who met me, that there was still another bit of news concerning me of which I was ignorant. I finally learned that it was rumored that I had died from my fall; and this rumor spread so rapidly and so obstinately that, more than two weeks after I had become aware of it, the king himself and the queen spoke of it as of something certain. In announcing this happy bit of news the *Avignon Courier,* according to what someone had the concern to write me, did not fail on this occasion to give a preview of the tribute of outrages and indignities which are being prepared in the form of a funeral oration in memory of me after my death.[16]

This news was accompanied by an even more unusual circumstance which I learned of only by chance and which I have not been able to learn about in any detail. It is that they had at the same time started a subscription for printing the manuscripts they would find in my home. By that I understood that they were keeping a collection of fabricated writings available just for the purpose of attributing them to me right after my death: for to think they would faithfully print any of those they would actually find is a folly that cannot enter into the mind of a sensible man and from which fifteen years of experience have only too well protected me.

These observations, made one after the other and followed by many others which were scarcely less astonishing, caused my imagination, which I had believed to be calmed down, to become alarmed all over again. And this black darkness with which they relentlessly surrounded me rekindled all the dread it naturally inspires in me. I wore myself out making a thousand commentaries on it all and trying to understand the mysteries they rendered inexplicable for me. The only constant result of so many enigmas was to confirm all of my previous conclusions, to wit, that my personal fate and that of my reputation have been so fastened by the connivance of the whole present generation that no effort on my part could free me, since it is completely impossible for me to transmit any bequest to other ages without making it pass in this age through the hands of those interested in suppressing it.

But this time, I went further. The accumulation of so many fortuitous circumstances, the elevation of all of my cruelest enemies favored, so to speak, by fortune; all those who govern the state, all those who direct public opinion, all the people in official positions, all the men of influence, picked and culled as it were from among those who have some secret animosity against me in order to concur in the common plot; this universal agreement is too extraordinary to be purely fortuitous. If there had been a single man who had refused to be an accomplice to it, a single event which had gone against it, a single unforeseen circumstance which had been an obstacle to it, any of that would have been enough to make it fail. But all the acts of will, all the unlucky events, fortune and all its revolutions have made firm the work of men. And such a striking concurrence, which borders on the prodigious, cannot let me doubt that its complete success is written among the eternal decrees. Swarms of individual observations, either in the past or in the present, so confirm me in this opinion that I cannot prevent myself from henceforth considering as one of those secrets of Heaven impenetrable to human reason the same work that until now I looked upon as only a fruit of the wickedness of men.

This idea, far from being cruel and rending to me, consoles me, calms me, and helps me to resign myself. I do not go as far as St. Augustine who would have consoled himself to be damned if such had been the will of God. My resignation comes, it is true, from a less disinterested source, but one no less pure and to my mind, more worthy of the perfect Being whom I adore. God is just; He wills that I suffer; and He knows that I am innocent. That is the cause of my confidence; my heart and my reason cry out to me that I will not be deceived by it. Let me, therefore, leave men and fate to go their ways. Let me learn to suffer without a murmur. In the end, everything must return to order, and my turn will come sooner or later.

NOTES

1. The account in the Fifth Walk of his sojourn on St. Peter's Island and the discussion in the Seventh Walk of his various botanical forays in the neighborhood of Neuchâtel suggest that Rousseau is thinking here of the years 1762-66. Although it was a period marked by vexing incidents and general distress, beginning as it did with the forced departure from France and ending with the attempt to find a peaceful haven in England, Rousseau did enjoy long moments of great joy during these years.

2. As he states a little later, Rousseau was living on Rue Platrière, now known as Rue Jean-Jacques Rousseau, during the period of time in which the *Reveries* was composed. This street is not far from St. Eustache Church. Rousseau would have taken the Rue du Chemin-Vert from the Rue de la Contrescarpe (now known as Boulevard Beaumarchais) up to the heights where Père Lachaise Cemetery is now situated and then gone across the fields to the village of Charonne.

3. The *Picris hieracioides* is commonly known as hawkweed.

4. The *Buplevrum falcatum* is commonly known as hare's ear.

5. The *Cerastium aquaticum* is commonly known as chickweed or mouse-ear chickweed.

6. Rousseau also seems to be suggesting a psychological return here, for he uses an awkward expression which carries a hint of returning to

oneself. Literally, he says: "I was coming back from them to myself" *(je m'en revenais).*

7. This is probably the name of a cabaret located in the district called La Haute Borne (see n. 8).

8. La Haute Borne was the name of an area and of the street which was the continuation of the Rue du Ménilmontant after the intersection of the Rue du Bas Popincourt. The lower part of the Rue du Ménilmontant is now called the Rue Oberkampf, and the Rue du Bas Popincourt is now called Rue Saint-Maur.

9. Rousseau is referring to the old Enclosure of the Temple (Enclos du Temple) where the Priory of the Knights Templars, a military and religious order formed in Jerusalem in 1118 and abolished in 1313, and the Tower of the Temple were located. Today, only the Square du Temple remains, the Tower and the Priory having been demolished in 1811.

10. Because of the different measures prevailing in various regions and provinces, the league had no precise length in eighteenth-century France. There is some agreement, however, that it was roughly equivalent to four kilometers, that is, to about two and one-half miles, and the distance from the Square du Temple to Rousseau's home on the Rue Platrière or Rue Jean-Jacques Rousseau is almost two kilometers.

11. Apparently, a special kind of lock had been placed on Rousseau's door at the street so that anyone wishing to visit him had to ask the neighbors how to get into the building. See *Dialogues, OC* 1, p. 713 and note: "They keep track of everyone who asks to see [me]. . . ." The note then explains: "For that purpose they have set up a newspaper vendor across the street from my door and a lock on the door, which they keep shut, so that anyone who wants to enter my building is forced to ask the neighbors, who have their instructions and orders."

In both passages, Rousseau refers to this lock as a *secret.* According to Littré, the word refers to special springs used for different purposes so that one might speak of the *secret* of a mechanism or of a lock. This very sentence of Rousseau's is cited as an example of how the word is used. See Émile Littré, *Dictionnaire de la Langue Française* (Paris: Hachette, 1958), vol. 6; cf. also Joseph Botterman, "Essai sur les Combinaisons Méchaniques, Supplément à l'Art du Serrurier," in *Description des arts et Métiers* (Neuchâtel: Imprimerie de la Société Typographique, 1783), vol. 19.

12. Jean-Charles-Pierre Lenoir (1732-1807) was appointed lieutenant general of police in Paris in 1774 and resigned in 1785. During his administration, many improvements were made in the city of Paris, notably the continuous lighting of the streets.

13. Charlotte Chaumet d'Ormoy (1732-91) was the author of several short stories; the comic opera *Zelmis, ou la Jeune Sauvage;* and two novels, *Les Malheurs de la Jeune Émilie* and *La Vertu Chancelante, ou la*

Vie de Mademoiselle d'Amincourt. Although she became a member of the academy of the Arcades de Rome under the name of Laurilla, Mme d'Ormoy had no great literary reputation.

14. The title of the book is *Les Malheurs de la Jeune Émilie pour Servir d'Instruction aux Âmes Vertueuses et Sensibles* (Paris: Dufour, 1777).

On pp. ix-x of the *Introduction,* Mme d'Ormoy wrote: "The desire to inspire the young people of my own sex with sensitivity and virtues is the second motive that pushed me to publish such a weak product, since I am very thoroughly persuaded that a woman should never write. M. Rousseau even thinks that a man should do so only when he is forced to; however, the public would have lost a great deal had he not written; I know no one whose soul is more sensitive; he is a sage who has freed himself from all needs. He is happy, and his philosophy is uncommon. I confess that this famous man is my hero; but since the praise of his virtues is above what a vulgar pen can do and since the pen of a woman is too slight a stylus to draw his portrait with, I will be quiet and will be content to admire him, while rendering him from the bottom of my heart all the homage due him. His modesty must forgive me for this; the more he disdains flattery, the more he must accept the language of truth."

15. The note mentioned by Rousseau is contained in only one edition of the book, a copy of which exists in the Rare Book Collection of the Bibliothèque Nationale in Paris.

Mme d'Ormoy's novel depicts the aristocracy as dissolute and vicious, but the harshness of her indictment suffers from her failure to offer vivid descriptions and to develop her characters fully. At one point in the book, a young nun recites her life story to Emily and in doing so asserts the injustice and the insensitivity of the sons of the aristocracy. The note referred to by Rousseau occurs just after the following, where the nun's recital is balanced by the description of a noble young man who befriended her and was one of her suitors before she took her vows. This young man, Dorimant, is presented as an exception to every generalization about the other sons of the artistocracy:

"I have blamed myself since then for all the bad treatment my vanity caused Dorimant to suffer. This respectable friend rendered me such great services that I shall never forget them. I promised to give you a description of him. Here it is:

"He did not stand out in a notable way; he was ugly. But in hearing him speak, you easily forgot his ugliness; a great deal of wit corrected nature's errors. His character basically consisted in great sweetness; filled with a most uncommon honesty and great compassion, he tended to the poor, especially those who, in spite of their toil and the sweat of their brow, did not have enough to eat.

"He performed his good deeds in hovels off in the countryside. Often he would help poor wretches reduced to the condition of animals, eating

grass as their only food; or others who had only a miserable cot which
was frequently seized from them because they did not have enough to
pay their taxes."

The missing note begins here, at page 149 of the text. (However, due to
a printing error, the page is actually numbered 159.) In the volume of the
Rare Book Collection, there is a sheet with the directions: "after the
word 'taxes [*impôts*],' p. 149, read the following: 'This man who cannot
feed himself owes a tax to his king. How will he pay it? Without pity,
they will reduce him to utter poverty: the tears of a mother and of the
children by whom he is surrounded do not touch tax collectors' hearts.
Humph! How could their hearts be touched! They answer for money
they have not received by being deprived of their own freedom.

'If sovereigns only knew all the evil that is done in their name, they
would shudder at being kings. Royalty should be desired only for the
felicity of the people, and that is the business of a virtuous king. But it is
very difficult for truth to penetrate all the way to the throne. They are
careful to turn away those who might tell the truth: the king's people is
dying of hunger, but they are depicted to him as being happy.

'My dear Emily, I am going to give you an example of this. A lord of
the court (the Marquis de Souvré), a great lover of truth was with the
king (Louis XV) at a time when bread was very expensive. The people of
the court had assured his Majesty that morning that the price of bread
had dropped. This prince, whose heart was sensitive, showed his joy
about this to his dear friend when he came in; the Marquis de Souvré,
astonished that they had tried to dupe the king, began to run toward the
door; the king, completely baffled by his actions, said to him:

"Where are you going?"

"Sire, I am going to hang my head butler immediately; again today he
charged me more for bread."

'You could not tell the truth in a more pleasant way nor better
enlighten your ruler about the things being hidden from him. It is always
the king's fault if he is deceived: he has only to go out in public. The cries
of joy at his appearance will tell him what he wants to learn; if the voices
are mute, the people are not happy; they can speak to their king only by
their silence. Usually, kings shape our virtues. We pattern ourselves after
the person who holds the reins of the government. Under a virtuous
king,° virtues are in a renaissance, and honest people are anxious to
gather around the throne. To find virtuous people, you must look for
them in modest situations. Virtue hides itself; it is incapable of acquiring
anything by plotting or begging. You get to know a man in happiness and
misfortune. Reverses in no way strike down his courage. Vice alone
terrifies him; and if somebody who is jealous of his reputation uses
slander to get the homage he deserves, he does not bother to justify

himself and lets only his virtues speak. Cato the censor, who was accused forty times and always absolved, was the author of seventy condemnations. This proves that the good man is always justified, whatever interest people may have in blackening his name. With such men, we would see Trajans or Tituses be born again, and they would make their people happy.' " (The asterisk is in Mme d'Ormoy's text and is reproduced at the end of the passage in this manner: °Louis XVI.)

In the *Dialogues*, Rousseau likewise claimed that this note was part of the plot and intended to bring public blame upon him. *OC* 1, pp. 891-92 and note.

16. In the edition of December 3, 1776, the *Courrier d'Avignon* reports the following news from Paris as of November 21, 1776:

"M. Rousseau who often walks about alone in the countryside was knocked over a few days ago by one of those Great Danes that run before fast moving carriages. He is alleged to be very sick from this fall, but his lot of having been crushed by dogs cannot be deplored too much. Now that gives rise to fine reflections about the vicissitudes of human affairs!"

However, the article to which Rousseau was probably alluding in this passage is the news from Paris as of December 12, 1776, which appeared in the December 20, 1776 issue of the *Courrier d' Avignon:*

"M. Jean-Jacques Rousseau has died from the after-effects of his fall. He lived in poverty; he died in misery; and the strangeness of his fate accompanied him all the way to the tomb. It pains us that we cannot speak about the talents of this eloquent writer; our readers must sense that the abuse he made of those talents imposes the most rigorous silence on us now. There is every reason to believe that the public will not be deprived of his life story and that even the name of the dog who killed him will be found."

When giving the news from Paris as of December 21, the issue of December 31 corrected the earlier false report:

"Two Swedes arriving in Paris for the first time asked the toll-collector at the city gates: 'Where does M. Fontenelle live?' The latter did not know. 'How can that be,' the two foreigners retorted 'you are French and you do not know where M. Fontenelle lives? Oh what Barbarians!' If these Swedes are not dead, what epithets would they hurl at a man who falsely announces the death of M. Rousseau? Most surely, they would call him even worse names. But if this man lived 150 leagues from the Capital he would want to clear himself from a bitter reproach and he would very likely reply to these foreigners: Gentlemen, I am terribly sorry if I injured an eloquent writer and over-alarmed the public on his behalf; but my error is quite involuntary. I was deceived by people living in the same city as he. M. Rousseau lives far away from the whirlwind of the world which makes and passes on news; they said he was dead; they wrote me that; they made a funeral eulogy that I did not copy; I am guilty due to error, not due to intention; I therefore hasten to announce to my readers that his accident will have no after-effects and that he enjoys good health. So then perhaps these foreigners, being gentle, honest, and good, will forgive my error in light of the confession I make of it."

THIRD WALK

"I continue to learn while growing old."

Solon frequently repeated this line in his old age.[1] There is a
sense in which I could also say it in mine, but what experience has
made me acquire these past twenty years is a very sad bit of
knowledge: ignorance is still preferable. Adversity is undoubtedly
a great teacher, but it charges dearly for its lessons; and the profit
we draw from them is frequently not worth the price they have
cost. Besides, before we have obtained all this learning by such
tardy lessons, the occasion to use it passes. Youth is the time to
study wisdom; old age is the time to put it into practice. Experience always instructs, I admit; but it is profitable only for the time
we have left to live. Is the moment when we have to die the time
to learn how we should have lived?

Humph! What benefit do I get from such late and painfully
acquired insights concerning my fate and concerning other people's passions, whose work it is? By coming to know men better, I
have only felt better the misery into which they have thrust me;
and while this knowledge has shown me all their snares, it has not
enabled me to avoid any. If only I had been able to preserve that
stupid, but pleasant, trustfulness which made me the prey and
plaything of my noisy friends for so many years and kept me from
having the least suspicion of all their plots, even though I was

27

bound up in them. I was their dupe and victim, it is true, but I thought myself loved by them; and, attributing to them as much friendship for me as they had inspired in me for them, my heart rejoiced. Those sweet illusions are destroyed. The sad truth that time and reason have unveiled to me by making me sense my misfortune has made me see that there was no remedy for it and that all that was left was for me to resign myself to it. Thus, all the experience proper to my age is useless for me now in this condition and of no benefit for the future.

We enter the lists at our birth; we leave them at death. What use is it to learn to handle our chariot better when we are at the end of the race? There is nothing more to think about then except how we will get out of it. If there is any study still appropriate for an old man, it is solely to learn to die; and this is precisely what we study least at my age. At this point, we think of anything but that. All old men hang on to life more than children and leave it with more reluctance than youngsters. That is because, all their toils having been for this very life, they see at its end that they have wasted their labors. All their cares, all their goods, all the fruits of their toilsome nights—they leave everything when they pass away. They have not dreamed of acquiring anything during their life that they might carry away at their death.

I told myself all that when it was time to tell it to myself; and if I have not put my reflections to better use, it is not for lack of making them in time or of having mulled them over thoroughly. Cast from childhood into the whirlwind of the world, I soon learned from experience that I was not made to live in it and that in it I would never reach the state my heart felt a need for. Ceasing, therefore, to seek among men the happiness I felt incapable of finding in their presence, my ardent imagination readily jumped beyond the interval of my life which had barely begun— as though from a terrain which was foreign to me—to settle down in a quiet resting place where I could anchor myself.

This feeling, nourished by education from the time of my childhood and reinforced during my whole life by this long web of miseries and misfortunes which has filled it, has at all times made me seek to know the nature and the destination of my being in a more interested and careful manner than I have found any other man seek to do. I have seen many who philosophized much more learnedly than I, but their philosophy was, so to speak, foreign to them. Wanting to be more knowledgeable than others, they studied the universe in order to know how it was ordered, just as they would have studied some machine they might have perceived—through pure curiosity. They studied human nature to be able to speak knowingly about it, but not in order to know themselves; they toiled in order to instruct others, but not in order to enlighten themselves within. Several of them only wanted to do a book, any book, provided it was well received. When theirs was done and published, its argument no longer interested them in any way, unless it were to make others adopt it and to defend it in case it were attacked; but for the rest, they drew nothing from it for their own use and were not even concerned whether this argument were false or true—provided it was not refuted. As for me, when I desired to learn, it was in order to know and not in order to teach. I have always believed that before instructing others, it was necessary to begin by knowing enough for oneself; and of all the studies I have tried to undertake during my life in the midst of men, there is hardly any I could not just as well have undertaken alone on a desert island to which I might have been confined for the rest of my days. What we ought to do depends a lot on what we ought to believe; and in everything which is not connected with the first needs of nature, our opinions are the rule of our actions. According to this principle, which has always been my own, I have sought frequently and for a long time to know the true end of my life in order to direct its use and I soon became consoled about being so inept at skillfully handling myself in this world when I sensed that this end should not be sought in it.

Born into a family in which morals [2] and piety reigned, raised subsequently with tenderness in the home of a minister full of wisdom and religion, from the time of my most tender childhood I have received principles, maxims—others would say prejudices—which have never completely deserted me.[3] Given into my own keeping while still a child and enticed by caresses, seduced by vanity, lured by hope, forced by necessity, I became a Catholic, but I always remained a Christian; and soon won over by habit, my heart became sincerely attached to my new religion.[4] The instructions and examples of Mme de Warens [5] made me firmer in this attachment. The rural solitude in which I passed the flower of my youth, the study of good books to which I completely gave myself up, reinforced in her presence my natural disposition to affectionate feelings and rendered me devout almost in the manner of Fénélon.[6] Secluded meditation, the study of nature, and contemplation of the universe force a solitary person to lift himself up incessantly to the author of things, to search with tender concern for the purpose in everything he sees and the cause of everything he feels. When my fate threw me back into the torrent of the world, I no longer found anything in it which could flatter my heart for a moment. Longing for my sweet leisure followed me everywhere and made everything apt to lead to fortune or honors that could be found within my reach seem indifferent and disgusting. Uncertain in my anxious desires, I hoped for little; I obtained less. And, in the very rays of prosperity, I felt that were I to obtain everything I thought I was seeking, I would in no way have found this happiness for which my heart was avid, but did not know how to recognize. Thus, everything contributed to detach my affections from this world, even before the misfortunes which were destined to alienate me from it completely. I reached the age of forty, wavering between indigence and good fortune, between wisdom and aberration, full of vices induced by habit but without any bad propensity in my heart, living according to chance without any principles determined by my reason, and inadvertent about my duties without scorning them, yet often without being fully cognizant of them.

From the time of my youth, I had set this age of forty as the terminal point for my efforts to succeed and as the one for all of my vain ambitions. I was fully resolved once this age was reached that whatever situation I might be in, I would struggle no longer to get out of it and would spend the remainder of my days living from day to day without ever again concerning myself about the future. The moment having come, I executed this plan without difficulty; and even though my fortune then seemed to want to take a turn for the better, I renounced it not only without regret but with actual pleasure. In releasing myself from all those lures and vain hopes, I fully gave myself up to carelessness and to the peace of mind which always constituted my most dominant pleasure and most lasting propensity. I forsook the world and its pomp; I renounced all finery: no more sword, no more watch, no more white stockings, gilding, or headdress; a very simple wig, a good coarse cloth garment; and, better than all that, I eradicated from my heart the cupidity and covetousness which give value to everything I was forsaking. I resigned the post I then held, for which I was in no way suited,[7] and began to copy music at so much a page, an occupation which had always greatly appealed to me.

I did not restrict my reform to external things. I felt that this reform was such as to require another of opinions, undoubtedly more painful but more necessary; and, resolved not to do it twice, I undertook to submit my inner self to a severe examination which would regulate it for the rest of my life just as I wanted to find it at my death.

A great revolution which had just taken place in me; another moral world which was unveiling itself to my observations; men's insane judgments, whose absurdity I was beginning to feel, without yet foreseeing how much I would be victimized by them; the ever growing need for some good besides literary vainglory whose vapor had hardly touched me before I was already disgusted by it; the desire, in short, to follow for the rest of my course a less uncertain route than the one I had just spent the finest half on—everything forced me to this great review for which I had long felt the need. I undertook it, therefore, and I neglected nothing within my power to carry the enterprise out well.

It is from this epoch that I can date my complete renunciation of the world and this intense desire for solitude which has not forsaken me since. The task I was undertaking could be carried out only in absolute seclusion; it required long and peaceful meditations that the tumult of society does not permit. This forced me to take up another way of life for a while, one in which I was subsequently so comfortable that, having since then interrupted it only when forced to and for a short time, I have taken it up again wholeheartedly and have restricted myself to it without difficulty whenever I could. Afterward, when men reduced me to living alone, I found that by sequestering me to make me miserable, they had done more for my happiness than I had ever been able to do.

I gave myself up to the toil I had undertaken with a zeal proportionate both to the importance of the matter and to the need I felt I had of it. I was living then among modern philosophers who hardly resembled the ancient ones. Instead of removing my doubts and ending my irresolution, they had shaken all the certainty I thought I had concerning the things that were most important for me to know. Ardent missionaries of atheism and very imperious dogmatists, there was no way that they would, without anger, put up with anyone daring to think other than they did about any point whatever. I had often defended myself quite feebly, due to hatred for dispute and little talent for sustaining it. But I never adopted their dismal doctrine. And this resistance to such intolerant men—who had their own interests, moreover—was not the least of the causes which stirred up their animosity.

They had not persuaded me, but they had troubled me. Their arguments had shaken me without having ever convinced me; I found no good reply to them, but I felt there must be one. I accused myself less of error than of ineptitude, and my heart replied to them better than my reason.

Finally I said to myself: will I let myself be tossed about eternally by the sophisms of better speakers when I am not even sure that the opinions they preach and are so eager to make others adopt are really their own? The passions which govern their doctrines and their interest in having this or that believed make it impossible to penetrate what they themselves believe. Can one expect good faith among the leaders of a faction? Their philosophy is for others; I need one for me. Let me look for it with all my strength while there is still time, so that I will have a set rule of conduct for the rest of my days. Here I am in the full maturity of age, in all the strength of my understanding. I am already beginning to decline. If I continue to wait, I will no longer have the use of my strength for my delayed deliberation. My intellectual faculties will have lost some of their agility. I will not do as well what I can do today in the best possible way. Let me seize this favorable moment. It is the epoch of my external and material reform; let it also be that of my intellectual and moral reform. Let me settle my opinions and my principles once and for all, and let me be for the remainder of my life what I will have found I ought to be after having carefully thought it over.

I carried out this project slowly and with various fresh starts, but with all the effort and all the attention of which I was capable. I felt intensely that the tranquility of the remainder of my days and my total lot depended on it. At first I found myself in such a labyrinth of encumbrances, difficulties, objections, twistings, and darkness that, twenty times tempted to abandon everything, I was ready to renounce such a futile quest and to abide by the rules of common prudence in my deliberations without seeking for anything more in principles I had so much trouble unraveling. But this very prudence was so foreign to me, I felt myself so unlikely to acquire it, that to take it for my guide was nothing other than to want to seek—across seas and storms, without a rudder or compass—an almost inaccessible lighthouse which pointed out no harbor for me.

I persisted. For the first time in my life I had courage, and to its success I owe having been able to endure the horrible fate which from that time began to envelop me without my having had the least suspicion of it. After the most ardent and sincere seeking that has perhaps ever been made by any mortal, I determined for my whole life all the sentiments [8] important for me to have; and though I may have deceived myself in my conclusions, I am at least sure that my error cannot be imputed to me as a crime, for I made every effort to keep myself from it. To be sure, I have no doubt but what the prejudices of childhood and the secret wishes of my heart made the scale lean to the side the most consoling for me. It is difficult to keep ourselves from believing what we so ardently desire, and who can doubt that most men's interest in admitting or rejecting the judgments of the next life determines their faith and does so according to their hope or fear. All of that could dazzle my judgment, I agree, but not alter my good faith, for I feared deceiving myself about anything. If everything depended on the use made of this life, it was important for me to know it so that I could at least turn it to the best account within my power while there was still time and not be a complete dupe. But given the way I felt myself disposed, what I had to dread most in the world was risking the eternal lot of my soul to enjoy the goods of this world which have never appeared very worthwhile to me.

I confess again that I did not always satisfactorily remove all these difficulties which had bothered me and about which our philosophers had so often battered my ears. But, resolved to settle once and for all these matters human intelligence has so little hold over and finding impenetrable mysteries and insoluble objections on all sides, I adopted for each question the sentiment which seemed to me the best established by direct means and the most believable in itself without paying attention to objections I could not resolve, but which were refuted by other no less strong objections in the opposite system. A dogmatic tone about these matters is suitable only to charlatans, but it is important to have one's own feeling and to choose it with all the maturity of judgment one can put into it. If we fall into error in spite of that, we could not justly suffer the penalty, since we would not be at fault. That is the unshakable principle which serves as the basis of my security.

The result of my painful seeking was approximately that which I have since set down in the "Profession of Faith of the Savoyard Vicar," [9] a work vilely prostituted and profaned among the present generation but which may one day make a revolution among men, if good sense and good faith are ever reborn among them.

Since then, having remained content with the principles I had adopted after such a long and reflective meditation, I have made them the immovable rule of my conduct and faith without bothering myself any longer about the objections I had not been able to resolve or about those I had not been able to foresee and which presented themselves anew to my mind from time to time. They sometimes bothered me, but never shook me. I have always said to myself: those are all only metaphysical quibbles and subtleties which have no weight next to the fundamental principles adopted by my reason, confirmed by my heart, and which all carry the seal of inner assent in the silence of the passions. In matters so much greater than human understanding, will an objection I cannot resolve overturn a whole body of doctrine so solid, so well integrated and formed with so much meditation and care, so very suited to my reason, to my heart, to my whole being, and reinforced by the inner assent I feel to be lacking in all the others? No, vain arguments will never destroy the congruity I perceive between my immortal nature, the constitution of this world, and the physical order I see reigning in it. In the corresponding moral order, whose arrangement I discovered by my seeking, I find the supports I need to endure the miseries of my life. In any other arrangement I would live without resource and die without hope. I would be the most unhappy of creatures. Let me hold then to this one, which alone suffices to render me happy in spite of fortune and men.

Do not this deliberation and the conclusion I drew from it seem to have been dictated by Heaven itself to prepare me for the fate which awaited me and to enable me to endure it? What would I have become, what would I yet become during the frightful periods of anguish which awaited me and the unbelievable situation I am reduced to for the rest of my life, if—having remained without a refuge where I could escape from my implacable persecutors, without compensation for the disgrace to which they submit me in this world, and without hope of ever obtaining the justice due me—I had seen myself completely surrendered up to the most horrible lot any mortal has undergone on earth? While, serene in my innocence, I imagined only esteem and benevolence for me among men and while my open and confiding heart poured itself out to friends and brothers, traitors silently entwined me with nets forged in the pits of Hell. Taken unawares by the most unforeseen of all misfortunes and those most terrible for a proud soul, dragged through the mud without ever knowing by whom or for what, thrust into an abyss of ignominy, enveloped in horrible darkness through which I discerned only sinister objects, I was

floored by the first surprise attack; and I would never have recovered from the despondency this unforeseen kind of misfortune
cast me into had I not stored up reserves of strength ahead of time
in order to pick myself up from my fall.

Only after years of agitation, when my spirits were finally
restored and I began to be myself again, did I feel the worth of
the resources I had stored up for adversity. Settled on all the
things it was important for me to judge, I saw—when I compared
my maxims to my situation—that I was giving far more importance to the insane judgments of men and to the petty events of
this short life than they possessed. Since this life is only a series of
ordeals, it mattered little what these ordeals were like provided
the effect they were destined for resulted from them; and consequently, the greater, stronger, and more multiplied the ordeals,
the more advantageous it was to know how to endure them. All of
the most intense pains lose their strength for anyone who sees the
great and sure compensation for them, and the certainty of this
compensation was the principal fruit I had drawn out of my
preceding meditations.

It is true that in the midst of the innumerable outrages and
immeasurable indignities by which I felt myself overwhelmed on
all sides, intervals of worry and doubt occasionally arose to shake
my hope and trouble my tranquility. The powerful objections I
had not been able to resolve then presented themselves to my
mind more forcefully to finish striking me down precisely at those
times when, overburdened by the weight of my fate, I was ready
to give way to discouragement. Frequently, new arguments I
heard came back to mind in support of those which had already
tormented me. Ah! I said to myself then, when my heart was
constricting so as to suffocate me, who will keep me from despair
if my lot is so horrible that I no longer see anything but idle
fancies in the consolations my reason furnished me; if thus de-
stroying its own work it overturns the whole support of hope and
confidence it had stored up for me in adversity? What kind of a
support are illusions which delude me alone in the whole world?
The whole present generation sees only errors and prejudices in
the sentiments with which I alone nourish myself. It finds truth

and evidence in the system opposed to mine. It even seems
incapable of believing that I adopt my own in good faith; and
although I give myself up to it wholeheartedly, even I find it has
insurmountable difficulties which are impossible for me to resolve
but which do not prevent me from persisting in it. Am I then
alone wise, alone enlightened, among mortals? To believe that
this is the way things are, is it sufficient that they suit me? Can I
put enlightened trust in appearances which have nothing solid in
the eyes of other men and which would seem illusory even to me
if my heart did not confirm my reason? Would it not have been
better to engage my persecutors with equal weapons by adopting
their maxims than to remain prey to their attacks because of the
idle fancies of my own maxims, without acting to repulse them? I
believe myself wise, but I am only a dupe, a victim, and a martyr
of a vain error.

How many times in these moments of doubt and uncertainty
was I ready to abandon myself to despair! If I had ever spent an
entire month in this state, my life and I would have been done for.
But although these crises used to occur quite frequently, they
have always been short; and now even though I am not yet
completely free of them, they are so rare and so fleeting that they
do not even have the strength to disturb my calm. They are light
worries which affect my soul no more than a feather which falls
into the river can alter the water's current. I felt that to put the
same points I had previously settled into question all over again
presupposed that I had new insights, a more formed judgment, or
more zeal for the truth than at the time of my seeking. Since none
of these is or can apply to my case, there could be no solid reason
for me to prefer opinions which tempted me in a moment of
overwhelming despair but which would only augment my misery
to feelings adopted in the vigor of age, in complete maturity of
mind, after the most reflective examination, and in times when
the calm of my life left me no other dominant interest than that of
knowing the truth. Today, when my heart is constricted from
distress, my soul weighed down by vexations, my imagination
terrified, and my head troubled by the many frightful mysteries
which surround me; today, when all of my faculties, weakened by

old age and anxieties, have lost all of their spring shall I wantonly deprive myself of all the resources I had stored up? Shall I place more trust in my declining reason, thereby making myself unjustly unhappy, than in my full and vigorous reason, thereby getting compensation for the evils I suffer without having deserved them? No, I am not wiser, more learned, or of better faith than when I settled all those great questions. I was not unaware then of the difficulties I allow myself to be troubled by today. They did not stop me, and if some new ones arise which have not yet been perceived, they are the sophisms of a subtle metaphysics which is unable to weigh the eternal truths admitted at all times by all wise men, recognized by all nations, and engraved on the human heart in indelible characters. While meditating about these matters, I knew that human understanding, circumscribed by the senses, could not embrace them in their full extent. I therefore limited myself to what was within my reach, without getting myself involved in what went beyond it. This decision was reasonable; I embraced it previously and held myself to it with the assent of my heart and of my reason. On what grounds would I renounce it today when so many powerful reasons ought to keep me attached to it? What danger do I see in following it? What profit would I find in abandoning it? By adopting the doctrine of my persecutors, would I also adopt their morality? This rootless and fruitless morality which they pompously display in books or in some striking scene on the stage without any of it ever penetrating the heart or the reason? Or else this other secret and cruel morality, the inner doctrine of all of their initiates, for which the other only serves as a mask, which is the only one they follow in their conduct, and which they have so skillfully practiced with respect to me? This purely offensive morality is of no use for defense and is good only for aggression. How would it be of use to me in the condition to which they have reduced me? My innocence alone sustains me in my misfortunes; and how much unhappier would I make myself if, ridding myself of this single but powerful resource, I substituted wickedness for it? Would I reach their level in the art of harming; and were I to succeed, from what evil would the one I might do them relieve me? I would lose my self-esteem and gain nothing in its place.

Reasoning in this way with myself, I succeeded in no longer allowing myself to be shaken in my principles by captious arguments, by insoluble objections, or by difficulties which went beyond my reach and perhaps beyond that of the human mind. My own mind remains as firmly tempered as I was able to make it and has become so well accustomed to resting there in the shelter of my conscience that no foreign doctrine, old or new, can any longer move it or trouble my rest for an instant. Fallen into mental languor and heaviness, I have forgotten even the reasonings on which I grounded my belief and my maxims, but I will never forget the conclusions I drew from them with the approval of my conscience and of my reason, and I hold to them henceforth. Let all the philosophers come cavil in opposition: they will waste their time and labors. For the rest of my life, with regard to everything, I hold to the course I took when I was in more of a condition to choose well.

Serene in this disposition, I find in it, along with self-contentment, the hope and the consolation I need in my situation. It is not possible that a solitude so complete, so permanent, so sad in itself, that the ever perceptible and ever active animosity of the whole present generation, and that the indignities this generation incessantly overwhelms me with will not sometimes throw me into despondency. Faltering hope and discouraging doubts still return from time to time to trouble my soul and to fill it with sadness. At that moment, unable to perform the mental operations needed to reassure myself, I must recall my former resolutions. The cares, the attention, the heartfelt sincerity that I applied in forming them come back to my mind then and restore all of my confidence. Thus, I refuse all new ideas as baleful errors which have only a false appearance and are good only to trouble my rest.

Confined thus within the narrow sphere of my former knowledge, I do not share with Solon the happiness of being able to learn each day while growing old and I even ought to keep myself from the dangerous pride of wanting to learn what I am hence-forth unable to know well. But if few acquisitions remain for me to hope for in the way of useful insights, very important ones remain for me to make in the way of the virtues necessary for my condition. In that regard, it is time to endow and adorn my soul with learning it might carry away with it when, delivered from this body which clouds and blinds it and seeing truth without a veil, it will perceive the wretchedness of all the knowledge our false learned men are so vain about. It will bemoan the moments wasted in this life trying to acquire that knowledge. But patience, sweetness, resignation, integrity, and impartial justice are goods we carry away with ourselves and with which we can perpetually endow ourselves, not fearing that even in death they would lose their worth for us. It is to this unique and useful study that I devote the rest of my old age. I will be happy if by the progress I make with myself I learn to leave life not better, for that is not possible, but more virtuous than I entered it!

NOTES

1. Cf. Plutarch *Lives of Illustrious Men: Solon* 2.2 and 31.3; also Plato *Republic* 536c-d, *The Lovers* 133c, and *Laches* 188b and 189a.

Rousseau was apparently using the Jacques Amyot translation of Plutarch; see *Les Vies des Hommes Illustres: Solon* 3 and 65 ("Bibliothèque de la Pléiade"; Paris: Gallimard, 1951), vol. I, pp. 173 and 211. Actually, Plutarch quoted Solon as saying: "I continue to learn many things while growing old."

2. The French word is *moeurs* and connotes both morals in a precise sense and manners in a very general sense. Each time this word occurs, the way in which it is understood will be mentioned.

3. When Rousseau was ten years old, he and his cousin were put into the home of Pastor Jean-Jacques Lambercier to be educated. See *Confessions*, Book I, *OC* 1, pp. 12-24. Jean-Jacques Lambercier (1676-1738) was the pastor of the village of Bossey, a little village close to Geneva, from 1708 until his death.

4. After running away from Geneva in 1728, shortly before his sixteenth birthday, Rousseau sought refuge with M. de Pontverre who was the priest in the nearby village of Confignon. M. de Pontverre sent Rousseau on to Annecy and the home of Mme de Warens (see n. 5). The

Bishop of Annecy, Michel-Gabriel de Rossillon, then sent Rousseau to Turin where he was instructed in the Roman Catholic faith and eventually received as a member of that faith. See *Confessions*, Book II, *OC* 1, pp. 45-70.

5. Françoise-Louise de la Tour (1699-1762) married Sébastian-Isaac de Loys, lord of Vuarrens or Warens, at Lausanne in 1713 and left him in 1726. She took refuge at Évian and secured the help of Victor Amédée, king of Sardinia. Shortly thereafter she converted to the Roman Catholic faith and moved to Annecy. See *Confessions*, Book II and Book V, *OC* 1, pp. 49-50 and 197-98. For a fuller statement about Rousseau's relationship with Mme de Warens, see Tenth Walk.

6. François de Salignac de La Motte Fénélon (1651-1715) became archbishop of Cambrai in 1694. Shortly afterward, he was condemned for heresy by the Holy Court of Rome because his theological teachings placed too much emphasis on a mystical experience of God's presence. In the heated debate which preceded the condemnation, these views were characterized as a doctrine of pure love and labeled "quietistic" by Fénélon's detractors. In his book *Explication des Maximes des Saints sur la Vie Intérieure*, Fénélon gives the best account of these views. Although he submitted to the condemnation, Fénélon maintained his interest in mysticism and subsequently developed a mystical theology which has never been condemned by the church.

In this reference to Fénélon, Rousseau seems to be thinking of the popular notion of Fénélon's early mysticism.

7. Shortly after the success of the *First Discourse*, Rousseau began to think about changing his way of life. At that time, he was working as a secretary for Mme Dupin and her stepson, Charles-Louis Dupin de Francueil. M. de Francueil was a great benefactor of Rousseau and in his role as a receiver general of finances appointed Rousseau as cashier of finances. This is the post for which Rousseau did not think he was suited and which he resigned at the moment of his major reform. The account of his reform in dress given here is very similar to that given in the *Confessions*, Books VIII and IX, *OC* 1, pp. 356, 361-63, and 416-18; see also *Confessions*, Book VII, *OC* 1, pp. 293-94 and 342 for an account of his deeper relationship with M. de Francueil. In the second letter to M. de Malesherbes, Rousseau speaks of this same reform; *OC* 1, pp. 1135-1137.

Here, as elsewhere, Rousseau's dating is approximate. Since the reform took place in 1750 or 1751 and Rousseau was born in 1712, this could not have been after he reached forty.

8. This is a literal translation of the French word *sentiments*. Although the word is sometimes used to mean opinions or beliefs, as in the present context, it is so important to the central theme of the *Reveries*—Rousseau's identification of happiness as "the sentiment of existence" *(le*

sentiment de l'existence)—that, with one exception (see Fifth Walk, n. 13), it will always be translated as "sentiment" or "feeling."

9. In the *Émile,* Rousseau introduced Émile to religious matters by having a Savoyard priest speak of his own religious views. Rousseau supposedly heard this very teaching from a priest when he was slightly older than Émile. See *Émile,* Book IV, *OC* 4, pp. 558-635.

Much of the public furor over the *Émile* can be traced to the reaction which Catholics and Protestants alike had to this religious teaching and to what they took to be its political implications.

FOURTH WALK

Of the small number of books I still occasionally read, Plutarch is the author who grips and benefits me the most. He was the first I read in my childhood, he will be the last I read in my old age; he is almost the only author I have never read without gaining something. The day before yesterday, I was reading in his moral works the treatise "How to Profit from One's Enemies." [1] The same day, while arranging some pamphlets sent to me by their authors, I came across one of the journals of Father Rosier on the title page of which he had written these words: *"Vitam vero impendenti, Rosier."* [2] Too familiar with the turns of phrase of these gentlemen to be fooled by this one, I understood that by that semblance of politeness he had meant to be cruelly ironic toward me. But based on what? Why this sarcasm? What could I have done to warrant it? To profit from the lessons of the good Plutarch, I resolved to devote the walk of the following day to examining myself on lying and I came to it quite confirmed in the previously held opinion that the "know thyself" of the temple of Delphi was not as easy a maxim to follow as I had believed in my *Confessions.*

The following day, having set off to carry out this resolution, the first idea which came to me when I began to collect my thoughts was that of a dreadful lie I told in my [3] early youth, the memory of which has troubled me all my life and even comes in

43

my old age to sadden my heart again, already distressed as it is in so many other ways. This lie, in itself a great crime, must have become an even greater one because of its consequences—of which I have always been unaware, but which remorse has made me suppose as cruel as possible. However, considering only how I was disposed when telling it, this lie was simply an effect of mortification; and far from originating from an intention to harm her who was the victim of it, I can swear by Heaven that in the very instant this invincible shame tore it from me, I would joyfully have shed all my blood to turn the consequences on myself alone.[4] This is a delirium I can explain only by saying, and this is what I think and feel, that in that instant my timid natural temperament subjugated all the wishes of my heart.

The memory of this unfortunate act and the inextinguishable regrets it left me have inspired in me a horror for lying that should have preserved my heart from this vice for the rest of my life. When I adopted my motto, I felt deserving of it and I did not doubt I was worthy of it when, due to the phrase of Father Rosier, I began to examine myself more seriously.

Then, scrutinizing myself more carefully, I was quite surprised at the number of things of my own invention I recalled having passed off as true at the same time that, inwardly proud of my love for truth, I was sacrificing my security, my interests, and myself to it with an impartiality of which I know no other example among human beings.

What surprised me the most was that in recalling these fabrications, I felt no true repentance for them. I, in whose heart nothing offsets the horror of a falsehood, I, who would brave punishments if it were necessary to lie to avoid them—by what strange inconsistency did I thus lie with gaiety of heart, unnecessarily, without profit, and by what inconceivable contradiction did I feel not the least regret, I, who for fifty years have not ceased to be afflicted by remorse for a lie? I have never become inured to my faults. Moral instinct has always guided me well; my conscience has preserved its initial integrity; and even if it had been altered by bending to my interests, how—having preserved all its rectitude on those occasions when a man, forced by his passions, may at least excuse himself for his weakness—does it lose its rectitude only with regard to indifferent matters for which there is no excuse for vice? I saw that the accuracy of the judgment I had to make about myself on this point depended upon a solution to this problem and, after having thoroughly examined it, this is the manner in which I managed to explain it to myself.

I remember having read in a Philosophy Book [5] that to lie is to conceal a truth we ought to make manifest. From that definition, it indeed follows that to withhold a truth we have no obligation to declare is not to lie: but does he who, not content with not telling the truth in such a case, says the opposite, lie or not? According to the definition, we could not say that he lies. For if he gives counterfeit money to a man to whom he owes nothing, he undoubtedly deceives this man, but he does not rob him.

Two questions arise here for examination, each one very important. The first, when and how we owe the truth to another, since we do not always owe it. The second, whether there are cases in which we may innocently deceive. I am well aware that this second question is entirely settled: negatively in books, where the most austere morality costs the author nothing; affirmatively in society, where the morality of books is considered idle chatter impossible to put into practice. So let me leave these mutually contradicting authorities and seek to resolve these questions for myself by my own principles.

General and abstract truth is the most precious of all goods. Without it, man is blind; it is the eye of reason. By it, man learns to direct himself, to be what he ought to be, to do what he ought to do, to head toward his true end. Particular and individual truth is not always a good; it is sometimes an evil, very often an indifferent thing. The things important for a man to know and of which he must be aware to achieve happiness are perhaps not very numerous. But however numerous they are, they are a good which belongs to him, which he has a right to demand wherever he may find it, and which we cannot keep from him without committing the most iniquitous of all robberies, since it is one of those goods common to all and one whose disclosure does not deprive the person who makes it.

As for truths which have no usefulness whatever, neither for instruction nor in practice, how could they be a good which is owed, since they are not even a good? And since property is founded only on usefulness, where there is no possible usefulness, there can be no property. We can claim a piece of ground, however barren, because we can at least live on the soil. But whether an idle fact, indifferent in all regards and without consequence for anybody, be true or false is of no interest to anyone. In the moral order, nothing is useless, any more than in the physical order.[6] Nothing of that which is good for nothing can be owed; for a thing to be owed, it is necessary that it be, or that it may be, useful. Thus, the truth owed is that which concerns justice, and this sacred name of truth is debased if applied to vain things whose existence is indifferent to all and knowledge of which is useless for anything. Truth stripped of every kind of possible usefulness cannot therefore be a thing owed, and consequently he who suppresses it or disguises it does not lie at all.

But are there any of these truths so perfectly sterile as to be in every way useless for everything? That is another matter to discuss, to which I will come back shortly. As for now, let us go on to the second question.

Not to say what is true and to say what is false are two very different things, but the same effect can nonetheless result from them, for the result is assuredly quite the same every time that this effect is null. Wherever the truth is indifferent, the opposing error is also indifferent; from whence it follows that in such a case he who deceives by saying the opposite of the truth is no more unjust than he who deceives by not declaring it; for with useless truths, error is no worse than ignorance. Whether I believe the sand at the bottom of the sea to be white or red matters no more to me than being unaware of what color it is. How could we be unjust when we harm no one, since injustice consists only in the wrong done to someone else?

But to settle these questions in this summary manner still does not furnish me any sure, practical rule without many preliminary explanations necessary for applying it accurately in all cases which may present themselves. For if the obligation to tell the truth is founded only on its usefulness, how will I make myself the judge of this usefulness? Very often, what is to one person's advantage is to another person's prejudice; private interest is almost always opposed to public interest. How should we conduct ourselves in such cases? Must what is useful to an absent person be sacrificed to what is useful to the person to whom we are speaking? Must the truth which profits one person while harming another be kept quiet or uttered? Must we weigh everything we say only on the scale of the public good or only on that of distributive justice? And am I confident of understanding all the relationships of the matter well enough so as to apply the insights I possess only according to rules of equity? Moreover, in examining what we owe others have I sufficiently examined what we owe ourselves and what we owe truth for its own sake? If I do no harm to another in deceiving him, does it follow that I do none to myself, and is it sufficient to be never unjust in order to be always innocent?

How many embarrassing discussions we could easily extricate ourselves from by saying: let us always be truthful, whatever comes of it. Justice itself is in the truth of things; a lie is always iniquity; error is deceit whenever we set forth that which is not as the rule of what we ought to do or believe. And whatever consequence results from the truth, we are always blameless when we have told it, because we have put nothing of our own in it.

But that is to settle the question without answering it. The issue was not to declare whether it would always be good to tell the truth, but whether we were always under an equal obligation to do so; and according to the definition I was examining, supposing that we had no obligation, to distinguish the cases in which truth is strictly owed from those in which we can remain quiet about it without injustice and disguise it without lying. For I have found that such cases really existed. The issue, then, is to seek a sure rule for recognizing and accurately determining those cases.

But where can this rule and the proof of its infallibility be come by? . . .[7] In all difficult questions of morality like this, I have always found myself better off answering them according to the dictates of my conscience than according to the insights of my reason. Moral instinct has never deceived me: until now, it has remained sufficiently pure in my heart that I can trust it; and if in my conduct it sometimes remains silent in the face of my passions, it soon regains its dominion over them [8] in my memories. It is there that I judge myself with perhaps as much severity as I will be judged by the sovereign judge after this life.

To judge men's speeches by the consequences they produce is usually a poor way to assess their worth. Apart from the fact that these consequences are not always perceptible or easy to recognize, they vary infinitely, as do the circumstances surrounding these speeches. Only the intention of the speaker gives them their worth and determines their degree of malice or goodness. To say what is false is to lie only when there is an intent to deceive; and even an intent to deceive, far from always being joined to an intent to harm, sometimes has an entirely different goal. Still, to make a lie innocent it is not enough that there be no express intent to harm; there must, in addition, be certainty that the error into which those spoken to are thrown can harm neither them nor anyone in any way whatever. It is rare and difficult to come by such certainty; thus it is difficult and rare for a lie to be perfectly innocent. To lie for our own advantage is deceit; to lie for the advantage of another is fraud; to lie in order to harm is slander and is the worst kind of lie. To lie without profit or prejudice to ourselves or another is not to lie: it is not a lie; it is a fiction.

Fictions which have a moral purpose are called allegories or fables; and as their purpose is or must be only to wrap useful truths in easily perceived and pleasing forms, in such cases we hardly care about hiding the *de facto* lie, which is only the cloak of truth; and he who merely sets forth a fable as a fable in no way lies.

There are other purely idle fictions such as the greater part of stories and novels which, containing no truthful instruction, have no purpose but amusement. Stripped of all moral usefulness, their worth can be assessed only in terms of the intention of the one who invents them; and when he forcefully sets them forth as real truths, we can scarcely deny that they are true lies. But who has ever had great scruples about those lies and who has ever seriously reproached those who make them? If, for example, there is any moral purpose in the *Temple de Gnide* [9] it is thoroughly obfuscated and spoiled by voluptuous details and lascivious images. What has the author done to cover it with a gloss of modesty? He has pretended that this work was the translation of a Greek manuscript and has fashioned the story about the discovery of this manuscript in the manner most likely to persuade his readers of the truth of his tale. If that is not a very positive lie, then let someone tell me what lying is. But who has thought to accuse the author of a crime for this lie or to call him a deceiver for it?

In vain will it be said that it is only a joke; that the author, though insisting on it, did not wish to persuade anyone; that, in effect, he persuaded no one; and that the public did not doubt for a moment that he was really the author of the supposedly Greek work of which he passed himself off as the translator. I will reply that if it had no purpose, such a joke was only a very silly and childish prank; that a liar lies no less when he insists, even though he does not persuade; that it is necessary to differentiate between the learned public and the hordes of simple, credulous readers whom the story of the manuscript, narrated by a serious author with the appearance of good faith, really deceived and who fearlessly drank from a goblet of ancient form the poison of which they would at least have been suspicious had it been presented to them in a modern vessel.

Whether or not these distinctions are found in books, they occur no less in the heart of every man who keeps good faith with himself and who does not want to permit himself anything for which his conscience might reproach him. For to say a false thing to one's own advantage is to lie no less than to say it to the prejudice of another, even though the lie might be less criminal. To give an advantage to one who ought not to have it is to disturb order and justice; to attribute falsely to ourselves or to another an act from which praise or blame, inculpation or exoneration, might result is to do an unjust thing. Now everything which, contrary to the truth, hurts justice in any way whatsoever is a lie. That is the exact limit: but everything which, though contrary to truth, in no way concerns justice is only fiction; and I confess that anyone who blames himself for a pure fiction as if it were a lie has a more delicate conscience than I.

What we call white lies are real lies, because to deceive to the advantage either of another or of ourselves is no less unjust than to deceive to our detriment. Whoever praises or criticizes contrary to the truth lies whenever a real person is involved. If it involves an imaginary being, he can say whatever he wants about it without lying, unless he judges the morality of the facts he invents and judges falsely: for if he does not then lie about the fact, he lies against moral truth—a hundred times more respectable than that of facts.

I have seen some of these people whom the world calls truthful. All their truthfulness is exhausted in idle conversations where they faithfully cite places, times, and persons; where they do not allow themselves any fiction, do not embroider any circumstances, and exaggerate nothing. In everything not touching their self-interest, they are of the most inviolable fidelity in their narrations. But if it involves speaking about some affair which concerns them or of narrating some fact which touches them closely, all the colors are used so as to present things in the light most advantageous to them. And if a lie is useful to them and they abstain from telling it themselves, they skillfully suggest it and arrange things so that it is adopted without it possibly being imputed to them. Thus wills expediency; good-bye truthfulness.

The man I call *truthful* [10] does just the opposite. In perfectly indifferent things, the truth the other man then respects so strongly concerns him very little; and he will scarcely have scruples about amusing a group of people with contrived facts from which no unjust judgment results, either for or against anyone living or dead. But every speech which leads to profit or hurt, esteem or scorn, praise or blame for someone, contrary to justice and truth, is a lie which will never approach his heart, his mouth, or his pen. He is solidly *truthful,* even against his self-interest, although he prides himself little enough on being so in idle conversations. He is *truthful* in that he seeks to deceive no one, is as faithful to the truth which indicts him as to the truth which honors him, and never deceives for his advantage or to harm his enemy. The difference, then, between my *truthful* man and the other man is that the world's is very rigorously faithful to every truth which costs him nothing, but not beyond that, whereas mine never serves it so faithfully as when it is necessary to sacrifice himself for it.

But it might be objected: how can this laxness accord with that ardent love for truth for which I glorify him? Is that love false, then, since it admits so much alloy? No, it is pure and true. But it is only an emanation of the love of justice and never wants to be false, even though it is often fictitious. Justice and truth are two synonymous words in his mind, and he takes the one for the other indifferently. The holy truth his heart adores does not consist in indifferent deeds and useless names, but in faithfully rendering to each one what is owed in things which are truly his own, in imputing good or bad, in making retributions of honor or blame, praise and [11] disapproval. He is not false with respect to someone else, either because his sense of equity keeps him from it and because he does not want to harm anyone unjustly, or in his own favor, because his conscience keeps him from it and because he could not appropriate for himself what is not his own. Above all, he is jealous of his self-esteem; this is the good he can least get along without and he would feel a real loss in acquiring the esteem of others at its expense. He will, therefore, sometimes lie about indifferent things without scruple and without believing he is lying, but never to hurt or profit another or himself. In all that pertains to historic truths, in all that relates to men's conduct, to justice, to sociability, and to useful insights, he will keep himself and others from error as much as it depends on him. Any lie other than that is not one according to him. If the *Temple de Gnide* is a useful work, the story about the Greek manuscript is only a very innocent fiction; it is a lie very worthy of punishment, if the work is dangerous.

Such were my rules of conscience about lying and truth. My heart followed these rules mechanically before my reason had adopted them, and moral instinct alone applied them. The criminal lie of which poor Marion [12] was the victim has left me with ineradicable remorse which for the whole rest of my life has preserved me not only from every lie of this kind but from all those which could in any way whatever affect another person's interest and reputation. By thus generalizing the exclusion, I have exempted myself from weighing the advantage and prejudice exactly and from marking the precise limits of the harmful lie and of the white lie; in considering the one and the other as blameworthy, I have forbidden myself both.

In this, as in all the rest, my temperament has greatly influenced my maxims or rather my habits. For I have scarcely acted according to rules or in anything scarcely followed any other rule than the impulses of my natural temperament. It never occurred to me to tell a premeditated lie. I have never lied for my self-interest, but I have frequently lied out of shame in order to extricate myself from an embarrassing situation with respect to things which were indifferent or which at the most concerned me alone when, having to keep up a discussion, the slowness of my ideas and the aridity of my conversation forced me to resort to fictions so as to have something to say. When I absolutely have to speak and amusing truths do not come to mind soon enough, I concoct fables so as not to remain mute. But in inventing these fables, I take as much care as I can that they not be lies, that is to say, that they hurt neither the justice nor the truth owed and that they be only fictions indifferent to everyone and to me. It would certainly be my desire to substitute at least a moral truth for the truth of the facts, that is to say, to portray effectively the affections natural to the human heart and always to set forth some useful instruction, to make of them, in a word, moral tales or allegories. But more presence of mind than I have and more facility of speech would be needed to be able to make the babble of conversation benefit instruction. Its pace, more rapid than my ideas and almost always forcing me to speak before thinking, has frequently suggested to me foolish and inappropriate things of which my reason disapproved and which my heart disavowed as soon as they escaped from my mouth, but which, rushing ahead of my own judgment, could no longer be corrected by its censure.

It is still by this first, irresistible impulse of temperament that, in unforeseen and rapid moments, shame and timidity often wrest from me lies in which my will has no part at all, but which somehow rush ahead of it because of the need to reply at the moment. The deep impression of my memory of poor Marion can always fully restrain those which might be harmful to others, but not those which can serve to save me from some embarrassing situation when it is a question of myself, even though this is no less against my conscience and principles than those which might influence the lot of another.

I swear to Heaven that if in the following instant I could withdraw the lie which exculpates me and tell the truth which burdens me without bringing a new insult on my head by my retraction, I would wholeheartedly do it. But the shame of thus catching myself at fault still holds me back, and I repent my fault very sincerely without, however, daring to remedy it. An example will explain better what I wish to say and will show that I lie neither due to interest nor self-love, even less due to envy or spite, but solely due to embarrassment and mortification, sometimes knowing very well that this lie is recognized as such and serves me in no way at all.

Some time ago M. Foulquier persuaded me, against my normal practice, to bring my wife along for a dutch-treat dinner with him and his friend Benoit at Madame Vacassin's, who was a restaurant keeper; she, along with her two daughters, also dined with us.[13] In the middle of the dinner, the eldest, who had recently married and was pregnant, ventured to ask me brusquely, staring at me all the while, if I had had any children. Blushing up to my eyes, I replied that I had not had this good fortune. She smiled mischievously while looking at the rest of the group. All that was not very obscure, even for me.

It is first of all clear that this reply is in no way the one I should have wished to make, even if I had intended to deceive; for, given the disposition in which I saw her who addressed the question to me, I was very sure that my negative reply would change nothing in her opinion on this point. They expected this negative reply; they even provoked it so as to enjoy the pleasure of having made me lie. I was not dolt enough not to sense that. Two minutes later, the reply I should have made came to me of itself: "Now that is hardly a discreet question for a young lady to ask a man who has passed his life as a bachelor." By speaking in this way, without lying and without having to blush from any admission, I would have placed the laughers on my side and I would have given her a little lesson which naturally ought to have made her a little less impertinent in questioning me. I did nothing of the sort; I in no way said what should have been said; I said what should not have been said and which could serve me in nothing. Thus it is certain that neither my judgment nor my will dictated my reply, but that it was the mechanical effect of my embarrassment. Previously, I did not have this embarrassment and I would admit my faults with more frankness than shame, because I did not doubt that people saw what redeemed them and what I felt inside myself. But a mischievous eye distresses and disconcerts me: in becoming more unfortunate, I have become more timid, and I have never lied except due to timidity.

I never felt my natural aversion for lying better than when I was writing my *Confessions;* for it is there that temptations would have been frequent and strong, however little my propensity might have carried me to that side. But far from having kept silent about anything or concealed anything which went against me, by a twist of mind which I have difficulty explaining to myself and which perhaps comes from my estrangement from all imitation, I felt myself more readily inclined to lie in the contrary sense by accusing myself with too much severity than by excusing myself with too much indulgence; and my conscience assures me that one day I will be judged less severely than I have judged myself. Yes, with some proudness of soul, I declare and I feel that in that writing I have carried good faith, veracity, and frankness as far, further even—at least I believe so—than any other man has ever done. Feeling that the good surpassed the evil, it was in my interest to say everything; and I said everything.

I have never said less; I have sometimes said more, not with regard to facts but with regard to circumstances, and this kind of lie was the effect of a delirious imagination rather than an act of will. I am even wrong to call it a lie, for none of these additions was one. I wrote my *Confessions* when I was already old and disgusted with the vain pleasures of life, all of which I had sampled and whose emptiness my heart had thoroughly felt.[14] I wrote them from memory. This memory often failed me or only furnished me imperfect recollections, and I filled in the gaps with details which I dreamed up, details which supplemented these recollections, but which were never contrary to them. I liked to dwell upon the happy moments of my life, and I sometimes embellished them with ornaments that tender regrets furnished me. I spoke of things I had forgotten as it seemed to me they must have been, as they had perhaps been in effect, never contrary to the way I recalled that they had been. I sometimes lent foreign charms to the truth, but I never replaced it with a lie so as to palliate my vices or ascribe virtues to myself.

If, without thinking about it and by an involuntary movement, I sometimes hid my deformed side and depicted my good side, these reticences have been well compensated for by other more bizarre reticences which often made me remain more assiduously silent about the good than about the evil. This is a peculiarity of my natural temperament which it is quite excusable for men not to believe but which, entirely unbelievable as it is, is no less real. I have often told the evil in all its baseness. I have rarely told the good in all its charm and I have often been completely silent about it because it honored me too much and because in making my *Confessions,* I would appear to have made my eulogy. I described my youthful years without vaunting the happy qualities with which my heart was gifted and even suppressing the deeds which placed them too much in evidence. Here, I recall two from my early childhood, both of which indeed came to mind while I was writing but both of which I rejected solely for the reason I have just mentioned.[15]

Almost every Sunday I used to go spend the day at Les Pâquis at the house of M. Fazy, who had married one of my aunts and who had a cotton print works there.[16] One day I was in the drying house in the calender room, and I was looking at the printing cylinders: their gleam had caught my eye. Tempted to put my fingers on them, I was contentedly running them along the glossy

side of the cylinder when young Fazy, having slid inside the
wheel, gave it a half-quarter turn so skillfully that he got only the
tips of my two longest fingers; but it was enough for them to be
crushed at the tip and for both fingernails to remain there. I let
out a piercing cry, Fazy instantly turned the wheel back, but my
fingernails remained nonetheless attached to the cylinder and the
blood streamed from my fingers. Fazy, dismayed, cried out,
jumped out of the wheel, embraced me, and implored me to hush
my cries, adding that he was done for. At the height of my
suffering, his own touched me; I calmed myself; we went to the
carp pond where he helped me wash my fingers and stop my
bleeding with moss. Tearfully he begged me not to tell on him; I
promised him not to and kept my promise so well, that more than
twenty years later, no one knew what accident had scarred two of
my fingers; for they have always remained so. I was kept in bed
for more than three weeks and was unable to use my hand for
more than two months, but insisted all the while that a large
stone, in falling, had crushed my fingers.

> *Magnanima menzogna! or quando è il vero*
> *Sì bello che si possa a te preporre?* [17]

This accident was even more painful for me due to the circumstances, for it was the period of the drills when the bourgeoisie
was made to perform maneuvers, and we had formed a squad of
three other children of my age, with whom I was supposed to
perform the drill in uniform with the company from my neighborhood. I had the sorrow of hearing the company drummer with my
three comrades passing under my window while I was in bed.

My other story is very similar, but comes from a more advanced
age.

I was playing pall-mall at Plain-Palais with one of my comrades
named Pleince.[18] We quarreled about the game, fought with each
other, and during the fight he hit my bare head with such a well-
placed mallet blow that with a stronger hand he would have
knocked my brains out. I fell instantly. I have never in my life
seen an agitation similar to that of this poor boy upon seeing my

blood streaming through my hair. He thought he had killed me. He threw himself on me, embraced me, and squeezed me tightly as he burst into tears and uttered piercing cries. I returned his embrace with all my strength, while crying like him in a confused emotion which was not without some tenderness. Finally, he began to try to stop my continued bleeding; and seeing that our two handkerchiefs would not suffice, he led me to his mother who had a little garden near there. This good lady almost fainted upon seeing me in this state. But she was able to remain strong enough to bandage me; and after having bathed my wound well, she applied iris petals soaked in brandy, an excellent vulnerary much used in our region. Her tears and those of her son penetrated my heart to such an extent that for a long time I considered her as my mother and her son as my brother until having lost sight of both, I forgot them little by little.

I kept the same secret about this accident as about the other, and a hundred others of the same nature have happened to me in my life which I was not even tempted to speak about in my *Confessions,* so little was I seeking a way there to show off the good I felt to be part of my character. No, when I have spoken against the truth which was known to me, it has only been with respect to indifferent things and due more either to the embarrassment of speaking or to the pleasure of writing than to any motive of self-interest or of advantage or prejudice for another. And anyone who reads my *Confessions* impartially, if that ever happens, will sense that the admissions I make there are more humiliating and more painful to make than those about a greater evil which would be less shameful to admit and which I have not admitted because I have not done any.

From all these reflections, it follows that the commitment I made to truthfulness is founded more on feelings of uprightness and equity than on the reality of things, and that in practice I have more readily followed the moral dictates of my conscience than abstract notions of the true and the false. I have frequently concocted fables, but very rarely lied. In following these principles, I have given others many openings to criticize me. But I have wronged no one at all, and I have never given myself any more of an advantage than was due me. It is solely in that, it seems to me, that truth is a virtue. In every other respect it is only a metaphysical entity for us from which neither good nor evil results.

I do not, however, feel my heart to be sufficiently satisfied with these distinctions as to believe myself entirely irreprehensible. In weighing so carefully what I owed others, have I sufficiently examined what I owed myself? If it is necessary to be just to others, it is necessary to be true to oneself: that is an homage an honest man should render to his own dignity. When the sterility of my conversation forced me to make up for it with innocent fictions, I erred, because to amuse someone else, we should in no way degrade ourselves; and when, carried away by the pleasure of writing, I added invented ornaments to real things, I erred even more, because to adorn truth with fables is, in effect, to disfigure it.

But what makes me more inexcusable is the motto I had chosen. This motto obligated me more than any other man to a strict commitment to the truth, and it was not enough for me to sacrifice my interest and my inclinations to it in all things; I should also have sacrificed my weakness and my timid natural temperament to it. I should have had the courage and the strength to be truthful always, on every occasion, and never to let fictions or fables come out of a mouth and a pen which had been specifically dedicated to the truth. That, indeed, is what I should have said to myself upon adopting this proud motto and should always have repeated to myself as long as I dared to keep it. Never has falseness dictated my lies to me; they have all come from weakness; but that excuses me very little. With a weak soul we can at the most preserve ourselves from vice; but to dare to profess great virtues is to be arrogant and rash.

Those indeed are the reflections which would probably never have come to my mind if Father Rosier had not suggested them to me. It is undoubtedly very late to make use of them; but at least it is not too late to set my error straight and bring my will back in line: for henceforth that is all that depends on me. In this, then, and in all similar things, Solon's maxim [19] is applicable to all ages, and it is never too late to learn, even from one's enemies, to be wise, true, modest, and to presume less of oneself.

NOTES

1. Plutarch *Moralia:* "How to Profit from One's Enemies." In trying to explain himself to M. de Malesherbes, Rousseau spoke about the influence Plutarch had on him: "When I was six, I got my hands on Plutarch; by the time I was eight, I knew him by heart; I had read all of his novels [namely, *The Lives of Illustrious Men*], and they caused me to shed buckets of tears before the age in which the heart becomes interested in novels. From that reading, my heart acquired this heroic and romantic bent which has done nothing but increase until now and which has made me completely disgusted with everything, except that which resembled my fantasies." *Four Letters to M. de Malesherbes* 2, *OC* 1, p. 1134. See also *Confessions,* Book I, *OC* 1, p. 9: "Plutarch, above all, was my favorite author." And in the *Dialogues, OC* 1, p. 819, Rousseau said of Jean-Jacques: "Plutarch's [*Lives of*] *Illustrious Men* was his first reading at an age when children rarely know how to read."

2. This Latin phrase, "to the one who consecrates his life to truth," was used to dedicate the copy of the journal to Rousseau. It is a modification of the verse from Juvenal *(Satires* 4.91) which Rousseau took as his motto: *vitam impendere vero,* that is, "to consecrate one's life to truth." He first used the motto in the *Letter to M. d'Alembert;* see *Politics and the Arts, Letter to M. d'Alembert on the Theatre,* trans. Allan Bloom (Ithaca: Cornell University Press, 1960), p. 131 and note. Just before presenting Émile with the religious teaching which he placed in the mouth of a Savoyard priest, Rousseau assured the reader that he was mindful of his motto; see *Émile,* Book IV, *OC* 4, p. 558 and Third Walk. Similarly, when he published the *Letters Written from the Mountain* in 1764, he placed this motto on the title page.

More than likely, Rousseau's phrase, "one of the journals of Father Rosier," is a reference to the August 1776 issue of *Observations sur la Physique,* edited by Father Jean Rozier. (Although Rozier is the correct spelling of the name, Rousseau consistently spelled it "Rosier." I have preserved his spelling in the text.) Father Rozier may have sent this issue of the journal to Rousseau because it contained an announcement about the formation of a Society for the Arts in Geneva accompanied by an announcement that each year the society would sponsor a contest for essays written in response to questions "whose solution appears most important for improving Arts and Economics" and would give an award for the best essay; see *Observations sur la Physique* (August 1776), pp. 145-51.

Father Jean Rozier (1734-93) was ordained as a Jesuit and was primarily interested in botany and agriculture. An author of many books on these subjects, he became editor of the *Journal de Physique et d'Histoire Naturelle* in the late 1760s and changed its title to *Observations sur la Physique, sur l'Histoire Naturelle, et sur les Arts* in 1771.

3. Reading *ma* with the manuscript.

4. Rousseau is referring to the time shortly after his religious conversion when he was still in Turin and employed in the household of the Comtesse de Vercellis. In the confusion following her death, Rousseau stole one of her ribbons; he claimed that he stole it as a keepsake. The ribbon was declared missing by the chambermaid of the comtesse and found among Rousseau's personal effects. Interrogated before all the members of the household, Rousseau's mortification led him to deny having stolen the ribbon and to insist that a young kitchen maid, Marion (whose name is mentioned later in this walk), had given it to him. He persisted adamantly in his tale and told it so convincingly that Marion's denials were not believed; because of the doubt about the true culprit, both Rousseau and Marion were dismissed. Evidence that this lie did haunt him throughout his life is that it is presented in the *Confessions* as one of the three great and painful confessions he felt obliged to make as proof of his veracity. Cf. *Confessions,* Book II, *OC* 1, pp. 80-87, esp. pp. 84-87; also *Confessions,* Books I and III, *OC* 1, pp. 15-18 and 129.

5. Rousseau's capitalization.

6. This and the next two sentences are found on the margin of the manuscript.

7. Rousseau's punctuation.

8. Reading *elles* with the manuscript.

9. Montesquieu published the *Temple de Gnide (Temple of Cnidus)* in 1725. He took every possible precaution to keep the work from being attributed to him. Cnidus, located in Caria in Asia Minor, was devoted to the worship of Aphrodite; the temple contained a famous statue of her by Praxiteles. See Pliny *Natural History* xxxvi. 4.20.

10. Rousseau's emphasis here and throughout the paragraph.

11. Reading *et* with the manuscript.

12. See n. 4.

13. Nothing is known of M. Foulquier, and except for the assertion that the person referred to here as Dame Vacassin was really named Vaucassin, nothing is known of her. For this assertion, see Comte Antoine-Joseph Barruel-Beauvert, *Vie de J.-J. Rousseau* (London, 1789), p. 377.

All that is known of M. Benoit is that he handled the manuscripts relating to music for the posthumous edition of Rousseau's works. According to letters discovered by Spink, the manuscript of the *Reveries* was altered at Benoit's insistence: since it was he who had introduced Foulquier to Rousseau, he felt slighted by being referred to here only as Foulquier's friend and prevailed upon the Marquis de Girardin, at whose home in Ermenonville Rousseau died and who had possession of the manuscript of the *Reveries* for some time, to strike the words *son ami* (his friend) from this passage. That emendation has now been corrected. See J.-J. Rousseau, *Les Rêveries du Promeneur Solitaire*, ed. J. S. Spink (Paris: Société des Textes Français Modernes, 1948), p. 78, note 2, and pp. xlv-xlvi.

Rousseau's wife was Marie-Thérèse Le Vasseur (1721-1801). They lived together from 1745 until Rousseau's death in 1778 and were married in 1768; see Preface, pp. xiv and xvii.

14. For some time prior to 1761, Marc-Michel Rey, Rousseau's editor, had been urging him to write his memoirs (see First Walk, n. 11), but Rousseau did not actually begin to write them until 1764, when he was at least fifty-two years old.

15. From here until the end of the Walk, the handwriting in the manuscript is small and almost cramped, as though Rousseau added this section afterward.

16. Antoine Fazy (1681-1731) became a resident of Geneva in 1701. He had learned how to manufacture printed cotton in Holland and founded his own factory at Les Pâquis in 1706. Les Pâquis was a few miles north of the city walls on the lake at that time; today, it is part of Geneva.

17. Torquato Tasso, *Jerusalem Delivered* 2.22:

> Magnanimous lie! Now when is the truth so
> beautiful that it can be preferred to thee?

The context should be examined.

18. Pall-mall is something like croquet: a ball of boxwood was hit with a wooden mallet toward a raised ring at the end of an alley, the object being to drive the ball through the ring with the fewest number of strokes.

Plain-Palais is a large esplanade that has been part of Geneva since its earliest days. Located between the Rhône and the Arve rivers, Plain-Palais was outside the southern walls of the city at the time of Rousseau's youth and could be reached by the Porte Neuve. What exists of the esplanade today is a large area somewhat resembling a parallelogram bordered by the Avenue du Mail, the Avenue Henri Dunant, and the Boulevard Georges Faron.

Nothing is known of Rousseau's friend Pleince.

19. See Third Walk, n. 1.

FIFTH WALK

Of all the places I have lived (and I have lived in some charming ones),[1] none has made me so truly happy nor left me such tender regrets as St. Peter's Island in the middle of Lake Bienne. This small island, which is called Hillock Island in Neuchâtel, is quite unknown, even in Switzerland. As far as I know, no traveler mentions it. However, it is very pleasant and singularly placed for the happiness of a man who likes to cut himself off; for although I am perhaps the only one in the world whose destiny has imposed this on him as a law, I cannot believe myself to be the only one who has so natural a taste—even though I have not found it in anyone else thus far.

The banks of Lake Bienne are wilder and more romantic than those of Lake Geneva, because the rocks and woods border the water more closely; but they are not less cheerful. If the fields and vineyards are less cultivated, and if there are fewer towns and houses, there is also more natural greenery, more meadows, grove-shaded retreats, more frequent contrasts, and more variety in the terrain. As there are no large thoroughfares suitable for coaches on these happy shores, the countryside is seldom frequented by travelers; but it is interesting for solitary contemplators who like to delight in the charms of nature at leisure and collect their thoughts in a silence troubled by no noise other than the cry of eagles, the intermittent chirping of a few birds, and the rushing of torrents as they fall from the mountain. This beautiful basin almost circular in form has two small islands in its center, one inhabited and cultivated, almost half a league around; the other smaller, uninhabited, and uncultivated, and which will ultimately be destroyed because earth is constantly taken away from it to repair the destruction waves and storms make to the large one. Thus it is that the substance of the weak is always used for the advantage of the powerful.

On the island there is only a single house, but a large, pleasant, and comfortable one which, like the island, belongs to Bern Hospital and in which a tax collector lives with his family and servants. He maintains a large farmyard, a pigeon house, and fishponds. Despite its smallness, the island is so varied in its terrain and vistas that it offers all kinds of landscapes and permits all kinds of cultivation. You can find fields, vineyards, woods, orchards, and rich pastures shaded by thickets and bordered by every species of shrubbery, whose freshness is preserved by the adjacent water. A high terrace planted with two rows of trees runs the length of the island, and in the middle of this terrace a pretty reception hall has been built where the inhabitants of the neighboring banks gather and come to dance on Sundays during harvests.

This is the island on which I sought refuge after the stoning at Môtiers.[2] I found the sojourn on it so charming, I led a life there so suitable to my temper that, resolved to end my days there, I had no worry other than their not letting me execute this project which did not fit in with the one of transporting me to England—a project whose first effects I was already feeling.[3] Because of the forebodings that troubled me, I wanted them to make this refuge a perpetual prison for me, to confine me to it for life, and—removing every possibility and hope of getting off it—to forbid me any kind of communication with the mainland so that being unaware of all that went on in the world I might forget its existence and that it might also forget mine.

They let me spend scarcely two months on this island,[4] but I would have spent two years there, two centuries, and the whole of eternity without being bored for a moment, even though besides my helpmate, I had no companionship there other than that of the tax collector, his wife, and his servants, who in truth were all very worthy people but nothing more; but that was precisely what I needed. I consider these two months the happiest time of my life, so happy that it would have contented me for my whole existence without the desire for another state arising for a single instant in my soul.

Now what was this happiness and in what did its enjoyment consist? From the description of the life I led there, I will let all the men of this century guess at it. The precious *far niente* [5] was the first and the principal enjoyment I wanted to savor in all its sweetness, and all I did during my sojourn was in effect only the delicious and necessary pursuit of a man who has devoted himself to idleness.

The hope that they would ask for nothing better than to leave me in this isolated spot where I had ensnared myself on my own, which it was impossible for me to leave without help and surely without being noticed, and where I could have communication or correspondence only by the assistance of the people who surrounded me, this hope, I say, led me to hope I would end my days there more peacefully than I had spent them until then. And the idea that I would have time to adapt myself to it in complete leisure caused me to begin by not adapting at all. Transported there abruptly, alone, and destitute, I had my housekeeper, my books, and my few furnishings brought over, one after the other. And I had the pleasure of unpacking nothing, leaving my boxes and my trunks as they had arrived and living in the abode in which I counted on finishing my days as in an inn I would have to leave on the following day. All things, such as they were, went along so well that to want to arrange them better would have been to spoil something. Above all, one of my greatest delights was to leave my books well packed up and to have no writing table. When wretched letters forced me to take up a pen to reply, I grudgingly borrowed the tax collector's writing table and then hastened to return it, in the vain hope of not needing to borrow it again. Instead of depressing papers and heaps of old books, I filled my room with flowers and dried plants; for I was then in my first

botanical fervor for which Dr. d'Ivernois [6] had given me an inclination and which soon became a passion. Wanting no more
toilsome work, I needed something amusing which would please
me and require only as much trouble as a lazy man likes to take. I
set about doing the *Flora petrinsularis* [7] and describing all the
plants of the island, without omitting a single one, in sufficient
detail to occupy myself for the rest of my days. It is said that a
German did a book about a lemon peel; I would have done one
about each stalk of hay of the meadows, each moss of the woods,
each lichen that carpets the rocks; in short, I did not want to
leave a blade of grass or a plant particle which was not amply
described. As a result of this fine project, every morning after
breakfast, which we all had together, I would go off, a magnifying
glass in hand and my *Systema naturae* [8] under my arm, to visit a
district of the island, which I had divided into small squares for
this purpose, with the intention of covering them one after the
other in each season. Nothing is more singular than the raptures
and ecstasies I felt with each observation I made on plant structure and organization, as well as on the role of the sexual parts in
sporulation, which was then a completely new system for me. I
was enchanted to discover generic features of which I previously
had not the slightest idea and to verify them on common species,
while waiting for rarer ones to offer themselves to me. The fork-
ing of the two long stamens of the self-heal, the spring of those of
the nettle and the pellitory, the explosion of the fruit of the
balsam and the pod of the boxwood, a thousand little games of
sporulation which I observed for the first time, filled me with joy
and I went around asking whether one had seen the horns of the
self-heal plant like La Fontaine asking whether one had read
Habakkuk.[9] At the end of two or three hours I would come back
laden with an ample harvest, a stock with which to amuse myself
after lunch in the lodging in case of rain. I would use the rest of
the morning to go with the tax collector, his wife, and Thérèse to
visit their workers and their crops, quite often joining my hand
with theirs in work; and often the residents of Bern who came to
see me found me perched in large trees, girdled with a sack that I
would fill with fruits and then lower to the ground with a rope.

My morning exercise and the good temper which is inseparable
from it made the pause for lunch very enjoyable. But when it took
too long and good weather beckoned, I could not wait so long.
While they were still at the table, I would slip away and go throw
myself alone into a boat that I rowed to the middle of the lake
when the water was calm; and there, stretching myself out full-
length in the boat, my eyes turned to heaven, I let myself slowly
drift back and forth with the water, sometimes for several hours,
plunged in a thousand confused, but delightful, reveries which,
even without having any well-determined or constant object,
were in my opinion a hundred times preferable to the sweetest
things I had found in what are called the pleasures of life. Often,
warned by the setting of the sun that it was the hour of retreat, I
would find myself so far from the island that I was forced to work
with all my might to get back before nightfall. Other times,
instead of heading out to open water, I took pleasure in gliding
along the verdant banks of the island where the limpid waters and
fresh shadows often induced me to bathe. But one of my most
frequent sailings was from the large to the small island. There I
would debark and spend the afternoon, sometimes in very limited
promenades through great round-leaved sallow, alder-buckthorn,
willow weed, shrubs of every sort, and sometimes setting myself
on the summit of a sandy knoll covered with grass, common
thyme, flowers, even cockscomb and clover that had most likely
been sown there some time ago and were very suitable for hous-
ing rabbits which could multiply in peace there without fearing
anything and without doing any harm. I passed this idea on to the
tax collector who had male and female rabbits brought from
Neuchâtel, and in great pomp his wife, one of his sisters, Thérèse,
and I went to settle them on the small island where they began to
breed before my departure and where they will undoubtedly have
thrived, if they have been able to withstand the rigor of the
winters. The founding of this little colony was a festival. The pilot
of the Argonauts [10] was no prouder than I, leading the company
and the rabbits in triumph from the large island to the small. And
I noted with pride that the tax collector's wife, who dreaded
water excessively and always felt uncomfortable upon it, em-

barked under my leadership with confidence and showed no fear during the crossing.

When the lake was too rough for boating, I would spend my afternoon wandering over the island searching right and left for plants, sometimes sitting down in the most cheerful and solitary nooks to dream at my ease and sometimes on terraces and knolls to let my eyes wander over the superb and breathtaking view of the lake and its shores, crowned on one side by the nearby mountains and on the other spread out onto rich and fertile plains over which my sight extended all the way up to the more distant, bluish mountains which blocked it.

When evening approached, I would come down from the heights of the island and gladly go sit in some hidden nook along the beach at the edge of the lake. There, the noise of the waves and the tossing of the water, captivating my senses and chasing all other disturbance from my soul, plunged it into a delightful reverie in which night would often surprise me without my having noticed it. The ebb and flow of this water and its noise, continual but magnified at intervals, striking my ears and eyes without respite, took the place of the internal movements which reverie extinguished within me and was enough to make me feel my existence with pleasure and without taking the trouble to think. From time to time some weak and short reflection about the instability of things in this world arose, an image brought on by the surface of the water. But soon these weak impressions were erased by the uniformity of the continual movement which lulled me and which, without any active assistance from my soul, held me so fast that, called by the hour and agreed-upon signal, I could not tear myself away without effort.

After supper, when the evening was fine, we would all go for a little walk together on the terrace to breathe in the air and the freshness of the lake. We would relax in the pavilion, laugh, chat, sing some old song which was easily as good as the modern rigmarole, and finally go to bed content with our day desiring only a similar one the next day.

Leaving aside unexpected and importunate visits, this is the way I spent my time on this island during my sojourn there. Tell me now what is so alluring about it as to arouse such intense, tender, and lasting regrets in my heart that at the end of fifteen years [11] it is impossible for me to think of that cherished abode without each time feeling myself carried away again by waves of desire.

In the vicissitudes of a long life, I have noticed that the periods of sweetest enjoyment and most intense pleasures are, nevertheless, not those whose recollection most attracts and touches me. Those short moments of delirium and passion, however intense they might be, are, even with their intensity, still only scattered points along the path of life. They are too rare and too rapid to constitute a state of being; and the happiness for which my heart longs is in no way made up of fleeting instants, but rather a simple and permanent state which has nothing intense in itself but whose duration increases its charm to the point that I finally find supreme felicity in it.

Everything is in continual flux on earth. Nothing on it retains a constant and static form, and our affections, which are attached to external things, necessarily pass away and change as they do. Always ahead of or behind us, they recall the past which is no longer or foretell the future which often is in no way to be: there is nothing solid there to which the heart might attach itself. Thus, here-below we have hardly anything but transitory pleasure. As for happiness which lasts, I doubt that it is known here. In our most intense enjoyments, there is hardly an instant when the heart can truly say to us: *I would like this instant to last forever.*[12] And how can we call happiness a fleeting state which leaves our heart still worried and empty, which makes us long for something beforehand or desire something else afterward?

But if there is a state in which the soul finds a solid enough base to rest itself on entirely and to gather its whole being into, without needing to recall the past or encroach upon the future; in which time is nothing for it; in which the present lasts forever without, however, making its duration noticed and without any trace of time's passage; without any other sentiment of deprivation or of enjoyment, pleasure or pain, desire or fear, except that alone of our existence, and having this sentiment alone fill it completely; as long as this state lasts, he who finds himself in it can call himself happy, not with an imperfect, poor, and relative happiness such as one finds in the pleasures of life, but with a sufficient, perfect, and full happiness which leaves in the soul no emptiness it might feel a need to fill. Such is the state in which I often found myself during my solitary reveries on St. Peter's Island, either lying in my boat as I let it drift with the water or seated on the banks of the tossing lake; or elsewhere, at the edge of a beautiful river or of a brook murmuring over pebbles.

What do we enjoy in such a situation? Nothing external to ourselves, nothing if not ourselves and our own existence. As long as this state lasts, we are sufficient unto ourselves, like God. The sentiment of existence, stripped of any other emotion, is in itself a precious sentiment of contentment and of peace which alone would suffice to make this existence dear and sweet to anyone able to spurn all the sensual and earthly impressions which incessantly come to distract us from it and to trouble its sweetness here-below. But most men, agitated by continual passions, are little acquainted with this state and, having tasted it only imperfectly for a few moments, preserve only an obscure and confused idea of it which does not let them feel its charm. It would not even be good in the present structure of things that, avid for these sweet ecstasies, they should become disgusted with the active life their ever recurring needs prescribe to them as a duty. But an unfortunate person who has been cut off from human society and who can no longer do anything here-below useful and good for another or for himself can find compensations for all the human felicities in this state, compensations which fortune and men could not take away from him.

It is true that these compensations cannot be felt by all souls nor in all situations. The heart must be at peace and no passion come to disturb its calm. The one who experiences them must be favorable to them, as must be the conjunction of the surrounding objects. What is needed is neither absolute rest nor too much agitation, but a uniform and moderated movement having neither jolts nor lapses. Without movement, life is only lethargy. If the movement is irregular or too strong, one is awakened. By reminding us of the surrounding objects, it destroys the charm of the reverie and tears us away from within ourselves, bringing us instantly back under the yoke of fortune and men and returning us to an awareness [13] of our misfortunes. An absolute silence leads to sadness. It offers an image of death. Then the assistance of a cheerful imagination is necessary and comes naturally enough to those whom Heaven has favored. Movement which does not come from outside then occurs inside us. One rests less, it is true, but also more pleasurably, when light and sweet ideas only skim the surface of the soul, so to speak, without disturbing its depths. Only enough ideas are needed to remember our own self while forgetting all our troubles. This kind of reverie can be enjoyed wherever we can be quiet, and I have often thought that in the Bastille—even in a dungeon where no object would strike my sight—I would still have been able to dream pleasurably.

But admittedly that was done better and more pleasurably on a fertile and solitary island, naturally closed off and separated from the rest of the world, where nothing but cheerful images came to me; where nothing recalled depressing memories to me; where the society of the small number of inhabitants was gentle and sweet, without being so interesting as to occupy me continuously; where I could, in short, give myself up all day long to the preoccupations of my liking or to luxurious idleness, without hindrance and care. It was undoubtedly a perfect occasion for a dreamer who, knowing how to nourish himself with pleasurable fancies in the middle of the most unpleasant objects, could satiate himself with them at his ease by making everything which really struck his senses come together in them. Upon emerging from a long and sweet reverie, upon seeing myself surrounded by greenery, flowers, and birds, and letting my eyes wander in the distance on the romantic shores which bordered a vast stretch of crystal-clear water, I assimilated all these lovely objects to my fictions; and finally finding myself brought back by degrees to myself and to what surrounded me, I could not mark out the point separating the fictions from the realities; it was this thorough conjunction of everything which made the absorbed and solitary life I led during this beautiful sojourn so dear to me. If it could only occur again! If

I could only go end my days on this beloved island without ever coming off it or ever seeing there any inhabitant of the continent to remind me of all the different calamities they have taken pleasure in heaping on me for so many years! They would soon be forever forgotten. Undoubtedly, they would not likewise forget me. But what would that matter to me, provided they had no way to come there to disturb my rest? Delivered from all the earthly passions the tumult of social life engenders, my soul would frequently soar up above this atmosphere and commune in advance with the celestial intelligences whose number it hopes to augment in a short while. I know men will be careful not to give me back such a sweet refuge when they did not want to leave me there. But at least they will not prevent me from transporting myself there each day on the wings of my imagination and from enjoying for a few hours the same pleasure as if I were still living there. The sweetest thing I would do would be to dream there at my ease. In dreaming that I am there, do I not do the same thing? I do even more: to the allure of an abstract and monotonous reverie, I join charming images which make it more intense. In my ecstasies, their objects often eluded my senses. Now the deeper my reverie is, the more intensely it depicts them to me. I am often more in the midst of them and even more pleasantly so than when I was really there. The misfortune is that to the extent that my imagination cools this comes with more labor and does not last as long. Alas! it is when we begin to leave our skin that it hinders [14] us the most.

NOTES

1. Rousseau's parentheses.
2. Rousseau's house in Môtiers was attacked in the middle of the night of September 6, 1765, by people throwing rocks. The damage was so extensive and the hostile intention so evident that he left Môtiers as soon as possible.
After fleeing from Montmorency on June 9, 1762, Rousseau had gone to Yverdon to visit his old friend Daniel Roguin. Although Roguin eventually persuaded him to remain in Yverdon, even offering him a little house in his garden, the authorities would not permit him to stay there.

Yverdon was within the territory of Bern and thus subject to the Senate of Bern, which ordered that Rousseau be expelled from all of its territory by July 9.

Roguin's niece, Madame Julie-Ann-Marie Boy de la Tour, then offered Rousseau her son's house in Môtiers. Located in the Val-de-Travers, Môtiers was part of the county of Neuchâtel and under the sovereignty of Frederick II. Rousseau was given permission to stay in Môtiers and about a year later was even provided with a letter of naturalization. However, shortly after the publication of the *Letters Written from the Mountain*, the people of Môtiers began to show hostility toward Rousseau. This hostility culminated in the September 6 attack on his house. See *Confessions*, Books XI and XII, *OC 1*, pp. 587-637.

3. David Hume took an interest in Rousseau's difficulties from the beginning, either because of his friendship with Comtesse Marie-Charlotte de Boufflers and Marquise Marie-Madeleine de Verdelin, ladies who were on warm terms with Rousseau, or because of his acquaintance with the Encyclopédistes. At any rate, he communicated an offer of hospitality to Rousseau by means of Mme de Boufflers and Mme de Verdelin and wrote Rousseau a number of times to renew his offer. Rousseau finally went to England in 1766, accompanied by Hume. Sometime later he quarreled violently with Hume and eventually left England convinced that the whole attempt to induce him to seek refuge in England was part of the plot to discredit and harass him and that all those who had urged him to go to England were members of the plot. He arrived in London on January 13, 1766 and returned to France on May 25, 1767.

4. Rousseau arrived at St. Peter's Island on September 12, 1765. On October 16, the Petit-Conseil of Bern ordered him to leave the island and the territory. Despite his request that he be held in captivity on the island, he was ordered to leave immediately and did so on October 25. See *Confessions*, Book XII, *OC 1*, pp. 646-48. Rousseau's account of his sojourn on St. Peter's Island in the *Confessions*, Book XII, *OC 1*, pp. 637-48 (see Appendix B of this work), should be compared with the account given here.

5. Italian expression: "to do nothing" or "doing nothing."

6. Jean-Antoine d'Ivernois (1703-65) was a medical doctor and botanist; he made a catalogue of the flora of the Neuchâtel Jura Mountain region. Rousseau made his acquaintance at Môtiers in 1764, and d'Ivernois introduced him to botany and to the work of Linnaeus (see n. 8).

7. That is to say, the flora of St. Peter's Island. Books about the flora of a region were frequently given such titles.

8. Carl Linnaeus (1707-78) is famous for having introduced efficient procedures for the naming and classifying of plants and animals at a period when rapid discoveries of new species were occurring. In 1735 his major work on the naming and classifying of plants, *Systema naturae*, appeared.

9. Rousseau has substituted the Book of Habakkuk for the Book of Baruch. Apparently, Racine once tried to instill religious sentiment in La Fontaine, but succeeded only in inspiring him with a passion for Baruch. In describing La Fontaine and the incident, Racine's son, Louis, says:

"Either he simply would not speak or else would want to speak only about Plato, whom he had carefully studied in Latin translation. He sought to know about the ancients by conversation and benefited from conversing with my father who sometimes gave him selections from Homer to read in Latin translation. There was no need to make him feel the beauty of it; he seized it: everything which was beautiful struck him. One day my father took him to vespers and, noticing that the service seemed too long for him, gave him a volume of the Bible containing the lesser prophets so as to occupy him. He fell upon the prayer for Jews in Baruch and, his admiration for Baruch driving away his restlessness, he said to my father: 'Baruch was a real genius. Who was he?' The next day and for several days afterwards, whenever he met someone he knew in the street, after the customary greetings he would raise his voice and say: 'Have you read Baruch? He was a real genius.' " *Mémoires sur la Vie et les Ouvrages de Jean Racine* in *Oeuvres Complètes de Jean Racine* (Paris: Lefèvre, 1820), vol. 1, pp. cxl-cxli.

10. The Argonauts were the warriors who sailed to Colchis under the leadership of Jason in quest of the Golden Fleece.

11. The interval is really only twelve years, for the Fifth Walk was probably written in 1777.

12. Rousseau's emphasis.

13. Literally, "to the sentiment" *(au sentiment)*.

14. The verb is *offusquer* (literally, "to obfuscate") and has been translated elsewhere in the text as "to cloud."

SIXTH WALK

There is hardly any of our automatic impulses whose cause we could not find in our heart, if we only knew how to look for it.[1] Yesterday, crossing the new boulevard to go look for plants on the Gentilly side of the Bièvre, I made a turn to the right in coming up to the Enfer tollgate and, getting out into the countryside, I went along the road to Fontainebleau up to the bluffs beside this little river.[2] In itself, this route was of no significance; but on recalling that I had automatically made the same detour several times, I looked within myself for its cause and I could not keep from laughing when I managed to unravel it.

At a corner of the boulevard near the Enfer tollgate exit, there is a woman who sets up a stand every day in the summer to sell fruit, herb tea, and rolls. This woman has a very nice, but lame little boy who, hobbling along on his crutches, goes about quite graciously asking passersby for alms. I had become slightly acquainted with this little fellow; each time I passed, he did not fail to come pay his little compliment, always followed by my little offering. At first I was charmed to see him; I gave to him very good heartedly and for some time continued to do so with the same pleasure, quite frequently even prompting and listening to his little prattle which I found enjoyable. This pleasure, having gradually become a habit, was inexplicably transformed into a kind of duty I soon felt to be annoying, especially because of the

74

preliminary harangue to which I had to listen and in which he never failed to call me Monsieur Rousseau many times, to show that he knew me well. But to the contrary, that only taught me that he knew me no more than those who had instructed him. From that time on I passed by there less willingly and finally I automatically got in the habit of making a detour when I came close to this crossing.

That is what I discovered by reflecting on it; for until then, none of this had clearly entered my thoughts. This observation recalled to me a multitude of others, one after the other, which entirely convinced me that the true and primary motives of most of my actions are not as clear even to me as I had long imagined. I know and feel that to do good is the truest happiness the human heart can savor; but it is a long time now since this happiness has been put out of my reach, and it is not in such a wretched lot as mine that one can hope to perform wisely and fruitfully a single really good action. The greatest care of those who rule my fate having been to make everything appear only false and deceptive to me, an occasion for virtue is never anything but a lure they hold out to draw me into the snare they want to enlace me in. I know that; I know that the only good which might henceforth be within my power is to abstain from acting, from fear of doing evil without wanting to and without knowing it.

But there were happier times when, following the impulses of my heart, I could sometimes make another heart content; and I owe myself the honorable testimony that, whenever I was able to savor this pleasure, I found it sweeter than any other. This tendency was intense, true, pure, and nothing in my most secret inner self ever belied it. However, I have often felt the burden of my own good deeds by the chain of duties they later entailed. Then the pleasure disappeared, and the continuation of the very attentiveness which had charmed me at first no longer struck me as anything but an almost unbearable annoyance. During my brief moments of prosperity, many people appealed to me; and despite the multitude of favors they asked of me, none of them was ever turned away. But from these first good deeds, which my heart poured out effusively, were forged chains of subsequent liabilities

I had not foreseen and whose yoke I could no longer shake off. In the eyes of those who received them, my first favors were only a pledge for those which were supposed to follow; and as soon as some unfortunate man had hooked me with my own good deed, that was it from then on. This first free and voluntary good deed became an unlimited right to all those he might need afterward, without even my lack of power being enough to release me from his claim. That is how very delightful enjoyments were transformed into onerous subjections for me ever afterward.

However, these chains did not appear very burdensome to me as long as I lived in obscurity, unknown to the public. But once my person was advertised by my writings—a serious fault without a doubt, but more than expiated by my misfortunes—from that time I became the general inquiry office for all destitute or self-styled destitute people; for all adventurers looking for dupes; for all those who, under the pretext of the great authority they pretended to attribute to me, wanted to influence me in some manner or another. It is then that I came to understand that all natural tendencies, including beneficence itself, carried out or followed imprudently and indiscriminately in society, change their nature and frequently become as harmful as they were useful in their first direction. A number of cruel experiences changed my original inclinations little by little; or rather, eventually confining them within their true limits, they taught me to follow my tendency to do good less blindly, when it served only to favor the wickedness of others.

But I regret these experiences in no way, since through reflection they have given me new insights into knowledge of myself and into the true motives for my conduct in a thousand circumstances I have so often deluded myself about. I saw that to do good with pleasure, it was necessary for me to act freely, without constraint, and that to take all the pleasure of a good act away from me, it was sufficient for it to become a duty for me. From then on the weight of obligation makes the sweetest enjoyments a burden for me, and as I have said in the *Émile*—or so I believe—I would have been a bad husband among the Turks at the hour that the public cry calls them to fulfill the duties of their condition.[3]

This is what greatly modifies the opinion I long had of my own virtue; for there is none at all in following our inclinations and in giving ourselves the pleasure of doing good when they lead us to do so. But virtue consists in overcoming them when duty commands in order to do what duty prescribes, and that is what I have been less able to do than any man in the world. Born sensitive and good, full of pity to the point of weakness, and feeling my soul exalted by everything which relates to generosity, I liked, even passionately liked, being humane, beneficent, and helpful, as long as only my heart was involved. I would have been the best and the most merciful of men if I had been the most powerful; and to extinguish any desire for vengeance within me, it would have sufficed for me to be able to avenge myself. I would even have been just against my self-interest without any difficulty, but I could not have resolved to be so against that of those who were dear to me. From the moment my duty and my heart were in conflict, the first was rarely the victor unless all I had to do was abstain. Then, I was strong for the most part. But to act against my inclination was always impossible for me. Whether it be men, duty, or even necessity commanding, when my heart is silent, my will remains deaf, and I am unable to obey. I see the evil which threatens me, and I allow it to occur rather than exert myself to forestall it. With effort, I sometimes start to, but this effort very quickly wearies and exhausts me; I am unable to continue. In everything imaginable, what I do not do with pleasure soon becomes impossible for me to do.

There is more. Constraint, though in harmony with my desire, suffices to annihilate it and to change it into repugnance, even into aversion, as soon as it functions too strongly; and that is what makes painful for me the good action which is demanded of me and which I did of my own accord when it was not demanded. A purely spontaneous good deed is certainly an action I love to perform. But when the one who has received it transforms it into a claim and exacts its continuation under penalty of his hatred, when he makes it a law for me to be his benefactor forever for my having at first taken pleasure in helping him, from that point annoyance begins and pleasure vanishes. What I do then when I yield arises from weakness and mortification, but good will is no longer in it; and far from applauding myself for it within, my conscience scolds me for doing good reluctantly.

I know that there is a kind of contract, and even the holiest of all, between the benefactor and the beneficiary. They form a sort of society with each other, more restricted than the one which unites men in general. And if the beneficiary tacitly pledges himself to gratitude, the benefactor likewise pledges himself to preserve for the other, as long as he does not make himself unworthy of it, the same good will he has just shown him and to renew its acts for him whenever he is able to and whenever it is required. Those are not stated conditions, but they are natural effects of the relationship which has just been set up between them. He who refuses a spontaneous favor the first time it is asked of him gives the one he has refused no right to complain. But he who, in a similar case, refuses the same person the same kindness he heretofore accorded him, frustrates a hope he has authorized him to conceive. He deceives and belies an expectation he has engendered. In this refusal, we feel an inexplicable injustice and greater harshness than in the other; but it is no less the effect of an independence the heart loves and renounces only with effort. When I pay a debt, it is a duty I fulfill; when I give a gift, it is a pleasure I give myself. Now, the pleasure of fulfilling our duties is one of those that only the habit of virtue engenders; those which come to us immediately from nature do not rise so high.

After so many sad experiences, I have learned to anticipate the consequences of my first constant impulses and I have often abstained from a good action I had the desire and the power to do, frightened of the subjection I would submit myself to afterward if I yielded to it without reflection. I have not always felt this fear. To the contrary, in my youth I obtained friends by my own good deeds. Even so, I have often sensed that those whom I benefited became friendly toward me through gratitude even more than through self-interest. But in this respect, as in all others, things completely changed countenance as soon as my misfortunes began. From that time on I have lived among a new generation that does not resemble the former at all, and with the change in the feelings of others toward me came a change in my own feelings toward them. The same people I saw in each of these two vastly different generations have, so to speak, adapted themselves to each one in succession.[4] Thus it is that the Comte des Charmettes,[5] for whom I had such a tender esteem and who liked me so sincerely, made his relatives bishops by becoming one of the workers in the Choiseulian maneuvers.[6] Thus it is that the good Father Palais,[7] formerly my debtor and my friend, a fine and honest boy in his youth, has procured himself a post in France by becoming treacherous and false with regard to me. Thus it is that Father de Binis,[8] who was my undersecretary in Venice and who always showed me the attachment and esteem which my conduct should naturally have inspired in him, was able to gain handsome benefits [9] at the expense of his conscience and of truth by opportunely changing language and demeanor in his self-interest. Moultou [10] himself has changed from white to black. From true and candid as they were at first, having become what they are, they have done as all the others; and simply because the times have changed, men have changed with them. Humph! how could I keep the same feelings for those in whom I find the opposite of what engendered those feelings? I do not hate them, because I cannot hate; but I cannot refrain from the scorn they merit or abstain from attesting to it.

Perhaps without noticing it I, too, have changed more than necessary. What natural temperament could resist a situation similar to mine without being altered? Convinced by twenty years of experience that everything in the way of happy dispositions which nature has put in my heart has been turned to the prejudice of myself or of others by my fate and by those who dispose of it, I can no longer consider a good action which they offer me to do as anything but a snare tendered me under which some evil is hidden.[11] I know that whatever the effect of the action might be, I will nonetheless have my good intention as a reward. Yes, this reward is undoubtedly still there, but the inner charm is no longer there; and as soon as this stimulant fails me, I feel only indifference and ice within myself. Certain that instead of performing a truly useful action I only act like a dupe, self-love's indignation joined to reason's disavowal inspires in me only repugnance and resistance, whereas in my natural condition I would have been full of ardor and zeal.

Some kinds of adversity elevate and strengthen the soul, but some strike it down and kill it; such is the one to which I am prey. Whatever small amount of bad leavening there might have been in my own soul, my adversity might have made it ferment excessively or have made me frenetic; but it has only made me ineffectual. Unable to do good either for myself or for others, I abstain from acting; and this condition, which is innocent only because it is compulsory, makes me find a sort of delight in yielding fully and without reproach to my natural inclination. I undoubtedly go too far, since I avoid occasions to act even where I see only good to do. But certain that I am not allowed to see things as they are, I abstain from judging according to their given appearances; and with whatever lure the motives for acting are covered, it is enough that these motives be left within my reach for me to be sure they are deceitful.

From childhood on, my fate seems to have tendered the first snare which long made me so apt to fall into all the others. I was born the most trusting of men, and for forty whole years this trust was never once betrayed.[12] Having suddenly fallen into another order of people and things, I stumbled into a thousand traps without ever noticing any of them; and twenty years of experience have barely sufficed to enlighten me about my lot. Once convinced that there was only lying and falseness in the dissembling way they fawned over me, I rapidly passed over to the other extreme: for when we have once abandoned our natural temperament, there are no longer any limits to hold us back. Ever since then I have been disgusted with men, and my will, concurring with theirs in this respect, keeps me even more removed from them than all their machinations do.

No matter what they do, this repugnance will never go to the point of aversion. In thinking about how they have made themselves dependent on me in order to make me dependent on them, they move me to real pity. If I am not unhappy, they are; and each time I turn back into myself, I always find them to be pitied.

Perhaps pride is still mingled with these judgments: I feel I am too much above them to hate them. At the very most they can concern me to the point of scorn, but never to the point of hatred: in short, I love myself too much to be able to hate anyone whatever. That would be to constrict or repress my existence, and I would rather extend it over the whole universe.

I prefer to flee them than to hate them. The sight of them affects my senses, and thereby my heart, with painful impressions brought on by the thousand cruel ways they stare at me; but the uneasiness ceases as soon as the object which causes it has disappeared. I become concerned about them quite in spite of myself because of their presence, but never because of remembering them. When I no longer see them, it is as if they did not exist.

I am not really indifferent about them, except in what relates to me; for in their relations among themselves, they can still concern and move me as would the characters in a drama I might see performed. My moral being would have to be annihilated for justice to become unimportant to me. The sight of injustice and wickedness still makes my blood boil. Acts of virtue in which I see neither boastfulness nor ostentation always make me quiver with joy and still wring sweet tears from me. But I must see and appreciate them myself, for after my own history I would have to be insane to adopt the judgment of men about anything whatever or to believe anything on the word of others.

If my face and my features were as perfectly unknown to men as my character and natural temperament are, I would still live in the midst of them without difficulty. Even association with them could please me as long as I were a complete stranger to them. Unrestrainedly indulging in my natural inclinations, I would still love them even if they never took any interest in me. I would practice a universal and perfectly disinterested benevolence toward them; but without ever forming any individual attachment and without bearing the yoke of duty, I would do unto them—freely and of myself—everything which, moved by their self-love and constrained by all their laws, they have so much difficulty doing.

If I had remained free, obscure, and isolated as I was made to be, I would have done only good; for I do not have the seed of any harmful passion in my heart. If I had been invisible and all-powerful like God, I would have been beneficent and good like Him. It is strength and freedom which make excellent men. Weakness and slavery have never made anything but wicked ones. If I had been the possessor of the ring of Gyges,[13] it would have freed me from dependence on men and made them dependent on me. In my castles in Spain, I have often asked myself what use I would have made of this ring; for it is surely here that the temptation to abuse would be close to the power to do so. Master of contenting my desires, able to do anything without anybody being able to fool me, what could I have reasonably desired? One thing alone: that would have been to see every heart content. Only the sight of public felicity could have affected my heart with a permanent feeling, and the ardent desire to contribute to it would have been my most constant passion. Always just without partiality and always good without weakness, I would have preserved myself both from blind distrust and from implacable hatred. For, seeing men as they are and easily reading to the depths of their hearts, I would have found few of them amiable enough to deserve all of my affections and few odious enough to deserve all of my hatred; and their very wickedness would have disposed me to pity them, due to the certain knowledge of the evil they do to themselves in wishing to do it to others. Perhaps in moments of lightheartedness, I would have been childish enough to perform an occasional miracle; but, perfectly disinterested with respect to myself and having only my natural inclinations as law, for a few acts of severe justice I would have performed a thousand merciful and equitable ones. Minister of Providence [14] and dispenser of its laws according to my power, I would have performed miracles wiser and more useful than those of the Golden Legend [15] and the tomb of St. Médard.[16]

On one point alone the ability to penetrate everywhere invisibly might have made me seek temptations I would have poorly resisted; and once straying onto these paths of aberration, where would I not have been led by them? To flatter myself that these advantages would not have seduced me or that reason would have stopped me from this fatal bent would be to understand nature and myself quite poorly. Sure of myself on every other count, that one alone would have done me in. Anyone whose power puts him above other men ought to be above human weaknesses; otherwise, this excess of strength will in effect serve only to put him below others and below what he himself would have been had he remained their equal.

All things considered, I believe I will do better to throw away my magic ring before it makes me commit some folly. If men persist in seeing me as the opposite of what I am and if the sight of me provokes their injustice, I must flee them to deprive them of this sight, not disappear from their midst. It is for them to hide themselves from me, to conceal their maneuvers from me, to flee the light of day, and to bury themselves in the earth like moles. As for me, let them see me if they can; so much the better. But that is impossible for them. They will never see in my place anyone but the Jean-Jacques [17] they have made for themselves and made to their heart's desire to hate at their ease. I would therefore be wrong to be affected by the way they see me. I ought to take no real interest in it, for it is not I whom they see in this way.

The conclusion I can draw from all these reflections is that I have never been truly suited for civil society where everything is annoyance, obligation, and duty and that my independent natural temperament always made me incapable of the subjection necessary to anyone who wants to live among men. As long as I act freely, I am good and do only good. But as soon as I feel the yoke either of necessity or of men, I become rebellious, or rather, recalcitrant; then I am ineffectual. When it is necessary to do what is opposite to my will, I do not do it at all, no matter what; I do not even do what accords with my will, because I am weak. I abstain from acting, for all of my weakness is with regard to action, all of my strength is negative, and all of my sins are of omission, rarely of commission. I have never believed that man's freedom consisted in doing what he wants, but rather in never doing what he does not want to do; and that is the freedom I have always laid claim to, often preserved, and most scandalized my contemporaries about. Because, as for them—busy, restless, ambitious, detesting freedom in others and not wanting any for themselves, provided that they sometimes do what accords with their will, or rather, that they dominate the will of others—they torment themselves their whole life long by doing what is loathsome to them; they omit nothing servile in order to command. Their wrong, then, was not to turn me out of society as a useless member, but to proscribe me from it as a pernicious member. For I admit that I have done very little good; but as for evil, my will has never in my life entertained it, and I doubt that there is any man in the world who has really done less of it than I.

NOTES

1. Rousseau added this sentence to the manuscript. It does not appear that he intended it to be a separate paragraph, for he made no attempt to set it apart in such a manner.

2. In Rousseau's time, the new boulevards were shaded avenues that ran from the Observatoire to the Hôtel des Invalides. Today they would consist of that part of Boulevard Raspail running from Place Denfert-Rochereau to Boulevard Montparnasse, Boulevard Montparnasse from that point on to its intersection with the Boulevard des Invalides, and the Boulevard des Invalides itself. The Enfer tollgate was a little north of what is now Place Denfert-Rochereau. The road to Fontainebleau was the Chemin du Petit-Montrouge, which is now the Avenue du Général Leclerc. Rousseau probably took the Rue d'Enfer (which would now correspond to the Boulevard Saint-Michel) and then, turning aside and crossing the Nouveau-Cours (which would today be that part of Boulevard Montparnasse running from Boulevard Raspail to Boulevard Saint-Michel), reached the Chemin du Petit-Montrouge which he could have followed to the bluffs of Gentilly along the Bièvre near what is today the site of the Cité Universitaire and the Parc de Montsouris. The Bièvre is now completely covered from Arcueil to the Pont d'Austerlitz.

3. To the best of my knowledge, this reflection occurs not in the *Émile*, but in the *Confessions*, Book V, *OC* 1, pp. 189-90.

4. The next two sentences are in the text itself, but have been crossed out with a red pencil, apparently by one of the early editors. The passage immediately after these two sentences—"Thus it is that Father de Binis . . . white to black"—is in the margin and has also been crossed out with a red pencil. This, too, seems to have been done by one of the early editors.

For a fuller account of their attempts to alter Rousseau's text, see Appendix A.

5. François-Joseph de Conzié (1707-89) was Comte des Charmettes and Baron d'Arenthon. In Chambéry he became friendly with Mme de Warens (see Third Walk, n. 5) and eventually persuaded her to become his neighbor at Les Charmettes. M. de Conzié had received a very fine education and had built up an excellent library. He became acquainted with Rousseau in 1734 or 1735 by taking music lessons from him, but music soon gave way to discussions about philosophical and literary questions as the acquaintance blossomed into a deep friendship. In the *Confessions*, Book V, *OC* 1, pp. 213-14, Rousseau spoke of M. de Conzié with affection and respect:

"Another friendship from the same period of time has not been extinguished and still lures me by that hope for temporal happiness which dies with such difficulty in the heart of man. M. de Conzié, a Savoyard nobleman, who was young and likable then, had the strange desire to learn music or rather to become acquainted with him who was teaching it. M. de Conzié was witty and had a taste for finer things, as well as a gentle disposition which was very appealing. Since I was very attracted to people in whom I found this quality, a friendship was soon formed. The germ of literature and philosophy which was beginning to ferment in my head and which needed only a little culture and emulation to develop completely found these in him."

However, sometime later, Rousseau added the following note in the margin of the Paris manuscript of the *Confessions:*

"I have seen him since and found him totally changed. Oh what a great magician M. de Choiseul is! None of my former acquaintances has escaped his metamorphoses." See also *Confessions*, Book VI, *OC* 1, pp. 232-33.

Two of M. de Conzié's cousins were bishops: Louis-François-Marc-Hilaire, bishop of Saint-Omer in 1766, then of Arras; and Joachim-François-Mamert, bishop of Saint-Omer in 1769 (after his brother went to Arras).

6. Étienne-François, Duc de Choiseul (1719-85) became the minister of foreign affairs in France in 1758; in 1761, he also became war minister and minister of the navy. For at least ten years he was the real ruler of France, and in the *Social Contract* (Book III, chap. vi, para. 9), Rousseau sought to praise him for his wise rulership by an oblique compliment:

"An essential and inevitable defect which will always place monarchical government beneath republican government is that in the latter the voice of the people almost never elevates anyone who is not enlightened and capable to the highest offices, and these men fill these offices with honor, whereas those who succeed in monarchies are most often only petty blunderers, petty knaves, and petty intriguers with petty talents, which enable them to rise to high offices in Courts, but which only serve to prove their ineptitude to the public as soon as they are appointed. The people is mistaken in this choice far less than a prince, and a man of true merit is almost as rare in a royal ministry as a fool at the head of a republican governmnent. Thus, when by some happy stroke of luck one of these men born to rule takes the helm of affairs in a monarchy that is almost ruined by these hordes of egregious administrators, we are completely surprised at the resources he discovers, and that marks an epoch in the history of the country."

Rousseau later came to believe that the Duc de Choiseul was offended rather than pleased by this remark and that joining with Mme de Boufflers, Mme de Verdelin (see Fifth Walk, n. 3), and others in the plot against Rousseau, he eventually became the leader of the whole group. Cf. *Confessions,* Books XI and XII, *OC* 1, pp. 553-54, 571, 577, and 653; Letter to M. de Saint-Germain of February 26, 1770, in *Correspondance Générale de J.-J. Rousseau,* ed. Théophile Dufour (Paris: Armand Colin, 1933), vol. 19, pp. 235-44 and 251-56; and *Dialogues, OC* 1, pp. 925-26.

7. Father Palais was an organist from the Piedmont region of Italy whom Rousseau met in Chambéry between 1732 and 1734. He and Rousseau discussed music, and he played the harpischord at the concerts which were given at the home of Mme de Warens under Rousseau's direction. It is not known how he became obligated to Rousseau. See *Confessions,* Book V, *OC* 1, pp. 184-85.

8. Father de Binis had served as an undersecretary at the French embassy in Venice prior to Rousseau's arrival. During the time Rousseau held the post of secretary at the embassy (September 1743-August 1744), Father de Binis worked with him as an undersecretary. In the *Confessions,* Rousseau spoke of his generosity toward Father de Binis and of their good relationship. Nothing else is known of him. See *Confessions,* Book VII, *OC* 1, pp. 295 and 299.

9. Reading *beaux bénéfices* with the manuscript, but the words are nearly illegible.

10. Paul Moultou (1725-87) and Rousseau met in 1754 when Rousseau returned to Geneva for a visit. Rousseau was so moved by the republican spirit of the city that he decided to embrace the Protestant faith again and be readmitted as a citizen. Moultou became a pastor in 1755, but resigned from the ministry in 1762 to defend Rousseau when the *Émile* was condemned. Although Rousseau had some reservations about Moultou, he was very fond of him and in 1778, just a few months before his death, gave Moultou a number of manuscripts to be published only after his death. The following remark from the *Confessions* aptly illustrates these ambivalent feelings about Moultou:

"Of all these people, the one I expected more of was Moultou: he was a young man of the greatest promise because of his talents and his fully alert mind; I have always liked him, even though his conduct with respect to me has often been equivocal and even though he has been in contact with my cruelest enemies; but despite all that I cannot help considering him as being one day called upon to be the defender of my memory and the avenger of his friend." See *Confessions*, Book VIII, *OC* 1, p. 394; also pp. 392-93.

11. If the reference to "twenty years of experience" was meant literally, Rousseau must have considered his troubles to have begun even earlier than the condemnation of the *Émile*. (See First Walk, n.1.) His bitter quarrel with Mme d'Épinay in December 1757 and subsequent departure from the Hermitage was followed by a complete break with Grimm and by a public declaration that his friendship with Diderot was over (see *Preface* to the *Letter to M. d'Alembert*, trans. Allan Bloom [Ithaca: Cornell University Press, 1960], p. 7 and note). In later years, Rousseau viewed Grimm as particularly malevolent and blamed him as the major cause of his troubles. Cf. *Confessions*, Books IX and X, *OC* 1, pp. 474-501, esp. pp. 492-93; also *Dialogues*, *OC* 1, pp. 926-27; and in this work, see Preface pp. xiv-xvi.

When he left the Hermitage, Rousseau moved to a house offered him by the Prince de Condé in the garden of Mont-Louis near the village of Montmorency. Except for a brief stay at the Petit-Château of Montmorency belonging to the Maréchal de Luxembourg while the house at Mont-Louis was being repaired, Rousseau lived in this house until he was forced to leave France in 1762.

12. According to the story he told in the *Confessions*, Rousseau's trust was not betrayed until June 1754 when he was forty-two years old. At that time, he traveled to Geneva with Thérèse and an old friend, Jean-Vincent Capperonier de Gauffecourt (1691-1766). During the trip, Rousseau would frequently get out of the carriage and walk. After a few days, Thérèse insisted upon joining him. Although he tried to prevent her from doing so and scolded her for being so headstrong, she refused to ride in the carriage if he were not in it. Finally, Thérèse explained: whenever Rousseau got out to walk, his friend would try to seduce her by offering her his purse of money or by reading to her from an erotic book and showing her the pictures in it. Rousseau was overwhelmed by this incident and spoke of it in the following terms: "I must consider this trip as marking the first experience I had until the age of forty-two, which is how old I was then, that destroyed the completely trusting natural disposition with which I was born and had always followed without reserve or inconvenience." See *Confessions*, Book VIII, *OC* 1, pp. 390-91.

13. See Plato *Republic* 359d-360b. When the ring is first mentioned in the *Republic*, it is identified as a ring possessed by an ancestor of Gyges, the king of Lydia. This ancestor had found a corpse with a gold ring on its hand and had taken the ring. He soon discovered that by turning the

setting of the ring toward the inside of his hand, he would become invisible. Taking advantage of the ring's powers, he committed adultery with the king's wife, killed the king with her help, and made himself ruler. Later in the *Republic*, the ring is referred to again; it is then called the ring of Gyges (ibid., 612b).

Concerning Gyges, see Herodotus *The Histories* i. 8-14.

14. Rousseau's capitalization.

15. In about 1260, a Dominican monk by the name of Jacobus de Voragine made a compilation of the lives of the saints and of their miraculous deeds. Originally entitled *Historia sanctorum* or *Legenda sanctorum*, the compilation became so popular that by the fifteenth century it had earned the title *Legenda aurea* or *Golden Legend*.

16. The deacon François de Paris (1690-1727) was a fervent Jansenist who lived in a log cabin and suffered numerous hardships so that he could give his income to the poor. He was buried in the cemetery of the church of Saint-Médard. Around 1730, it was reported that many miraculous healings had occurred at his tomb. It was said that people would have convulsions at the tomb, predict the future, and then be cured. To attest to the miraculous character of these events, women submitted themselves to trials: they would be beaten, put on crosses, and stabbed with swords; allegedly, they were hurt by none of these trials. However, because of the disruption surrounding all of this activity and because of its potential harm, the authorities closed the cemetery in 1732.

17. The manuscript reads: "J.J."

SEVENTH WALK

The collection of my long dreams is scarcely begun, and I already feel it is near its end. Another pastime takes its place, absorbs me, and even deprives me of the time to dream. I give myself up to it with an infatuation which partakes of extravagance and which makes even me laugh when I think about it; but I give myself up to it nonetheless, because in my present situation, I no longer have any other rule of conduct than in everything to follow my propensity without restraint. I can do nothing about my lot. I have only innocent inclinations; and all the judgments of men being null for me henceforth, wisdom itself wills that in what remains within my reach I do whatever gratifies me, either in public or alone, without any rule other than my fancy and any limit other than the little strength I have left. Here I am, then, with grass as my only nourishment and botany as my only preoccupation. I was already old when I had my first smattering of it in Switzerland with Dr. d'Ivernois; and during my travels I had so happily looked for plants that I acquired a tolerable acquaintance with the vegetable kingdom. But having become more than a sexagenarian, having become sedentary in Paris, strength for extensive plant excursions beginning to fail me, and, moreover, sufficiently given up to my music copying so as not to need any other preoccupation, I had abandoned this pastime which I no longer needed. I had sold [1] my herbarium and my books, content

89

to see again from time to time the common plants I found on the outskirts of Paris during my walks. During this interval, the little that I knew was almost entirely erased from my memory, much more rapidly than it had become engraved upon it.

All of a sudden at the age of sixty-five plus, deprived of the little memory I used to have and of my remaining strength to wander around the countryside, without a guide, without books, without a garden, without a herbarium, here I am caught up again in this folly, but with still more ardor than I had in giving myself up to it the first time. Now I am seriously preoccupied with the prudent project of learning Murray's whole *Regnum vegetabile* ² by heart and of becoming acquainted with all the known plants on earth. Unable to buy any botany books again, I set myself the task of copying those lent to me. And, resolved to make another herbarium richer than the first, while waiting to put all the plants of the sea and the Alps and all the trees of the Indies in it, I begin, at least quite economically, with bird's-eye, chervil, borage, and common groundsel. I learnedly look for plants in my birdcage and with each new blade of grass I encounter, I say to myself with satisfaction: here is yet another plant.

I do not seek to justify the course I take in following this fancy. I find it very reasonable, persuaded that in my present position it is great wisdom and even great virtue to give myself up to pastimes which gratify me. It is the means of not letting any germ of revenge or hatred spring up in my heart; and, given my destiny, to still find delight in any amusement, it is surely necessary to have a natural temperament quite purified of all irascible passions. I thus avenge myself of my persecutors in my way: I would not know how to punish them more cruelly than to be happy in spite of them.

Yes, without a doubt, reason permits me, even commands me, to give myself up to every propensity which attracts me and which nothing prevents me from following. But it does not teach me why this propensity attracts me and what attraction I can find in a vain study done without profit, without progress, and which leads me—a doddering old man, who is already decrepit and sluggish and without aptitude or memory—back to the exertions of youth and the lessons of a schoolboy. Now this is a strange thing I would like to explain to myself. It seems to me that if it were thoroughly explained, it could throw some new light on this knowledge of myself I have consecrated my last moments of leisure to acquiring.

I have sometimes thought rather deeply, but rarely with plea- sure, almost always against my liking, and as though by force. Reverie relaxes and amuses me; reflection tires and saddens me; thinking always was a painful and charmless occupation for me. Sometimes my reveries end in meditation, but more often my meditations end in reverie; and during these wanderings, my soul rambles and glides through the universe on the wings of imagina- tion, in ecstasies which surpass every other enjoyment.

As long as I savored that enjoyment in all of its purity, every other preoccupation was always insipid to me. But when, once thrown into a literary career by foreign impulsions, I felt the fatigue of mental work and the importunity of an ill-fated re- nown, at the same time I felt my sweet reveries languish and cool. And soon forced, despite myself, to concern myself with my sad situation, only very rarely could I recapture those dear ecstasies which for fifty years had taken the place of fortune and glory and, without any other expense than that of time, had made me, in idleness, the happiest of mortals.[3]

In my reveries I even had to fear lest my imagination, fright- ened by my misfortunes, might finally turn its activity to this side and lest the continual sentiment of my troubles, gradually con- stricting my heart, crush me at last with its weight. In this condition an instinct which is natural to me, making me flee every depressing idea, imposed silence upon my imagination and, fixing my attention upon the objects which surrounded me, made me consider in detail for the first time the spectacle of nature which until then I had hardly contemplated except in a mass and in its wholeness.

Trees, shrubs, and plants are the attire and clothing of the earth. Nothing is so sad as the sight of a plain and bare coun- tryside which displays only stones, clay, and sand to the eyes. But enlivened by nature and arrayed in its nuptial dress amidst brooks and the song of birds, the earth, in the harmony of the three realms, offers man a spectacle filled with life, interest, and charm—the only spectacle in the world of which his eyes and his heart never weary.

The more sensitive a soul a contemplator has, the more he gives himself up to the ecstasies this harmony arouses in him. A sweet and deep reverie takes possession of his senses then, and through a delicious intoxication he loses himself in the immensity of this beautiful system with which he feels himself one. Then, all particular objects elude him; he sees and feels nothing except in the whole. Some particular circumstance must focus his ideas and close off his imagination for him to be able to observe the parts of this universe he was straining to embrace.

This is what naturally happened to me when my heart, constricted by distress, brought together and centered all its impulses around itself to preserve the remainder of warmth that was about to evaporate and be extinguished by the despondency into which I was gradually falling. I would wander at random through the woods and mountains, not daring to think for fear of stirring up my sufferings. My imagination, which rejects sorrowful objects, let my senses give themselves up to the light but delicious impressions of surrounding objects. My eyes incessantly strayed from one object to another, and in such a great variety it was impossible not to find something which would captivate them more and hold them for a longer time.

I delighted in this ocular recreation which in misfortune relaxes, amuses, distracts the mind, and suspends the troubled feeling. The nature of the objects greatly aids in this diversion and makes it more seductive. Fragrant odors, intense colors, the most elegant shapes seem to vie with each other for the right of capturing our attention. To give oneself up to such delicious sensations, it is necessary only to love pleasure. And if this effect does not occur for all those who perceive these objects, with some it is due to a lack of natural sensitivity and with most it is because their mind, too preoccupied with other ideas, only furtively gives itself up to the objects which strike their senses.

Yet another thing contributes to turning refined people's atten-

tion away from the vegetable realm: the habit of seeking only
drugs and remedies in plants. Theophrastus [4] had gone about it
otherwise, and we can regard this philosopher as the only botanist
of antiquity; therefore, he is almost unknown among us. But
thanks to a certain Dioscorides [5]—a great compiler of recipes—
and to his commentators, medicine has taken possession of plants
and transformed them into simples to such an extent that we see
in them only what we do not see in them at all, to wit, the
pretended virtues it pleases just anybody to attribute to them. We
do not imagine that plant structure might merit any attention in
itself. People who spend their life learnedly arranging shells rid-
icule botany as a useless study when we do not, as they say,
combine it with the study of properties; that is to say, when we do
not forsake the observation of nature, which does not lie at all and
which says nothing of all that to us, to yield to the sole authority
of men, who are liars and who assert many things we must
necessarily believe upon their word, itself most often founded on
the authority of others. Stop in a multicolored meadow to examine, one after the other, the flowers which make it gleam. Those
who see you doing this, taking you for a barber-surgeon's assis-
tant, will ask you for herbs to cure children's itches, men's sca-
bies,[6] or horses' glanders. This disgusting prejudice has been
partly destroyed in other countries, especially in England, thanks
to Linnaeus who has somewhat taken botany out of pharmacology
schools and brought it back to natural history and economic uses.
But in France, where this study has penetrated less among the
worldly people, they have remained so barbarous on this point
that a wit from Paris, seeing in London a connoisseur's garden full
of rare trees and plants, cried out as his sole praise: "That is a very
fine apothecary's garden." By this account, the first apothecary
was Adam, for it is not easy to imagine a garden better stocked
with plants than the Garden of Eden.

These medicinal ideas are assuredly not very suitable for making the study of botany pleasurable. They wither the diversity of
colors in the meadows and the splendor of the flowers, dry up the
freshness of the groves, and make greenery and shady spots insipid
and disgusting. All these charming and gracious structures barely

interest anyone who only wants to grind it all up in a mortar, and no one will go seeking garlands for shepherd lasses amidst purgative herbs.

All this pharmacology did not sully my pastoral images; nothing was further removed from them than infusions and poultices. While looking closely at fields, orchards, woods, and their numerous inhabitants, I have often thought that the vegetable realm was a storehouse of foods given to man and animals by nature. But it never crossed my mind to seek drugs and remedies in nature. I see nothing in her various products which indicates such a use to me, and had she prescribed this to us she would have shown us how to select them as she has done with victuals. I even feel that the pleasure I take in wandering through groves would be poisoned by the sentiment of human infirmities, if I were led to think about fever, stones, gout, or epilepsy. For the rest, I will not dispute the great virtues attributed to plants. I will only say that in supposing those virtues to be real, it is pure malice for the sick to continue to be so. For of the many sicknesses men give each other, there is not a single one which twenty different herbs do not completely cure.

This turn of mind, which always brings everything back to our material interest, which causes us to seek profit or remedies everywhere, and which would cause us to regard all of nature with indifference if we were always well, has never been mine. With respect to that, I feel just the opposite of other men: everything which pertains to feeling my needs saddens and spoils my thoughts, and I have never found true charm in the pleasures of my mind except when concern for my body was completely lost from sight. Thus, even if I were to believe in medicine and even if its remedies were pleasant, in concerning myself with them I would never find those delights which arise from pure and disinterested contemplation; and my soul could not rise up and glide through nature as long as I felt it holding to the bonds of my body. Besides, without ever having had great trust in medicine, I have had a great deal in doctors whom I esteemed, whom I loved, and whom I allowed to govern my carcass with full authority.

Fifteen years of experience have instructed me at my own expense; back now under the sole laws of nature, I have regained my original health through them. Were doctors to have no other grievances against me, who could be surprised at their hatred? I am the living proof of the futility of their art and the uselessness of their ministrations.

No, nothing personal, nothing which concerns my body can truly occupy my soul. I never meditate, I never dream more deliciously than when I forget myself. I feel ecstasies and inexpressible raptures in blending, so to speak, into the system of beings and in making myself one with the whole of nature. As long as men were my brothers, I made plans of earthly felicity for myself. These plans always being relative to the whole, I could be happy only through public felicity; and the idea of private happiness never touched my heart until I saw my brothers seeking theirs only in my misery. Then it became necessary to flee them so as not to hate them. Then, seeking refuge in mother nature,[7] I sought in her arms to escape the attacks of her children. I have become solitary or, as they say, unsociable and misanthropic, because to me the most desolate solitude seems preferable to the society of wicked men which is nourished only by betrayals and hatred.

Forced to abstain from thinking for fear of thinking about my misfortunes in spite of myself, forced to keep in check the remainders of a cheerful but languishing imagination which so much anguish could end up by frightening, forced to try to forget the men who overwhelm me with ignominy and insults for fear that indignation might finally embitter me against them, I am nevertheless unable to become entirely wrapped up in my own self, because in spite of my efforts, my expansive soul seeks to extend its feelings and existence over other beings. And I can no longer, as before, throw myself headfirst into this vast ocean of nature, because my weakened and slackened faculties no longer find objects sufficiently defined, sufficiently settled, sufficiently within my reach to which they can strongly attach themselves, and because I no longer feel myself vigorous enough to swim in the chaos of my former ecstasies. My ideas are now almost nothing but sensations, and the sphere of my understanding does not transcend the objects which immediately surround me.

Fleeing men, seeking solitude, no longer imagining, thinking even less, but gifted nonetheless with a lively temperament which saves me from listless and melancholy apathy, I began to busy myself with everything which surrounded me and by a quite natural instinct I preferred the most pleasant objects. In itself, the mineral realm has nothing lovely or attractive. Its riches, sealed up within the bosom of the earth, seem to have been removed from the sight of man so as not to tempt his cupidity. They are there, as though in reserve, to serve one day as a supplement to the true riches more within his reach and for which he loses taste to the extent that he becomes corrupted. Thus he must call on industry, labor, and toil to relieve his misery. He digs in the bowels of the earth. He goes to its center, at the risk of his life and the expense of his health, to seek imaginary goods in place of the real goods it freely offered him when he knew how to enjoy them. He flees the sun and the day which he is no longer worthy to see. He buries himself alive and does well, no longer deserving to live in the light of day. There, quarries, pits, forges, furnaces, an apparatus of anvils, hammers, smoke, and fire replace the gentle images of pastoral occupations. The wan faces of the wretches who languish in the foul fumes of the mines, of grimy ironsmiths, of hideous cyclopes are the spectacle the apparatus of the mines substitutes, in the bosom of the earth, for that of greenery and flowers, of azure sky, of amorous shepherds, and of robust plowmen on its surface.

It is easy, I confess, to go about picking up sand and stones with which to fill our pockets and our study, thereby affecting to be a naturalist. But those who devote and limit themselves to these sorts of collections are, ordinarily, wealthy ignoramuses who seek in them only the pleasure of ostentation. To make progress in the study of minerals, it is necessary to be a chemist and a physicist. It is necessary to perform tedious and costly experiments, to work in laboratories, to spend much money and time in the midst of charcoal, crucibles, furnaces, retorts, smoke, and suffocating fumes, always at the risk of life and often at the expense of health. From all this sad and tiresome toil much less knowledge than pride ordinarily results, and where is the most mediocre chemist who does not think he has penetrated all the great operations of nature because he has discovered, perhaps by chance, a few small tricks of the art?

The animal realm is more within our reach and is certainly even more deserving of being studied. But, after all, does this study not also have its difficulties, its encumbrances, its distasteful elements, and its labors, especially for a solitary person who can hope for no assistance from anyone either in his play or in his toils? How am I to observe, dissect, study, become acquainted with the birds in the air, the fish in the water, or the quadrupeds swifter than the wind and stronger than man, which are no more disposed to come offer themselves to my research than I to run after them to make them submit to it by force? Thus I would have snails, worms, and flies as a resource; [8] and I would spend my life gasping for breath as I chase after butterflies, impale poor insects, dissect mice when I could catch any, or the carrion of the beasts I might by chance find dead. The study of animals is nothing without anatomy. By it one learns to classify them, to distinguish the genera and the species. To study them according to their habits [9] and characteristics, it would be necessary to have aviaries, fishponds, cages; it would be necessary to force them, as best I could, to remain gathered together around me. I have neither the desire nor the means to hold them in captivity, nor the necessary agility to chase after them when they are at liberty. It will be necessary, then, to study them dead, to tear them apart, to bone them, to poke at leisure into their palpitating entrails! What a frightful apparatus is an anatomical amphitheater: stinking corpses, slavering and livid flesh, blood, disgusting intestines, dreadful skeletons, pestilential fumes! Upon my word, that is not where Jean-Jacques [10] will go looking for his fun.

Brilliant flowers, diverse colors of the meadows, fresh shady spots, brooks, thickets, greenery, come purify my imagination sullied by all those hideous objects. My soul, dead to all great impulses, can no longer be affected by anything but perceptible objects. I no longer have anything but sensations, and now it is only by them that pain or pleasure can reach me here-below. Attracted by the cheerful objects which surround me, I consider them, contemplate them, compare them, and eventually learn to classify them; and now I am all of a sudden as much a botanist as is necessary for someone who wants to study nature only to find continuous new reasons to love it.

In no way do I seek to instruct myself: it is too late. Besides, I have never seen that such knowledge contributes to life's happiness. But I seek to give myself sweet and simple pastimes which I can savor without labor and which distract me from my misfortunes. It costs me neither expense nor trouble to wander at random from herb to herb and from plant to plant to examine them, to compare their diverse characters, to take note of their similarities and differences, in sum, to observe the way plants are composed so as to follow the course and the operation of these living machines, to seek—sometimes with success—their general laws as well as the reason for and the end of their diverse structures, and to give myself up to the charm of grateful admiration for the hand which lets me enjoy all of that.

Plants seem to have been sown profusely on the earth, like the stars in the sky, to invite man to the study of nature by the attraction of pleasure and curiosity. But the heavenly bodies are set far away from us. Preliminary knowledge, instruments, machines, and very long ladders are needed to get to them and bring them within our reach. Plants are naturally within our reach. They are born under our feet and in our hands, so to speak; and if the smallness of their essential parts sometimes conceals them from plain view, the instruments which reveal them are much easier to use than those of astronomy. Botany is a study for an idle and lazy solitary person: a point and a magnifying glass are all the apparatus he needs to observe plants. He walks about, wanders freely from one object to another, examines each flower with interest and curiosity, and as soon as he begins to grasp the laws of their structure, he enjoys, in observing them, a painless pleasure as intense as if it had cost him much pain. In this idle occupation there is a charm we feel only in the complete calm of the passions, but which then alone suffices to make life happy and sweet. But as soon as we mingle a motive of interest or vanity with it, either in order to obtain distinction or to write books, as soon as we want to learn only in order to instruct, as soon as we look for flowers only in order to become an author or professor, all this sweet charm vanishes. We no longer see in plants anything but the instruments of our passions. We no longer find any true pleasure in their study. We no longer want to know, but to show that we know. And in the woods, we are only on the world's stage, preoccupied with making ourselves admired. Or else, restricting ourselves to armchair and garden botany at the most, instead of observing vegetation in nature, we concern ourselves only with systems and methods—an eternal matter of dispute which does not lead to an additional plant being known and throws no true light on natural history and the vegetable realm. That is the source of the hatreds and the jealousies that rivalry for fame excites among botanical authors as much as, and more than, among other learned men. Altering the nature of this lovely study, they transplant it to the middle of cities and academies where it withers no less than exotic plants in the gardens of connoisseurs.

Quite different dispositions have made this study a kind of passion for me which fills the void left by all those I no longer have. I clamber up rocks and mountains, I go deep into vales and woods in order to slip away, as much as possible, from the memory of men and from the attacks of the wicked. It seems to me that in the shade of a forest I am as forgotten, free, and peaceful as though I had no more enemies or that the foliage of the woods must keep me from their attacks just as it removes them from my memory; and in my foolishness I imagine that by not thinking about them, they will not think about me. I find so great a comfort in this illusion that I would give myself up to it entirely if my situation, my weakness, and my needs permitted it. The more profound the solitude in which I then live, the more necessary it is that some object fill the void; and those my imagination denies me or my memory pushes away are replaced by the spontaneous products that the earth, not violated by men, offers my eyes on all sides. The pleasure of going into an uninhabited area to seek new plants blots out the pleasure of escaping from my persecutors, and having arrived in places where I see no trace of men, I breathe more at my ease, as though I were in a refuge where their hatred no longer pursues me.

All my life I will remember a plant excursion I made one day near the Robaila, a mountain farm belonging to Justiciary Clerc.[11] I was alone; I went deep into the winding crevices of the mountain; and passing from wood to wood and boulder to boulder, I arrived at a retreat so hidden that I have never seen a more desolate sight in my life. Black pines were interspersed with prodigious beeches, several of which had fallen from old age and become interlaced with each other, thereby closing off this retreat with impenetrable barriers. The few openings left from this somber enclosure gave on to nothing but perpendicularly cut boulders and horrible precipices, which I dared to look over only by lying down on my stomach. The eagle owl, the sparrow hawk, and the osprey made their cries heard in the chasms of the mountain. However, some small birds, rare but known to me, tempered the dreadfulness of this solitude. There I found the *Dentaria heptaphyllos*,[12] the *Cyclamen*,[13] the *Nidus avis*,[14] the big *Laserpitium*,[15] and some other plants which charmed and absorbed me for a long time. But imperceptibly dominated by the strong impression of the surrounding objects, I forgot botany and plants. I sat down on a cushion of *Lycopodium*[16] and mosses and began to dream more at ease thinking that I was in a refuge unknown to the whole universe where persecutors would not unearth me. A flash of pride soon inserted itself into this reverie. I compared myself to those great travelers who discover an uninhabited island, and I said to myself with self-satisfaction: "Without a doubt, I am the first mortal to have penetrated thus far." I saw myself almost as another Columbus. While I preened myself with this idea, I heard, not far from me, a certain clanking I thought I recognized; I listened—the same noise was repeated and increased. Surprised and curious, I got up, burst through a thicket of brush on the side from which the noise was coming, and, in a little hollow twenty feet from the very place where I believed myself to have been the first to arrive, I saw a stocking mill.

I cannot express the confused and contradictory agitation I felt in my heart at this discovery. My first impulse was a feeling of joy to find myself back among humans when I had believed myself totally alone. But this impulse, occurring faster than lightning, soon gave way to a painful and more lasting feeling of being unable, even in the deepest recesses of the Alps, to escape from the cruel hands of men eager to torment me. For I was quite sure that there were perhaps not two men in this factory who were not initiates in the plot of which Pastor Montmollin [17] had made himself the leader and whose mainsprings he regulated from afar. I hastened to drive away this depressing idea and ended up laughing to myself about both my puerile vanity and the comic manner in which I had been punished for it.

But, after all, who would ever have expected to find a mill in a ravine? In the whole world, only Switzerland presents this mixture of wild nature and human industry. The whole of Switzerland is, so to speak, only a large city whose streets, wider and longer than the Rue St. Antoine, [18] are sown with forests, cut by mountains, and whose sparse and isolated houses have only English gardens as a link between them. With reference to this, I recalled another plant excursion that Du Peyrou, [19] d'Escherny, [20] Colonel de Pury, [21] Justiciary Clerc, and I had made some time ago on Mount Chasseron, from whose summit seven lakes can be seen. [22] We were told that there was only a single house on this mountain and we would surely not have guessed the profession of the person who inhabited it, had it not been added that he was a bookseller and one who even did a very good business in the region. [23] It seems to me that a single fact of this kind makes Switzerland better understood than all the descriptions of travelers.

Another of the same nature, or very nearly so, serves no less to make a quite different people understood. During my sojourn in Grenoble, [24] I frequently made little plant excursions outside the city with Squire Bovier, [25] a lawyer of that region—not that he loved or knew botany, but having made himself my personal bodyguard, he made it a law unto himself not to be a step away from me, if at all possible. One day we were walking along the

Isère in a spot completely full of thorny willows. I saw some ripe fruit on these shrubs; I was interested in tasting a few and, finding a bit of acidity in them that was very pleasant, I began to eat some of these berries to refresh myself. Squire Bovier stood along-side of me without imitating me and without saying anything. One of his friends came up and, seeing me pecking at these berries, said to me: "Hey, sir! What are you doing there? Don't you know this fruit is poisonous?" "This fruit is poisonous?" I cried out, completely surprised. "Without a doubt," he replied, "and everyone knows it so well that nobody in the region would think of eating them." I looked at Squire Bovier and said to him: "Why, then, didn't you warn me?" "Ah, sir," he replied to me in a respectful tone, "I didn't dare take that liberty." I began to laugh at this Dauphinois humility, but nonetheless put an end to my little snack. I was persuaded, as I still am, that any pleasant-tasting natural product cannot be harmful to the body, or is so, at least, only through excess. However, I confess that I watched myself a little for the remainder of the day, but I got off with no more than a little worry; I supped very well, slept better, and got up the next morning in perfect health, after having the day before swallowed fifteen or twenty berries of this terrible *hippophae*,[26] of which, according to what everyone told me in Grenoble the following day, even the smallest dose is poisonous. This adventure struck me as so funny that I never recall it without laughing at the unusual discretion of the lawyer, M. Bovier.

All of my botanical jaunts, the diverse impressions of the place in which the objects which struck me were located, the ideas that place brought forth in me, the incidents which were mingled with it, all of that has left me with impressions which are renewed by seeing the plants that I had looked for in those very places. I will never again see those beautiful landscapes, forests, lakes, groves, masses of rocks, or mountains whose sight has always touched my heart; but now that I can no longer roam about those happy regions, I have only to open my herbarium, and it soon transports me there. The fragments of the plants I collected there suffice to remind me of that whole magnificent spectacle. This herbarium is for me a diary of plant excursions which permits me to begin them again with a renewed pleasure and produces the effect of an optical illusion [27] which paints them anew before my eyes.

I am attached to botany by the chain of accessory ideas. Botany gathers together and recalls to my imagination all the ideas which gratify it more. The meadows, the waters, the woods, the solitude, above all, the peace and rest to be found in the midst of all that are incessantly retraced in my memory by my imagination. Botany makes me forget men's persecutions, their hatred, scorn, insults, and all the evils with which they have repaid my tender and sincere attachment for them. It transports me to peaceful habitats among simple and good people, such as those with whom I formerly lived. It recalls to me both my youth and my innocent pleasures; it makes me enjoy them anew and, quite often, still makes me happy in the midst of the saddest lot a mortal has ever undergone.

NOTES

1. Reading *vendu* with the manuscript.

2. Johannes-Andreas Murray (1740-91) was born in Stockholm and studied in Uppsala where he was encouraged by Linnaeus to devote his efforts to botany. He eventually became a professor of medicine and director of the botanical garden of the University of Göttingen. In 1774, he published *Linnaeus' Systema vegetabilium*, writing an introduction to that work; this introduction is the *Regnum vegetabile* referred to here. In general, Murray's botanical studies were pharmacological in nature and gave rise to similar kinds of research.

3. When the *Émile* was condemned by the French Parliament on June 9, 1762, and Rousseau was obliged to flee, he was "forced, despite [him]self, to concern [him]self with his sad situation." This event occurred slightly less than three weeks before his fiftieth birthday. Strange as it may seem for him to speak of having had reveries from his earliest childhood, it is quite consistent with the claims he made in the *Confessions* (Book I, *OC* 1, pp. 8-9) about the way his fertile imagination was developed in his early years.

"I felt before thinking; that is the common lot of mankind. I experienced it more than any other. I do not know what I did until I was five or six. I do not know how I learned to read. I only remember the first books I read and the effect they had on me. This is the time from which I date my uninterrupted awareness of myself. My mother had left some novels. My father and I began to read them after supper. At first it was only a question of using amusing books to gíve me practice in reading, but our interest in them soon became so intense that we took turns in reading one after the other without a break and would pass the night at this activity. We could never stop until the end of the volume. Sometimes when my father would hear the morning chirping of the sparrows, he would say, quite abashedly: 'let's go to bed; I am more of a child than you.'

"In a short while, I not only acquired extreme ease in reading and in understanding by this dangerous method, but a knowledge of the passions unique for my age. Although all the feelings were already known to me, I had no idea of things. I had thought about nothing; I had felt everything. These confused emotions, which I had experienced one after the other, in no way affected the reason I had not yet acquired. But they did furnish me a reason of a different stamp and gave me strange and fanciful notions of human life of which experience and reflection have never quite cured me.

"The novels were finished by the summer of 1719. The following winter, it was something else. My mother's library having been exhausted, we had recourse to that part of her father's which had come down to us. Fortunately, there were some good books to be found in it; and it could hardly have been otherwise, this library having been formed by a pastor, a true one—and one who was even learned, for that was the fashion then—but nonetheless a man of taste and of wit. *The History of the Church and of the Empire* by Le Sueur, Bossuet's *Discourse on Universal History,* Plutarch's *[Lives of] Illustrious Men, The History of Venice* by Nani, the *Metamorphoses* by Ovid, La Bruyère, Fontenelle's *Worlds,* his *Dialogues of the Dead,* and some volumes of Molière were carried into my father's workshop, and I read them to him every day while he worked. I formed a rare and, at this age, a perhaps unique taste for all this. Plutarch, above all, became my favorite author. The pleasure I had in constantly rereading him cured me slightly of the novels, and I soon preferred Agesilaus, Brutus, and Aristides to Orondates, Artamenes, and Juba. From these interesting readings, from the discussions between my father and myself to which they gave rise, was fashioned this free and republican spirit, this indomitable and proud character, impatient with any yoke and servitude, which has tormented me my whole life long in the situations the least likely to give it free scope. Incessantly busied with Rome and Athens; living, so to speak, with their great men; myself a native citizen of a republic and the son of a father whose love for his fatherland was his strongest passion, I became enflamed with it by his example; I believed myself Greek or Roman; I became the person whose life I was reading: struck by the narration of traits of constancy and intrepidation, my eyes sparkled and my voice boomed. One day while I was at the dinner table recounting the adventure of Scaevola, everyone was alarmed to see me put my hand forward and hold it over a heating plate so as to depict his deed."

In other passages of the *Confessions* (especially Book IX, *OC* 1, p. 435), Rousseau described how his fertile imagination and his reveries helped him see through the clouds that enveloped his age and allowed him to discern clearly the natural order he described in his writings:

"My decision taken, I threw myself wholeheartedly into my reveries and by dint of turning them over and over in my head, I finally found the sort of plan whose realization has been seen. Assuredly, that was the best that could be made of my follies: the love of the good which has never left my heart turned them toward useful objects which morality could use to its own advantage. My voluptuous canvases would have lost all their charms if the sweet color of innocence had been missing. A weak girl is an object of pity whom love can make interesting and who is often not less lovable. But who can bear the sight of fashionable morals without indignation and what is more revolting than the pride of an unfaithful wife who openly spurns all her duties while insisting that her husband be overwhelmed with gratitude because she grants him the favor of not wanting to be caught in the act? Perfect beings do not exist in nature, and their lessons are not accessible enough to us. But that a young person born with a heart as tender as it is honest should let herself be over-whelmed by love while still a girl and find the strength, once she is a married woman, to overcome it herself and become virtuous again, whoever says that such a canvas is scandalous in its totality and useless is a liar and a hypocrite; do not listen to him." Cf. also ibid., Books VIII and IX, pp. 388-89 and 426-27.

4. Theophrastus (ca. 372-287 B.C.E.) was born at Eresos in Lesbos. A student of Plato and Aristotle, he eventually succeeded Aristotle as head of the Lyceum. He was primarily interested in natural history and especially in botany. Two of his botanical writings have come down to us: *Enquiry into Plants* and *Aetiology of Plants*. He was perhaps the first to apply a system of classification to the vegetable world. However, he is best known to us not for his works on botany, but for his *Characters*.

5. Dioscorides Pedanius (fl. 60 C.E.) was born in Anazarbos near Tarsus in Cilicia and is known as a botanist, physician, and pharmacologist. His major work, *De Materia medica*, is a description of drugs derived from plant, animal, and mineral origins and of their uses. This five-volume work is especially important for its extensive description and systematic ordering of plants. Originally written in Greek, it was translated into several languages and commented on by the Greeks, the Latins, and the Arabs. Until the time of Rousseau, the fame of Dioscorides far surpassed that of Theophrastus.

6. Reading *gale* with the manuscript.

7. Literally, "at the home of the common mother" *(chez la mère commune)*.

8. Reading *ressource* with the manuscript.

9. The French word is *moeurs;* see Third Walk, n. 2. In this context, Rousseau obviously means the manners or habits of animals, not their morals.

10. The manuscript reads: "J.J."

11. Rousseau must have made this excursion sometime during his stay at Môtiers (see n. 17 and notes 19-22 with text). M. d'Escherny (see n. 20) identifies Justiciary Clerc as M. Leclerc and says that in addition to being a justiciary of the Val-de-Travers region, he was a country doctor and somewhat interested in botany; *Mélanges de Littérature, d'Histoire, de Morale et de Philosophie* (Paris: Bossange et Masson, 1811), vol. 3, p. 46. The farm of Justiciary Leclerc was probably located on the north slope of Mount Chasseron (see n. 22). Using the dialect of the region, Rousseau identifies it as a mountain farm *(montagne)*.

12. This is commonly known as the seven-leaved toothwort.

13. This plant is commonly known as the sowbread.

14. The full name of this plant is *Neottia nidus-avis,* otherwise known as the bird's-nest orchid.

15. Commonly known as the broad-leaved laserwort, this plant belongs to the *umbelliferae* family (see Second Walk, n. 4).

16. This plant is commonly known as the club moss.

17. Frédéric-Guillaume de Montmollin (1709-83) became pastor of Môtiers in 1742 and kept that position until his death. When Rousseau first arrived in Môtiers, he asked Montmollin for permission to receive communion; his request was granted after Rousseau agreed to a few formalities. Rousseau thought that he and Montmollin were on good terms and was therefore surprised when Montmollin came to him shortly after the publication of the *Letters Written from the Mountain* and asked him not to participate in the next communion service. When Rousseau refused this request, Montmollin sought to have him censured or excommunicated. The enterprise failed, and Montmollin apparently tried to use his pulpit to stir up the populace against Rousseau. In Rousseau's mind, Montmollin was primarily responsible for the events which forced him to leave Môtiers (see Fifth Walk, n. 2). See *Confessions,* Book XII, *OC* 1, pp. 604-36, esp. pp. 624-31.

18. In Rousseau's time, the Rue St. Antoine was an unusually wide and long street for Paris. It started at the Porte de St. Antoine next to the Bastille and ran past one side of the Place des Vosges or Place Royale and several large private houses in what was then a very fashionable section of the city.

19. Pierre-Alexandre Du Peyrou (1729-94) met Rousseau at Colonel de Pury's house (see n. 21) near Môtiers, and they became very close friends.

When Rousseau was on St. Peter's Island and having financial difficulties, Du Peyrou came to his aid by taking the place of the company that had just abandoned the publication of Rousseau's *Oeuvres Complètes*. Rousseau gave him all the necessary manuscripts and papers, including what had been completed until then of his memoirs, and asked only that Du Peyrou publish none of this until after his death. In return, Du Peyrou agreed to pay Rousseau an annuity for the rest of his life and acted as a general manager for Rousseau's other income. Rousseau's confidence in Du Peyrou was so complete that when he was eventually forced to leave St. Peter's Island, he placed his personal papers in his care.

After Rousseau's death, Du Peyrou, Moultou (see Sixth Walk, n. 10), and Girardin sold all the works which would be included in an "authentic collection of Rousseau's writings" to the Société Typographique de Genève, with the money from the sale going to Thérèse. In 1780, the Société Typographique began to publish Rousseau's works.

In the *Confessions*, Rousseau speaks very warmly of Du Peyrou and seems to have had only a passing doubt about his friend's sincerity; Books VI and XII, *OC* 1, pp. 226, 602-3, 631-39, and 652; see also Appendix B.

20. Comte François-Louis d'Escherny (1733-1815) first met Rousseau in Paris in 1762, but only established a friendship with him in Môtiers during the spring of 1764. In his later years, d'Escherny became a rather prolific author and published a book entitled *De l'Égalité* which he prefaced with a ringing praise of Rousseau. The third volume of his *Mélanges de Littérature* contains a long essay on Rousseau, "De Rousseau et des Philosophes du XVIII Siècle" ("On Rousseau and the Philosophers of the 18th Century") in which he speaks of the different botanical excursions he made with Rousseau and especially of this one; pp. 41-47 and 65-77.

21. Abraham de Pury (1724-1807) had served as an officer for the kingdom of Sardinia. Rousseau visited him frequently at his farm near Môtiers, and he was very helpful to Rousseau when Pastor Montmollin (see n. 17) was trying to bring excommunication proceedings against him. Cf. *Confessions*, Book XII, *OC* 1, pp. 602-3, 627-28, and 635.

22. From the top of Mount Chasseron (1,609 meters) in the Jura Mountain range, it is possible to see the lakes of Neuchâtel, Bienne, Morat, Geneva, Joux, Brenet, and Saint-Point.

23. According to a note that Du Peyrou put into the 1782 edition of the *Reveries*, the bookseller's house was actually on Mount Chasseral. Mount Chasseral, about as high as Mount Chasseron, is also in the Jura Mountain range near Neuchâtel.

24. After leaving England in 1767, Rousseau spent almost a year at Trye, which is near Gisors in Normandy, and then went to Grenoble for about a month (July 11-August 12, 1768). In August, he moved to Bourgoin, which is almost midway between Grenoble and Lyon. He stayed

there until the following January, when he moved to a farm in Monquin, a village just outside Bourgoin. Monquin was his residence from January 1769 until April 1770, when he went to Lyon for a short time and finally moved to Rue Platrière in Paris in June 1770.

25. Gaspard Bovier (1733-1836) was a lawyer in the Parliament of Grenoble. Rousseau's friends had asked Bovier's father to assist Rousseau during his visit to Grenoble and to help him find a place to live, if he decided to settle there. Bovier later wrote a lengthy account of the relations he had with Rousseau during his stay in Grenoble. This account, entitled "Journal du Séjour de Jean-Jacques Rousseau à Grenoble sous le Nom de Renou" ("Diary concerning Jean-Jacques Rousseau's Stay in Grenoble under the Name of Renou"), and a number of other documents relating to Rousseau's stay in Grenoble were published by Ernest Jovy as *Un Document Inédit sur le Séjour de Jean-Jacques Rousseau à Grenoble en 1768 [An Unpublished Document about Jean-Jacques Rousseau's Stay in Grenoble in 1768]* (Extract from the *Mémoires de la Société des Sciences et des Arts de Vitry-le-François;* Vitry-le-François: J. Denis, 1898). Although Jovy was the first to publish Bovier's own account, others had tried to defend Bovier against the implications of the story. For example, in his *Réflexions sur les Confessions de J.-J. Rousseau,* Joseph M.-A. Servan, a friend of Bovier's who was in Grenoble during Rousseau's sojourn, described Bovier's character and tried to show why the incident could not have taken place as Rousseau described it. His account appeared as an article in the *Journal Encyclopédie* of 1783 (pp. 17-44) and was published separately in Paris the same year. In 1852, Auguste Ducoin used Bovier's account to show the errors in Rousseau's story and its characterization of Bovier; *Particularités Inconnues sur Quelques Personnages des XVIII et XIX Siècles: I. Trois Mois de la Vie de Jean-Jacques Rousseau, Juillet-Septembre, 1768 [Unknown Details about Some Well Known Figures in the 18th and 19th Centuries: I. Three Months in the Life of Jean-Jacques Rousseau, July-September, 1768]* (Paris: Dentu et France, 1852).

26. This is the scientific name of the plant Rousseau referred to earlier as "thorny willows" *(saules épineux)*. It is also called the sea buckthorn and is a spiny shrub or small tree. The leaves are narrow and lance-shaped and are covered with silvery scales. Its fruit is round and pale orange and is grouped along the stem on short stalks.

According to Bovier's account of this incident, he had indeed asked Rousseau whether these berries were safe to eat and had been assured by him that they were. Bovier also insisted that no third person joined them during this excursion. See Jovy, *Un Document Inédit,* pp. 42-43.

M. Grieve's *A Modern Herbal* (Thetford: Lowe and Brydone, Ltd., 1931), p. 137, states that the plant is *Hippophae rhamnoides* and that its fruit, because of a pleasant-tasting acidity, is made into a jelly by the people of Tartary and into a fish sauce by the inhabitants of the Gulf of Bothnia. She adds, however, that the fruit is considered poisonous in some parts of Europe. The name, *Hippophae,* is derived from Greek words meaning "giving light to a horse," apparently because of its supposed powers for curing a certain kind of blindness in horses.

Rousseau's belief in the salubrity of pleasant-tasting natural products taken in moderation appears erroneous when the consequences of eating mushrooms or certain kinds of wild black cherries are considered. Rousseau may have made this generalization because he was thinking of alkaloids, which always have an unpleasant taste.

27. The French word is *optique.* This was an instrument something like a stereoscope that was very popular in the eighteenth century. It was a box fitted with a mirror and magnifying lens. The *optique* was used to look at vividly colored prints which took on a great variety of perspectives as they were viewed.

EIGHTH WALK

In meditating upon the dispositions of my soul during all the situations of my life, I am quite struck to see so little proportion between the different phases of my fate and the habitual feelings of well-being or uneasiness by which they affected me. My various, brief intervals of prosperity have left me almost no pleasant memory of the intimate and permanent manner in which they affected me. Conversely, during all the miserable moments of my life, I constantly felt myself filled with tender, touching, delightful sentiments which, pouring a salutary balm over the wounds of my broken heart, seemed to transform its suffering into pleasure. And separated from the memory of the evils I felt at the same time, only the gentle memory of those sentiments comes back to me. It seems to me that I have savored the sweetness of existence more, that I have really lived more, when my sentiments—drawn back around my heart, so to speak, by my fate—were not being wasted on all the objects of men's esteem which are of so little merit in themselves, but which are the sole concern of the people we believe to be happy.

When all was in order around me, when I was content with all that surrounded me and with the sphere in which I was to live, I filled it with my affectionate feelings. My expansive soul extended itself to other objects and, continually drawn outside myself by a thousand different kinds of fancies, by gentle attachments which continually busied my heart, I somehow forgot even myself.[1] I was entirely devoted to what was alien to me; and in the continual agitation of my heart, I experienced all the vicissitudes of human things. This stormy life left me neither peace within nor rest without. Happy in appearance, I had not one sentiment which could withstand the test of reflection and truly please me. I was never perfectly satisfied with others or myself. The tumult of the world made my head swim; solitude bored me; I needed to move around constantly; and I was comfortable nowhere. I was, however, entertained, welcomed, well received, and treated with affection everywhere. I had not one enemy, no one ill-disposed toward me, no one envious of me. Since people sought only to do me favors, I often had the pleasure of doing favors for many people myself. And, without wealth, without employment, without a protector,[2] without great talents that were either well developed or well known, I enjoyed the advantages which went along with all that. And I saw nobody in any station whose lot appeared preferable to mine. What was I lacking, then, to be happy? I don't know, but I do know that I was not happy.

What am I lacking today to be the most unfortunate of mortals? Nothing of anything men have been able to do to make me so. And yet in this deplorable condition, I still would not change being or destiny with the most fortunate among them, and I still prefer to be myself in all my misery than to be any of those people in all their prosperity. Left only to myself, I feed, it is true, on my own substance; but it is not depleted. And I am sufficient unto myself, even though I ruminate on an empty stomach, so to speak, and though my withered imagination and my burned-out ideas furnish no more nourishment for my heart. My soul—clouded and obstructed by my organs—sinks down day by day and, [beneath the] weight of these heavy masses, no longer has enough vigor to thrust itself out of its old wrapping as it used to do.[3]

Adversity forces us to this turning in on ourselves; and that is perhaps what renders it most unbearable for the greater part of

men. As for me, who finds only faults for which to reproach
myself, I blame them on my weakness and console myself, for
premeditated evil never approached my heart.

However, unless I am stupid, how can I contemplate my situation for a moment without seeing that it is as horrible as they
have made it and without perishing from sorrow and despair? Far
from that, I, the most sensitive of beings, contemplate it and am
not disturbed by it; and without struggling or exerting myself, I
see myself almost with indifference in a condition whose sight
perhaps no other man could bear without horror.

How have I come to that? For I was quite far from this peaceful disposition when I first suspected the conspiracy in which I
had long been entangled without having noticed it at all. This
new discovery overwhelmed me. Infamy and betrayal caught me
unawares. What honest soul is prepared for such suffering? It
would be necessary that one deserve it in order to foresee it. I fell
into all the snares they placed along my path; indignation, fury,
delirium, took possession of me. I was completely disoriented. My
mind was overwhelmed. And in the horrible darkness in which
they did not cease to keep me immersed, I no longer perceived a
glimmer of light to guide me or a support or stay to steady myself
by and resist the despair which carried me away.

How could I live happily and serenely in this dreadful condition? I am, however, still in it and deeper so than ever. In it, I
have again found calm and peace. In it, I live happily and serenely. In it, I laugh at the incredible torments my persecutors
constantly give themselves in vain,[4] while I remain at peace,
busied with flowers, stamens, and childish things and do not even
think of them.

How was this transition made? Naturally, imperceptibly, and
without toil. The first surprise was frightful. I, who felt myself
worthy of love and esteem; I, who believed myself honored,
cherished, as I deserved to be; I saw myself suddenly misrepre-
sented as a dreadful monster the likes of which has never existed.
I saw a whole generation rush headlong into this strange opinion,
without explanation, without doubt, without shame, and without
my ever being able at the very least to get to know the cause of

this strange revolution. I struggled violently and only entangled myself more. I wanted to force my persecutors to explain themselves to me; they took care not to. After having unsuccessfully tormented myself for a long time, it was quite necessary to catch my breath. However, I always hoped. I said to myself: so stupid a blindness, so absurd a prepossession, will never be able to win over the whole human race. There are sensible men who do not share this delirium; there are just souls who detest knavery and traitors. Let me seek, I will perhaps eventually find a man; if I find him, they are confounded. I sought in vain; I have not found him. The league is universal, without exception, past all hope; and I am sure I will finish my days in this dreadful rejection without ever penetrating the mystery of it.

It is in this deplorable condition that, after lengthy anguish, instead of the despair which seemed bound to be my share in the end, I again found serenity, tranquility, peace, even happiness, since each day of my life reminds me with pleasure of the previous day and since I desire no other for the morrow.

What gives rise to this difference? A single thing: I have learned to bear the yoke of necessity without murmur. I was still forcing myself to [5] hold on to a thousand things, but now that they have all slipped away from me one after the other and I am left only to myself, I have finally regained my composure. Pressed on all sides, I dwell in equilibrium because, no longer attached to anything else, I depend only on myself.

When I rose up against opinion with so much ardor, I was still bearing its yoke without having noticed it. We want to be esteemed by the people we esteem; and as long as I could judge men, or at least some men, favorably, the judgments they held about me could not be uninteresting to me. I saw that the judgments of the public are often equitable. But I did not see that this very equity was the effect of chance, that the rules on which they base their opinions are drawn only from their passions or their prejudices, which are the work of their passions, and that even when they judge well, these good judgments still frequently arise from a bad principle—as when they feign to honor a man's merit because of some success,[6] not from a spirit of justice, but to seem impartial, while slandering the same man on other points with no qualms whatever.

But after long and vain research, I still saw them all, without exception, participating in the most iniquitous and absurd system an infernal mind could invent. I saw that with respect to me reason was banished from every head and equity from every heart. I saw a frenetic generation completely cede to the blind fury of its leaders against an unfortunate man who never did, willed, or rendered evil to anybody. After having sought ten years for a man in vain, I finally had to extinguish my lantern and cry out: "There are no more!" Then I began to see myself alone on earth and I understood that in relation to me my contemporaries were nothing more than automatons who acted only on impulse and whose action I could calculate only from the laws of motion.[7] Whatever intention, whatever passion, I might have supposed in their souls would never have explained their conduct with respect to me in a way I could have understood. Thus their interior dispositions ceased to be of any importance to me. I no longer saw in them anything but randomly moved masses, destitute of all morality with respect to me.

In all the evils which befall us, we look more to the intention than to the effect. A shingle falling off a roof can injure us more, but does not grieve us as much as a stone thrown on purpose by a malevolent hand. The blow sometimes goes astray, but the intention never misses its mark. Material suffering is what we feel least in the blows of fortune; and when the unfortunate do not know whom to blame for their misfortunes, they blame fate which they personify and to which they ascribe eyes and an intelligence to torment them intentionally. Thus it is that a gambler, vexed by his losses, becomes furious at he knows not whom. He imagines a fate which relentlessly and intentionally torments him and, finding fuel for his anger, he becomes irritated and inflamed against the enemy he has created for himself. The wise man, who sees only the blows of blind necessity in all the misfortunes which befall him, does not have this insane agitation. He cries out in his suffering, but without being carried away, without anger. He feels only the material blow of the evil to which he is prey, and the beatings he receives [8] injure his body in vain—not one reaches his heart.

It is a lot to have reached this point, but it is not all. If we stop here, we have indeed cut out the evil, but we have left the root. For this root is not in the beings who are alien to us, but in ourselves; and that is where we must exert ourselves to extract it completely. That is what I felt perfectly from the moment I began to turn back to myself. My reason showing me only absurdities in all the explanations I sought to give to what befalls me, I understood that the causes, the instruments, and the means of all that, unknown and inexplicable to me, ought not to matter to me. I understood that I ought to regard all the details of my fate as so many acts of pure fatality to which I ought not ascribe direction, intention, or moral cause. I understood that I had to submit to it without reasoning and without struggling, because that would be useless. I understood that since all I had yet to do on earth was to regard myself on it as a purely passive being, I ought not to use up, in futilely resisting my fate, the strength I had left to endure it. That is what I told myself; my reason and my heart acquiesced in it; and yet I still felt this heart of mine grumble. What gave rise to this grumbling? I sought for it and found it: it came from self-love which, after having become indignant about men, also rebelled against reason.

This discovery was not as easy to make as one might believe, for an innocent persecuted man considers his petty self-pride as pure love of justice for a long time. Still, once the true source is known, it can easily be dried up or at least diverted. Self-esteem is the greatest motive force of proud souls. Self-love, fertile in illusions, disguises itself and passes itself off as this esteem. But when the fraud is finally discovered and self-love can no longer hide itself, from then on it is no more to be feared; and even though we stifle it with difficulty, we at least easily overcome it.

I never had much of a bent for self-love, but this factitious passion had become magnified in me when I was in the world, especially when I was an author. I had perhaps even less of it than others, but I had it prodigiously. The terrible lessons I received soon confined it to its former limits. It began by revolting against injustice, but finished by disdaining it. By withdrawing into my soul and severing the external relations which make it demanding, by renouncing comparisons and preferences, it was satisfied with my being good in my own eyes. Then, again becoming love of myself, it returned to the natural order and delivered me from the yoke of opinion.

From that moment, I again found peace of soul and almost felicity. In whatever situation we find ourselves, it is only because of self-love that we are constantly unhappy. When self-love is quiet and reason speaks, reason eventually consoles us for all the bad things we have not been able to avoid. Reason annihilates them insofar as they do not immediately affect us; for by ceasing to be preoccupied with them, we are sure of avoiding their most poignant blows. They are nothing for the person who does not think about them. Offenses, acts of revenge, slights, insults, injustices are nothing for the person who, in the bad things he endures, sees only the bad itself and not any intention, for the person whose rank in his own esteem does not depend on the one others are willing to accord him. However men may wish to view me, they cannot change my being; and, regardless of their power and all their underhanded intrigues, I will continue to be what I am, whatever they might do and in spite of them. It is true that the way they are disposed to me influences my actual situation; the barrier they have placed between them and me deprives me of every source of subsistence and assistance in my old age and time of need. This barrier even makes money useless to me, because it cannot procure me the necessary services. There is no longer mutual exchange and assistance, no longer any correspondence between them and me. Alone in the midst of them, I have only myself as a source, and this source is very feeble at my age and in my present condition. These evils are great, but they have lost all their force for me since I have learned how to bear them without becoming irritated. The times in which true need makes itself felt are always rare. Foresight and imagination increase them, and as these feelings continue we worry and make ourselves unhappy. As for me, it matters little that I know I will suffer tomorrow; to be at peace, it is sufficient that I not suffer today. I am not affected by the evil I foresee, but only by the one I feel and that limits it considerably. Alone, sick, and forsaken in my bed, I can [suffer] [9] there from indigence, cold, and hunger without anybody caring. But what does it matter, if not even I care and if I become as little affected as the others about my destiny, whatever it may be? Is it nothing, especially at my age, to have learned to view life and death, sickness and health, wealth and misery, glory and infamy with the same indifference? All other old men are worried about everything; I am worried about nothing. Whatever may happen, I am completely indifferent to it; and this indifference is not the work of my wisdom; it is that of my enemies. Let me learn, therefore, to accept these advantages as compensation for the evils they do to me. In making me insensitive to adversity, they have done me more good than if they had spared me its blows. In not experiencing it, I might have always feared it; instead, by overcoming it, I no longer fear it.

In the midst of the things that hinder my life, this disposition delivers me up to my natural carefreeness almost as fully as if I were living in the most complete prosperity. Apart from the brief moments when I am recalled to the most distressing worries by the presence of objects,[10] all the rest of the time, given up by my inclinations to the affections which attract me, my heart is still nourished by the sentiments for which it was born and I enjoy them with the imaginary beings who produce and share them, as though these beings really existed. They exist for me who has created them, and I am not afraid they will betray or abandon me. They will last as long as my misfortunes themselves and will suffice to make me forget them.

Everything brings me back to the happy and sweet life for which I was born. I pass three-fourths of my life occupied with instructive and even agreeable objects in which I indulge my mind and my senses with delight, or with the children of my fancy whom I have created according to my heart and whose company sustains its sentiments, or with myself alone, satisfied with myself and already full of the happiness I feel to be due me. In all this, love of myself does all the work; self-love has nothing to do with it. This is not the case during the sorrowful moments I still pass in the midst of men—a plaything of their treacherous flattery, bombastic and derisive compliments, and honeyed malignity. No matter what I might try to do, self-love then comes into play. The hatred and animosity I discern through the coarse wrapping of their hearts tear my own heart apart with sorrow; and the idea of being taken for a dupe in this foolish way adds a very childish spite to this sorrow—the result of a foolish self-love whose complete folly I sense, but which I cannot overcome. The efforts I have made to become inured to these rude and mocking looks are unbelievable. A hundred times I have passed along the public walks and through the most frequented spots with the sole intention of inuring myself to those cruel taunts.[11] Not only have I not been able to succeed, I have not made any progress; and all my painful, but vain, efforts have left me as easy to disturb, to grieve, and to render indignant as before.

Dominated by my senses whatever I may do, I have never been able to resist their impulses; and as long as an object acts upon them, my heart does not fail to be affected. But these passing affections last only as long as the sensation which causes them. The presence of a hateful man violently affects me. But as soon as he disappears, the impression ceases. The instant I no longer see him, I no longer think about him. It matters little that I know he is going to pay attention to me; I cannot pay any attention to him. The evil I do not feel at this moment affects me in no way; the persecutor I do not see is nothing for me. I am aware of the advantage this position gives to those who dispense my fate. Let them dispense it, then, with no qualms whatever. I still prefer to have them torment me without resisting than to have to think about them so as to protect myself from their attacks.

The way my senses thus work upon my heart constitutes the sole torment of my life. The days I see no one I no longer think about my fate, I no longer feel it, I no longer suffer; I am happy and satisfied without distraction, without obstacle. But I can rarely escape any perceptible slight; and when I am least thinking about it, a gesture,[12] a sinister look I perceive, a venomous word I hear, an ill-disposed person I meet, is enough to overwhelm me. All I am capable of in such a case is very quickly forgetting and fleeing. The disturbance in my heart disappears with the object which has caused it, and I return to calm as soon as I am alone. Or if something does worry me, it is the fear of encountering some new cause of sorrow along my way. That is my only torment, but it suffices to alter my happiness. I reside in the middle of Paris. When I leave my home, I long for the countryside and solitude. But it is necessary to go so far to seek it that before I can breathe easily, I find a thousand objects along my path which constrict my heart, and half the day is passed in anguish before I have reached the refuge I am seeking. At least I am happy when they let me reach my destination. The moment I slip away from the retinue of the wicked is delightful; and as soon as I find myself under the trees and in the midst of greenery, I believe I am in an earthly paradise and I savor an inner pleasure as intense as if I were the happiest of mortals.

I remember perfectly that during my brief moment of prosperity these same solitary walks which are so delightful for me today were insipid and boring. When I was at someone's house in the country, the need to get some exercise and to breathe fresh air often made me go out alone; and sneaking away like a thief, I would go walk about the park or the countryside. But far from finding the happy calm I savor there today, I took along the disturbance of the vain ideas which had preoccupied me in the drawing room. Memory of the company I had left followed me into solitude. The fumes of self-love and the tumult of the world made the freshness of the groves seem dull and troubled the peace of the retreat. I fled deep into the woods in vain; an importunate crowd followed me everywhere and veiled all of nature to me. It is only after having detached myself from social passions and their sad retinue that I have again found nature with all its charms.

Convinced of the impossibility of containing these first involuntary motions, I gave up all my efforts to do so. Now, at each blow I let my blood boil. I let anger and indignation take possession of my senses. I yield this first explosion, that all my strength could neither stop nor delay, to nature. I try only to stop its consequences before it produces any effect. Flashing eyes, an inflamed face, trembling limbs, a throbbing heart—that is all purely physical, and reasoning can do nothing about it. But after having let our natural temperament have its first explosion, we can become our own master again as we regain our senses bit by bit. That is what I unsuccessfully tried to do for a long time, but with more luck at last. And ceasing to use up my strength by vainly resisting, I wait for the moment when I can conquer by letting my reason act; for it speaks to me only when it can make itself heard. Alas! What am I saying, my reason! I would be very wrong to honor it with this triumph, for it hardly plays a role in any of this. Everything comes out the same when a changeable temperament is irritated by an impetuous wind, but becomes calm again the instant the wind stops blowing. My ardent natural temperament irritates me; my indolent natural temperament pacifies me. I yield to all present impulses; every conflict sets off an intense and short motion in me. As soon as the conflict subsides, the motion ceases. Nothing imparted from outside can prolong itself in me. All the accidents of fortune, all the contrivances of men have little hold on a man thus constituted. To affect me with lasting sorrows, the impulse would have to be renewed each instant. For the intervals, however brief they may be, are enough for me to come back to myself. I am what men please, as long as they can act on my senses. But in the first instant of respite, I again become what nature wanted. Whatever they may do, this is my most constant condition and the one through which, in spite of my fate, I savor a happiness for which I feel myself constituted. I have described this condition in one of my reveries.[13] It suits me so well that I desire nothing other than its duration and fear only to see it troubled. The evil that men have done me in no way bothers me. Only the fear of the evil they can still do to me is capable of disturbing me. But certain that they have no other new hold by which they can affect me with a permanent feeling, I laugh at all their intrigues and enjoy myself in spite of them.

NOTES

1. After the clause "I somehow forgot even myself," Rousseau had written: "But it seems to me that what takes place outside of us can only

offer passing distractions which let us fall back into this world impotent; and it is when we savor what is within ourselves and again find our soul in order, that we can draw forth truly sure enjoyment and savor a continuous happiness." These two sentences were then crossed out. The text of the rest of this paragraph and of the next paragraph is very difficult to decipher.

2. Reading *fauteur* with the manuscript.

3. This sentence is at the top of the folio and interrupts the first sentence of the following paragraph; that is, it comes after the words "forces us." The words "beneath the" have been added for sense.

4. Reading *en vain* with the manuscript.

5. In the manuscript, a new folio begins here. At the top of this folio, before the continuation of the text, are two sentences which are separated from each other and from the text by heavy black lines, but which are not crossed out:

"However sad the lot of my last days might be and whatever men might be able to do, when I have done what I ought, they will not prevent me from living and dying in peace."

"What I do know is that the Supreme Arbitrator is powerful and just, that my soul is innocent, and that I have not deserved my lot."

6. Reading *succès* with the manuscript.

7. The phrase from the beginning of the paragraph to this point has the sense of one long conditional sentence. Literally, it begins "But when . . ." and a conditional "when" *(quand)* is used to tie each subsequent clause to the preceding one. The apodosis begins at "Then I . . . ." For the sake of clarity, it was decided to omit the conditional conjunctions and to break the phrase into separate sentences. Although Rousseau's own punctuation broke the interdependence of the clauses, it did so without providing any answer to the conditional phrases. He also failed, contrary to all rules of grammar, to put an "I" before the verb "began."

8. Two readings are possible here because there is some doubt about what has been crossed out. Equally strong arguments can be given for reading "which reach him" as for "which he receives."

9. This word has been added because there is no verb in the manuscript here. Most French editors have inserted the word "die" *(mourir)*, but that seems too extreme given the context.

10. Rousseau broke the interdependence of these two clauses by making two sentences at this point.

11. Reading *burdes* as *bordes* or *bourdes;* see Roddier, ed., *Les Rêveries du Promeneur Solitaire* (Paris: Garnier Frères, 1960), p. 115, note 1.

12. Reading *un geste* with the manuscript.

13. See Fifth Walk, esp. pp. 68 and 70-71.

NINTH WALK

Happiness is a permanent condition which does not seem to be made for man here-below. Everything on earth is in constant flux, which permits nothing to take on a constant form. Everything around us changes. We ourselves change, and no one can be assured he will like tomorrow what he likes today. Thus, all our plans for felicity in this life are idle fancies. Let us take advantage of mental contentment when it comes; let us keep from driving it away by our own fault. But let us not make any plans to chain it up, for those plans are pure follies. I have seldom seen happy men, perhaps not at all. But I have often seen contented hearts; and of all the objects which have struck me, that is the one which has made me most content. I believe this is a natural consequence of the power my sensations have over my internal feelings. Happiness has no exterior sign; to recognize it, it would be necessary to see into the heart of the happy man. But contentment is read in the eyes, in the bearing, in the lilt of the voice, in the manner of walking, and seems to be transmitted to the one who perceives it. Is there a sweeter enjoyment than to see a whole people give itself up to joy on a holiday and every heart expand in the broad rays of pleasure which pass rapidly, but intensely, through the clouds of life? [1]

Three days ago Monsieur P.[2] came with extraordinary eagerness to show me the eulogy of Mme Geoffrin by M. d'Alembert.[3]

The reading was preceded by long and loud cackles of laughter about the ridiculous affectation of this piece and the silly puns of which he said it was full. Still laughing, he began to read. I listened to him with a serious manner which calmed him; and, seeing that I did not imitate him, he finally stopped laughing. The longest and most strained passage in this piece turned on the pleasure that Mme G. took in seeing children and making them chat. The author rightly drew from this inclination proof of a good natural temperament. But he did not stop there. He roundly accused all those who did not have the same fondness of having a bad natural temperament and of being wicked—to the point of saying that if those being led to the gallows or to the torture wheel were to be asked about it, all would acknowledge they had not loved children.[4] In that context, these assertions had a peculiar effect. Supposing all of that true, was this the occasion on which to say it and was it necessary to sully the eulogy of an estimable woman with images of tortures and wrongdoers? I easily understood the reason for this disagreeable contention. When Monsieur P. had finished reading, I extolled what had appeared good to me in the eulogy and added that the author, in writing it, had not so much friendship in his heart as hatred.

The next day, the weather being quite nice, though cold, I went for a walk all the way to the École-Militaire, expecting to find some mosses in full bloom there. On my way, I mused about the visit of the day before and about M. d'Alembert's pamphlet, in which I was pretty sure this discursive gloss had not been placed unintentionally. And the sole pretext of bringing this brochure to me, from whom they hide everything, sufficiently apprised me of its object. I had placed my children in the foundling home.[5] That was enough to let them misrepresent me as an unnatural father; and from that, pushing and pulling this idea, they had little by little drawn the consequence that I evidently hated children. Following in thought this chain of gradual changes, I admired the artfulness with which human industry is able to transform things from white to black. For I do not believe any man has ever loved to see little bambinos frolic and play together more than I. Frequently, in the street and on my walks, I stop to watch their mischief and little games with an interest I see no one share. The very day that Monsieur P. came, an hour before his visit, the two little du Soussoi children had visited me; they were my landlord's [6] youngest children, and the elder of the two was about seven. They had come up to hug me so good-heartedly, and I had returned their embrace so tenderly, that in spite of the disparity in our ages they had sincerely appeared pleased to be with me. As for me, I was carried away with joy to see that my old face had not repulsed them. The youngest even appeared to come back to me so willingly that, more of a child than they, I felt myself already begin to prefer him, and I saw him leave with as much sorrow as if he had belonged to me.

I understand that the reproach of having put my children in the foundling home has, with a little perversity,[7] easily degenerated into that of being an unnatural father and of hating children. However, it was the fear of a fate a thousand times worse for them and one otherwise almost inevitable which surely most determined me in this proceeding. Had I been indifferent about what would become of them, since I was incapable of raising them myself, in my situation, I would have had to let them be raised by their mother, who would have spoiled them, and by her family, who would have made monsters of them. I still shudder to think about it. What Muhammad made of ˙Zayd [8] is nothing compared with what would have been made of them on my account, and the snares that were set for me afterward regarding them sufficiently convince me that such a plan had been formed. In truth, I was then quite far from foreseeing those atrocious intrigues; but I knew that the least perilous upbringing for them was that of the foundling home, and I placed them in it. I would do it again, with much less doubt too, if I had to do it again; and I well know that no father is more tender than I would have been toward them, however little habit might have aided nature.

If I have made any progress in understanding the human heart, it is the pleasure I used to take in seeing and observing children which has earned me this understanding. In my youth, this same pleasure barred me somewhat from it, for I played with children so gaily and so good-heartedly that I scarcely dreamed about studying them. But when, growing old, I saw that my decrepit face bothered them, I abstained from pestering them and I preferred to deprive myself of a pleasure rather than disturb their joy. Content then with the satisfaction of watching their games and all their little activities, I have found compensation for my sacrifice in the insights these observations have made me acquire concerning the first and true impulses of nature of which all our learned men understand nothing. I have set down in my writings the proof that I busied myself with this research too carefully not to have done it with pleasure, and it would assuredly be the most unbelievable thing in the world that the *Héloïse* and the *Émile* were the work of a man who did not love children.

I [9] have never had presence of mind or facility of speech; but since my misfortunes, my tongue and my head have become more and more obstructed. The idea and the proper word both escape me, and nothing requires better discernment or more accurate choice of locutions than the remarks we make to children. What increases this obstruction even more for me is the attentiveness of the listeners, the interpretations and the weight they give to everything which comes from a man who, having written expressly for children, is supposedly bound to speak to them only by an oracle.[10] This extreme uneasiness and the ineptitude I feel trouble and disconcert me; I would be much more at ease standing before an Asian monarch than I am standing before a bambino with whom I have to babble.

Another disadvantage now keeps me more distant from them. And even though I still see them with the same pleasure since my misfortunes, I no longer have the same familiarity with them. Children do not like old age; the sight of decaying nature is hideous to their eyes. Their repugnance, which I perceive, grieves me; and I prefer to abstain from embracing them than to make them uneasy or disgusted. This motive, which acts only upon truly loving hearts, is nothing for all of our learned men and women. Mme Geoffrin troubled herself very little about whether children had any fun with her, as long as they amused her. But for me, this fun is worse than nothing. It is negative when it is not shared, and I am no longer in the circumstances [11] or of an age in which I would see the little heart of a child expand with mine. If that could happen to me again, this pleasure—having become rarer—would only be more intense for me. And I indeed experienced it the other morning in the way embracing the little du Soussoi children delighted me, not only because the maid who brought them did not greatly impose upon me and I therefore felt less need to watch myself in front of her, but also because the jovial manner in which they greeted me did not leave them and because they appeared to be neither displeased nor bored with me.

Oh! if I still had a few moments of pure affection which comes from the heart, were it only from a child still in a romper; if I could still see in some eyes the joy and contentment of being with me which I used to see so often or of which I would at least be the cause, for how many ills and sorrows would these short but sweet effusions of my heart not compensate me? Ah! I would not be obliged to seek among animals for the look of benevolence which is henceforth denied me among humans. I can judge about this on the basis of very few examples, but examples still dear to my memory. Here is one [12] which I would almost have forgotten in any other condition and which, by the impression it has made upon me, well depicts all my misery. Two years ago, having gone to walk in the vicinity of Nouvelle-France, I pushed further on; then, veering left and wanting to circle Montmartre, I crossed the village of Clignancourt.[13] I was walking along inattentively and dreaming, without looking around me, when all of a sudden I felt something seize my knees. I looked down and saw a little child of five or six years squeezing my knees with all his might while looking up at me in such a friendly and affectionate manner that I was inwardly moved, and I said to myself: "This is how I would have been treated by my own." I took the child in my arms, kissed him several times in a kind of rapture, and then continued on my way. As I was walking along, I felt something missing; a burgeoning need made me retrace my steps. I criticized myself for having left this child so brusquely. I thought I saw a sort of inspiration not to be disdained in his apparently spontaneous action. In short, yielding to temptation, I retraced my steps, ran up to the child, embraced him again, gave him something with which to buy some Nanterre rolls,[14] since a vendor happened to pass by, and began to make him prattle. I asked him where his father was; he pointed to a man who was hooping barrels. I was about to leave the child and go talk to him when I saw that I had been preceded by an evil-looking man who seemed to me to be one of those spies they keep constantly on my trail. While this man was whispering to him, I saw the eyes of the cooper fasten upon me attentively in a most unfriendly manner. This instantly constricted my heart, and I left the father and the child even more promptly than I had retraced my steps, but with a most unpleasant feeling which altered all my inclinations.

I have, however, felt them return often enough since then. Several times I have gone back through Clignancourt in the hope of seeing this child again, but I have seen neither him nor his father. And I have retained nothing more of this encounter but a somewhat bittersweet recollection, like all the emotions which from time to time still penetrate all the way to my heart and which a painful reaction always succeeds in pushing away.[15]

There is compensation for everything. If my pleasures are few and brief, I surely savor them more deeply when they come than if they were more familiar. I ruminate upon them, so to speak, by frequently remembering them; and, however few they might be, if they were pure and without mixture, I would perhaps be happier than I was in my prosperity. In extreme misery, we find that a little makes us rich. A beggar who finds one gold piece [16] is more moved by it than a rich man who finds a purse of gold. People would laugh if they were to see the impression made upon my soul by the least little pleasures like this which I can conceal from the vigilance of my persecutors. One of these pleasures occurred about four or five years ago, and I never recall it without feeling thoroughly delighted about having turned it to such good account.

One Sunday my wife and I had gone to dine at Porte Maillot. After dinner we crossed through the Bois de Boulogne as far as the Château de la Muette. There we sat down in the shade on the grass and waited for the sun to get lower so as to return quite

easily through Passy afterward. About twenty little girls led by a
sort of nun came, some to sit down, others to frolic, quite close to
us. While they were playing, a waferman with his drum and
board [17] passed by, looking for business. I saw that the little girls
greatly coveted the wafers, and two or three among them, who
apparently had a few pennies in their possession, asked for permission to play. As the governess was hesitating and arguing, I
called to the waferman and said: "Let all of these young ladies
spin, each in turn, and I will pay you for the whole thing." This
word spread a joy through the whole group which alone would
have more than reimbursed me, had I used up all my money.

As I saw that they were milling about somewhat confusedly,
with the consent of the lady in charge, I made them all line up on
one side and then pass over to the other side, one after the other,
as soon as they had made their spin. There were no blanks and at
least one wafer came to each of those who would have won
nothing, and thus no one could be absolutely discontented; but to
make the party still gayer, I secretly told the waferman to use his
ordinary skill in an opposite sense by making as many good spins
as possible occur and that I would make it up to him. Due to this
prearrangement almost a hundred wafers were distributed, although each girl had only a single spin; for on that point I was
unrelenting, not wanting anyone to take unfair advantage or to
show preferences which would produce dissatisfaction. My wife
gently persuaded those who had good spins to share with their
companions, by which means the distribution became almost
equal and the joy more general.

I begged the nun to spin also, quite fearful that she might
disdainfully reject my offer. She accepted it very graciously, made
a spin like the schoolgirls, and took what came to her without a
fuss. I was infinitely grateful to her for this and found in it a kind
of courtesy which greatly pleased me and which is quite as good, I
believe, as that of affected manners. During this whole operation,
disputes arose which were brought before my tribunal; and these
little girls, coming one after the other to plead their case, gave me
the opportunity to note that although not one of them was pretty,
the sweetness of some caused their homeliness to be forgotten.

We finally separated, very pleased with each other; and that afternoon was one of those of my life which I remember with the greatest satisfaction. Besides, the party was not ruinous. To the contrary, for the thirty copper coins it cost me at the most, I had more than a hundred gold pieces worth of contentment. So true is it that true pleasure is not measured by the expense and that joy is more a friend of pennies than of large gold coins. Several other times I have come back to the same place, at the same time, hoping to meet the little group there again; but that has never occurred.

This calls to mind another similar kind of amusement, the memory of which has remained with me from much longer ago. It was during the unfortunate time when, thrust in among the wealthy and the men of letters, I was sometimes reduced to sharing their sad pleasures. I was at the Château de la Chevrette for the master of the house's name day.[18] His whole family had come together to celebrate it, and all the pomp of noisy pleasures was put in motion for this purpose. Games, pageants, banquets, fireworks, nothing was spared. We had no time to catch our breath and instead of having fun, our heads were spinning. After dinner we went for a breath of air along the avenue; a sort of fair had been set up. There was dancing; the gentlemen deigned to dance with the peasant girls, but the ladies kept their dignity. Someone was selling gingerbread. A young man from the group took it into his head to buy some to throw, one after the other, into the middle of the crowd. And the others took so much pleasure in watching all these oafs rush headlong into each other, fight with each other, and knock each other over to get some gingerbread that they all wanted to procure the same pleasure for themselves. Gingerbread flying right and left, girls and boys running, piling up on each other, mangling each other—that appeared charming to everyone. I did as the others through mortification, although I did not find it as entertaining as they. But soon sick of emptying my pocket to get people crushed, I left the well-bred group and went off to walk alone through the fair. The variety of objects entertained me for a long time. Among others, I noticed five or six Savoyard boys around a little girl who still had a dozen sorry-

looking apples on her tray [19] of which she would very much have
liked to rid herself. For their part, the Savoyards would very
much have liked to rid her of them; but they had only two or
three pennies between them, and that was not enough to make a
great dent in the apples. This tray [20] was the garden of the
Hesperides for them, and the little girl was the dragon guarding
it.[21] This comedy entertained me for a long time; I finally resolved it by paying the little girl for the apples and having her
distribute them to the little boys. I then experienced one of the
sweetest sights which can gratify a man's heart, that of watching
joy united with the innocence of age spread all about me. For
even those who were looking on shared it as they watched it; and
I who shared this joy so cheaply had, in addition, that of sensing
that it was my handiwork.

In comparing this entertainment with the ones I had just left, I
felt with satisfaction the difference that separates healthy tastes
and natural pleasures from those which opulence engenders and
which are hardly anything but pleasures of mockery and exclusive
tastes engendered by scorn. For what sort of pleasure could one
take in seeing herds of men degraded by abject poverty pile up on
each other, choke each other, brutally mangle each other to grab
avidly at some pieces of gingerbread trampled underfoot and
covered with mud?

For my part, when I have carefully thought about the kind of
sensual pleasure I savored on these occasions, I have found that it
consisted less in a feeling of beneficence than in the pleasure of
seeing contented faces. This sight has a charm for me which, even
though it penetrates all the way to my heart, seems to be solely
one of sensation. If I do not see the satisfaction I cause, even
though I am sure of it, I only half enjoy it. It is even a disinterested pleasure for me which does not depend on the part I
might have in it. For in popular celebrations, the pleasure of
seeing gay faces has always eagerly attracted me. This expectation, however, has often been frustrated in France, where this
nation which claims to be so gay shows so little gaiety in its
amusements. I often used to go to dance halls to see the lower
classes dance; but their dances were so boring, their bearing so

doleful, so awkward, that I would leave more depressed than delighted. But in Geneva and in Switzerland, where laughter is not constantly wasted on foolish acts of malice, everything in the celebrations exudes contentment and gaiety; abject poverty does not bring its hideous face to them nor ostentation show its insolence. Well-being, brotherhood, and concord dispose hearts to expand; and often, in the raptures of innocent joy, strangers greet each other, embrace, and invite one another to enjoy the pleasures of the day. For me to enjoy these friendly celebrations, I do not need to be part of them. It is sufficient for me to see them. In seeing them, I share in them; and among so many gay faces, I am quite sure there is no heart gayer than mine.

Although that is only a pleasure of sensation, it certainly has a moral cause. The proof is that this same sight, instead of gratifying or pleasing me, can tear me apart with sorrow and indignation when I know that these signs of pleasure and joy on the faces of the wicked are only indications that their malice is satisfied. Innocent joy is the only one whose signs gratify my heart. Those of cruel and mocking joy break and afflict it, even though this joy has nothing whatever to do with me. Undoubtedly, these signs could not be exactly the same, since they come from such different principles. But they are, after all, equally signs of joy, and their perceptible differences are assuredly not proportionate to those of the impulses they stir up in me.

Those of sorrow and pain are even more poignant to me, to the point that it is impossible for me to endure them without being perturbed by emotions perhaps even more intense than those they represent. My imagination, strengthening sensation, makes me identify with the suffering being and often causes me more anguish than even he feels. A discontented face is still a sight impossible for me to endure, especially if I have reason to think that this discontentment concerns me. I am unable to say how many gold coins were extorted from me by the grumbling and sulking manner of valets who serve grudgingly in the houses into which I formerly had the foolishness to allow myself to be drawn and in which the servants always made me pay very dearly for the hospitality of the masters. Always too affected by discernible objects, especially by those which bear a sign of pleasure or pain, of benevolence or aversion, I allow myself to be drawn on by these external impressions, often without being able to avoid them except by flight. A sign, a gesture, a glance from a stranger, suffices to disturb my pleasures or to calm my troubles. I am my own only when I am alone. Apart from that I am the plaything of all those around me.

Before, when I saw only benevolence in everyone's eyes, or, at the worst, indifference in those to whom I was unknown, I lived in the world with pleasure. But today, when no less trouble is taken to point out my face to the people than to mask my natural temperament from them, I cannot set foot in the street without seeing myself surrounded by rending objects. With long strides, I rush to get to the country. As soon as I see greenery, I begin to breathe. Need anyone be astonished that I love solitude? I see only animosity on the faces of men, whereas nature always smiles at me.

It must be confessed, however, that I still feel pleasure in living in the midst of men as long as my face is unknown to them. But that is a pleasure which is scarcely allowed me. A few years ago, I still liked to walk through villages in the morning and see the laborers mending their flails or the women on their stoop with their children. There was something in this sight which touched my heart. I would sometimes stop, without being aware of it, to watch the little activities of these good people and I would feel myself sigh without knowing why. I do not know whether they saw me sensitive to this tiny pleasure and wanted to take even that from me, but from the change I notice on the faces as I pass by and from the way I am looked at, I am simply forced to understand that they have taken great care to remove this anonymity from me. The same thing happened to me, and in an even more conspicuous way, at the Invalides.[22] This fine establishment has always interested me. I never see, without tenderness and veneration, these groups of good old men who, like those of Lacedaemon, can say:

> Formerly, we were
> Young, valiant, and bold.[23]

One [24] of my favorite walks was around the École-Militaire, and I was pleased to meet here and there some disabled veterans who, having kept the old military decorum, saluted me as I passed by. This salute, which my heart returned a hundredfold, gratified me and augmented the pleasure I had in seeing them. As I am unable to hide anything that moves me, I often spoke about the disabled veterans and the way seeing them affected me. No more was needed. After a short time, I noticed that I was no longer unknown to them or, rather, that I was even more unknown to them, since they saw me with the same eye as the public. No more decorum, no more salutations. A repellent manner, a glowering look had taken the place of their earlier graciousness. The old frankness of their trade not allowing them to cover their animosity with a sneering and treacherous mask like the others, they openly showed me the most violent hatred; and such is the extreme of my misery that I am forced to distinguish in my esteem those who least disguise their fury from me.

Since that time I walk with less pleasure near the Invalides. However, as my feelings for them do not depend on theirs for me, I still do not see these former defenders of their fatherland without respect or interest. But it is quite hard for me to see myself so poorly repaid by them for the justice I render them. When by chance I meet one of them who has escaped the common instructions or who, not knowing my face, shows no aversion to me, the honest greeting of this single one makes up for the surly bearing of the others. I forget them so as to concern myself with him alone, and I imagine that he has a soul like mine, which hatred would not be able to penetrate. I had this pleasure again last year when crossing the water to go walk on the Île aux Cygnes.[25] A poor old disabled veteran was in the boat waiting for enough people to cross over. I stepped forward and told the boatman to leave. The water was rough, and the crossing was long. I almost dared not say a word to the veteran for fear of being rudely treated and rebuffed as usual, but his forthright manner reassured me. We chatted. He appeared to me a man of sense and of morals.[26] I was surprised and charmed by his open and affable tone. I was not accustomed to so much kindness; my surprise ceased when I learned he had only recently arrived from the provinces. I realized that they had not yet showed him my face and given their instructions. I took advantage of this anonymity to converse for a few moments with a man, and I felt, in the delight I found in it, how much the rarity of the most common pleasures is capable of augmenting their value. As he was stepping out of the boat, he got his two miserable pennies ready. I paid for the passage and begged him to put them away, trembling lest I rile him. That did not happen. To the contrary, he appeared moved by my attentiveness, and especially by that which I also had of helping him step out of the boat, since he was older than I. Who would believe I was enough of a child to weep with joy? I was dying to put a twenty-four copper piece in his hand for some tobacco; I never dared. The same shame which held me back has often prevented me from doing good works which would have filled me with joy and from which I have abstained only in deploring my foolishness. This time, after having left my old disabled veteran, I soon consoled myself by thinking that I would have acted against my own principles, so to speak, by mixing with honorable things a prize of money which degrades their nobility and sullies their disinterestedness. We must be eager to help those who need it, but in the ordinary business of life, let us allow natural benevolence and graciousness each do its work, without anything venal or mercenary ever daring to approach such a pure source to corrupt or vitiate it. They say that in Holland the people require payment to tell you the time and show you the way. Those who would thus traffic in the simplest duties of humanity must be a despicable people indeed.

I have observed that it is in Europe alone that hospitality is sold. In all of Asia they lodge you for nothing; I understand that one does not so easily find all ones comforts there. But is it nothing to say to oneself: "I am a man, received among humans; it is pure humanity which sets a table before me"? Small privations are endured without pain when the heart is treated better than the body.

NOTES

1. This first paragraph seems to have been added afterward. It is on the verso side of folio 17. On the recto side of folio 18 is the title of the Ninth Walk, and the Walk begins with the words "Three days ago . . . ."

2. This probably refers to Rousseau's fellow Genevan, Pierre Prévost (1751-1839), who visited Rousseau frequently during the last eighteen months of his life.

3. This eulogy was presented in the form of a letter to Condorcet; see *Lettre à M. de Condorcet sur Madame Geoffrin* in *Oeuvres Philosophiques, Historiques, et Littéraires de Jean Le Rond d'Alembert* (Paris: Jean-François Bastien, 1805), vol. 14, pp. 239-62.

Marie-Thérèse Rodet (1699-1777) married François Geoffrin at the age of fourteen. For almost thirty years, Mme Geoffrin reigned over one of the most popular *salons* in Paris. Her home on the Rue St. Honoré was constantly frequented by men of letters, artists, diplomats, and people of high rank, and she was on very good terms with d'Alembert as well as with other Encyclopédistes. In addition to a reputation for concern for others, Mme Geoffrin was known for her generosity, pleasant wit, and charm.

4. The passage in question reads:

"Madame Geoffrin had all the tastes of a sensitive and sweet soul. She loved children passionately. She never saw a single child without being moved to tenderness. She was interested in the innocence and weakness of this age. She loved to observe nature in them; nature which, thanks to our moral habits, is now seen only in childhood. She took pleasure in chatting with them and in asking them questions; and she would not permit their nurses to prompt them. 'I much prefer,' she would say to them, 'to hear the foolish things this child might say to me than those you might tell him to say. . . . I would like,' she would add, 'all those hapless souls about to be put to death for their crimes to be asked: "did you love children?" I am sure they would reply that they didn't.'

"By that you can see that she considered fatherhood as the sweetest natural pleasure. But the more sacred this pleasure was for her, the more she wanted it to be pure and free of difficulty. That is why she begged those of her friends who had little money not to marry. 'What will become of your poor children,' she would say to them, 'if they lose you too soon? Think about how horrible your last moments will be as you leave behind and in misery those who were dearest to you!' Some of those to whom she spoke in this way married despite her objections. They brought their little children to her. She cried, kissed them, and became their mother." See d'Alembert, *Lettre à M. de Condorcet*, pp. 244-45.

5. In the *Confessions*, Rousseau acknowledged that he had placed his

five children in the foundling home. The decision was not easy for him to make, and he returned to this problem on three different occasions. Each time he elaborated a little more on the considerations that led him to make the decision.

In Book VII, he explained that it was a normal practice in Paris at that time to put children in the foundling home:

". . . I patterned my way of thinking after the one I saw reigning among very likable and ultimately very decent people and said to myself: since this is the custom of the country, when you live in it, you should follow it. . . ." *OC* 1, p. 344; see also pp. 343-45.

In Book VIII, after a long and involved argument, he associated this action with the duty of a good citizen. However, he admitted that there was a fallacy in that reasoning and finally excused himself by the after-thought that his children would have been taught to hate him:

"While I was philosophizing about the duties of men, an event occurred which made me reflect more carefully about my own duties. Thérèse became pregnant for the third time. Too sincere with myself, too proud within to wish to contradict my principles by my actions, I began to examine the destiny of my children and my relationship with their mother according to the laws of nature, of justice, and of reason, and according to those of this religion which is pure, holy, and eternal like its Author. Men have sullied it while feigning a desire to purify it; and they have made it nothing more than a religion of words by their formulas, since it is very easy to prescribe what is impossible when we dispense with practicing it.

"If I was mistaken in my conclusions, nothing is more astonishing than the peace of soul with which I gave myself up to them. If I were one of these ill-bred men who are deaf to the sweet voice of nature and within whom no true sentiment of justice or humanity ever sprang up, this insensitivity would be very easy to comprehend. But this warmth of heart, this sensitivity which is so intense, this ease of forming attachments, this power with which they overwhelm me, these cruel rendings when it is necessary to break those attachments, this innate benevolence for my fellow men, this ardent love of the great, the true, the noble, the just; this horror of evil of any kind; this impossibility of hating, of harming, and of even wanting to; this tenderness, this intense and sweet emotion I feel at the sight of all that is virtuous, generous, likable—can all that ever be brought into accord in the same soul with the kind of depravity which causes the sweetest duties to be trampled underfoot without scruples? No, I feel it and loudly proclaim it: that is not possible. Not for a single moment of his life has Jean-Jacques been a man without feeling, without entrails—an unnatural father. I may have been mistaken, but not insensitive. If I were to give my reasons, I would say too much. Since they were able to seduce me, they could seduce many others. I don't want to expose the young people who might read me to letting themselves be fooled by the same error. I will content myself with saying that it was such that in giving my children over to a public upbringing due to an inability to raise them myself, in destining them to become workers and farmers rather than adventurers or seekers of fortune, I believed I was performing the act of a citizen and of a father; and I looked upon myself as a member of Plato's Republic. More than once since then, the sorrows of my heart have taught me that I was mistaken. But far from my reason having given me the same kind of lesson, I have often blessed Heaven for having in that way preserved them from their father's lot and from the lot that threatened them when I would have been forced to abandon them. If I had left them to Mme d'Épinay or to Mme de Luxembourg who—either due to friendship, generosity, or some other motive—later wanted to take care of them, would they have been happier, would they at least have been raised as decent people? I do not know; but I am certain they would have been brought up to hate, perhaps to betray, their parents: it is a hundred times better that they never knew their parents." *OC* 1, pp. 356-57; see also n. 8.

In Book IX, Rousseau explained that he did not want to let his children be raised by Thérèse's family:

"I shuddered at giving them over to this ill-bred family to be raised in an even worse way by them. The risks of being brought up in the foundling home were far less. This reason for the decision I took, stronger than all those I set forth in my letter to Mme de Francueil, was nonetheless the only one I dared not tell her. I preferred to be exonerated less from such a serious accusation and to spare the family of someone I loved. But just by considering the moral habits of her wretched brother, you can see that no matter what might have been said, I would never have exposed my children to receive an education and upbringing like his." *OC* 1, pp. 415-16.

6. Nothing is known about M. du Soussoi or his children.

7. Reading *tracasseries* with the manuscript.

8. According to Islamic tradition, Zayd was a slave of the prophet Muhammad who became so devoted to his master that he refused to accept his freedom when his father came to ransom him and take him home. Muhammad subsequently freed Zayd and adopted him as a son.

Voltaire drastically altered this traditional account in his play *Le Fanatisme, ou Mahomet le Prophète*. Whereas the traditional account suggests that Muhammad was guilty at the most of alienating Zayd's affection and of bringing him to forsake his filial obligations, Voltaire's Muhammad is an utter scoundrel who tricks Zayd into committing parricide and then kills him.

9. The passage that begins here and ends with the opening words of the next paragraph "from them. And . . ." is not in the manuscript.

However, it does occur in the first edition of the *Reveries* in 1782, and most editors agree that the passage was written on a loose piece of paper which has been lost.

10. Reading *oracle* with the manuscript.

11. Reading *les situations* with the manuscript.

12. Contrary to all rules of grammar, the word "one" is missing from the mauscript.

13. The area around the Rue du Faubourg-Poissonière between the Rue des Messagéries and the Rue La Fayette was known as Nouvelle-France because the barracks there originally housed soldiers sent off to the wars in Canada. There was also a well-known tavern called the Nouvelle-France located on the Rue du Faubourg-Poissonière near where Rue Montholon now intersects it.

Rousseau probably walked up the Rue Poissonière and continued on up the Rue du Faubourg-Poissonière keeping Montmartre on his left until he reached the little village of Clignancourt. He would then have come around behind Montmartre and back into the city.

14. Nanterre was famous for its salty rolls and little cakes.

15. Reading after "heart," *et qu'une réaction douloureuse finit toujours en les repoussant* with the manuscript.

16. The French word is *écu*. It was the smallest gold coin in use at that time, and was normally worth three livres or francs.

17. The face of the waferman's board was divided into numbered sections and had a large arrow that could be spun. He would beat his drum to attract a crowd and then let each child spin the arrow. The child then received as many of the sweet little cylinder- or cone-shaped wafers as the result of the spin determined.

18. The Château de la Chevrette was near Montmorency and belonged to Mme d'Épinay (see Preface, p. xv). It was not far from the Hermitage. Mme d'Épinay's husband was Denis-Joseph Lalive, lord of Épinay; his name day, that is, the day of Saint-Denis, after whom he was named, is October 9. For another account of this celebration, see *Confessions*, Book IX, *OC* 1, p. 465.

19. Reading *éventaire* with the manuscript.

20. See n. 19.

21. The Hesperides were the three daughters of Night: Aegle, Erythea, and Hesperethusa. The island on which they lived near Mount Atlas was a marvelous garden filled with trees bearing golden apples and was guarded by Ladon, a dragon with one hundred heads. Heracles killed the dragon and gathered the apples as one of his tasks.

22. The Hôtel des Invalides was built in 1670 as a home for wounded veterans.

23. See Plutarch *Lives of Illustrious Men: Lycurgus* 21.2. See also Plato *Laws* 664b-d.

24. According to the manuscript, this is a new paragraph.

25. The Île aux Cygnes was an island in the middle of the Seine that stretched from the Champ de Mars to the Esplanade des Invalides. It was joined to the left bank in the beginning of the nineteenth century.

26. The French word is *moeurs;* see Third Walk, n. 2.

TENTH WALK

Today, Palm Sunday, it is precisely fifty years since I first met Mme de Warens.[1] She was twenty-eight then, having been born with the century.[2] I was not yet seventeen,[3] and my burgeoning temperament, of which I was still unaware, gave new warmth to a heart naturally full of life. If it was not surprising that she could have benevolent feelings for an intense, but mild and modest young man with a pleasant enough face, it was even less surprising that a charming woman, full of wit and grace, could inspire in me, along with gratitude, more tender feelings which I did not perceive. But what is more unusual is that this first moment determined my whole life and by an inevitable chain of events shaped the destiny of the rest of my days. My soul, whose most precious faculties my organs had not developed, still had no fixed form. It awaited, with a sort of impatience, the moment which would give it that form. This moment, accelerated by our encounter, did not, however, come at once. And due to the simplicity of manners [4] which education had given me, I saw this delicious but fleeting state in which love and innocence inhabit the same heart prolonged in me for a long time. She had sent me away.[5] Everything called me back to her; I had to come back to her.[6] This return determined my fate, and for a long time yet before possessing her, I only lived in and for her. Ah! if I had sufficed for her heart as she sufficed for mine, what peaceful and delightful days we might have spent together! We did pass such days but how short and fleeting they were, and what a destiny followed them! No day passes but what I recall with joy and tenderness this unique and brief time of my life when I was myself, fully, without admixture and without obstacle, and when I can truly say that I lived. Almost like that praetorian prefect who, disgraced under Vespasian, went away to end his days peacefully in the country, I can say: "I have spent seventy years on earth and lived seven of them." [7] Without this short but precious time, I would perhaps have remained uncertain about myself. For, weak and without resistance all the rest of my life, I have been so troubled, tossed about, plagued by the passions of others that, almost passive in such a stormy life, I would have difficulty in unraveling what there is of my own in my own conduct. To such an extent hard necessity has unremittingly borne down upon me. But during those few years, loved by a woman full of desire to please and of gentleness, I did what I wanted to do, I was what I wanted to be; and through the use I made of my leisure, aided by her lessons and example, I was able to give to my still simple and new soul the form which better suited it and which it has always kept. Fondness for solitude and contemplation arose in my heart along with the expansive and tender feelings made to be its nutriment. Tumult and noise constrict and stifle them; calm and peace restore and exalt them. I need to collect myself in order to love. I induced "Mama" to live in the country. An isolated house on the slope of a valley was our refuge; and there, for a period of four or five years, I enjoyed a century of life and a pure and full happiness which covers with its charm everything dreadful in my present lot. I needed a friend suited to my heart; I possessed her. I had longed for the country; I obtained it. I could not bear subjection; I was perfectly free and better than free, for bound only by my affections, I did only what I wanted to do. All my time was filled with loving concerns or rustic occupations. I desired nothing but the continuation of such an enjoyable situation. My only worry was the fear it might not last for long; and this fear, born of the instability of our situation, was not without foundation. From then on I thought about how to take my mind off this worry and, at the same time, acquire resources to ward off its effect. I thought that a provision of talents was the surest resource against misery, and I resolved to use my leisure to put myself in a position, if it were possible, to give back one day to the best of women the help I had received from her.

NOTES

1. This Walk would thus have been written on April 12, 1778. In Book II of the *Confessions, OC* 1, pp. 48-49, Rousseau said that he met Mme de Warens (see Third Walk, n. 5) upon his arrival in Annecy on Palm Sunday, 1728.

2. In Book II of the *Confessions, OC* 1, p. 50, Rousseau identified the age of Mme de Warens in the same way: "She had been there six years when I came and was then twenty-eight, having been born with the century." As a matter of fact, Mme de Warens was born in 1699.

3. Since Rousseau was born on June 28, 1712 and since Palm Sunday fell on March 28 in 1728, he would not even have been sixteen years old at that time.

4. The French word is *moeurs;* see Third Walk, n. 2.

5. Following the advice of the bishop of Annecy, Mme de Warens persuaded Rousseau to go to Turin and be converted to the Roman Catholic faith. According to his account in the *Confessions,* Book II, *OC* 1, p. 55, he left Annecy on the Wednesday before Easter, that is, four days after his arrival. See also Third Walk, n. 4.

6. After his service in the de Vercellis household ended (see Fourth Walk, n. 4), Rousseau was brought into the household of the Comte de Gouvon and worked under the tutelage of his son. The comte and his son thought Rousseau had great promise and seemed desirous of training him for an eventual political career so that he could be of greater service to them, but Rousseau gave up this promising future to go off with a friend on an extravagant trip across the Alps and back to Annecy. In all, he spent a little more than a year in Turin. See *Confessions,* Book III, *OC* 1, pp. 92-103.

7. The context suggests that Rousseau is referring to the period of time spent in Les Charmettes from 1735 or 1736 until 1740 when he went to Lyon to tutor the sons of M. de Mably. See below, his reference to a "period of four or five years" and *Confessions,* Books V and VI, *OC* 1, pp. 218-67. At the very beginning of Book VI of the *Confessions,* in speaking of the period of time spent at Les Charmettes, Rousseau even asserted: "The brief happiness of my life begins here; the peaceful, but fleeting, moments which gave me the right to say that I have lived belong here."

However, using a quotation similar to this in his third letter to M. de

Malesherbes, Rousseau identified the period of his happiness as covering the years from the day he moved into the Hermitage in 1756 until the date of the letter, that is, January 26, 1762:

"My ills are nature's doing, but my happiness is my own doing. Whatever they might say about it, I have been prudent because I have been happy to the extent that my nature has let me be happy. I have not gone far away to seek my happiness; I have sought it in what surrounded me and found it there. Spartian says that Similis, a courtier under Trajan, having left the court and all his duties without any personal discontentment to go live peacefully in the country, had these words put on his tomb: 'I have inhabited the earth for seventy-six years and lived on it for seven.' That is what I can say in a certain respect, even though my sacrifice has been smaller. I only began to live on April 9, 1756." *OC* 1, p. 1138.

The praetorian prefect was Similis. He had been a centurion during the reign of Trajan and became a praetorian prefect under Hadrian. Dio is the source of the quotation about life and living; see Cassius Dio Cocceianus *Roman History* lxix. 22.2. In his comment about Similis being disgraced under Vespasian, Rousseau seems to have been thinking of Martius Turbo. Although Similis was never disgraced, Turbo was. While serving under Hadrian, Turbo had said of himself that a praetorian prefect should die on his feet and was therefore accused of imitating what Vespasian had said about an emperor dying.

INTERPRETATIVE ESSAY

I

Jean-Jacques Rousseau's last work, *The Reveries of the Solitary Walker*, is like none of his other works. Although it is auto-biographical in style, as are the *Dialogues*, the *Confessions*, the *Letter to Christophe de Beaumont*, and the *Four Letters to M. le Président de Malesherbes*, it stands apart from these works in that it has no explicit exculpatory goal nor any pervasive chronological order. According to Rousseau's own account of this work, it is meant to be nothing more than a record of his inner feelings or a barometer of his soul.[1] Moreover, he disclaims any intention of keeping this record for anyone other than himself. He insists that it is written only for himself and that it is intended to be a kind of comforting companion in his old age, a reminder of happier times and places.[2]

Rousseau's *Four Letters to M. le Président de Malesherbes*, written in the beginning of 1762, are quite different: manifestly intended for others, they represent Rousseau's first attempt to explain himself to another person.[3] The subtitle he placed on his own copy of the letters [4] and the topics he developed in them testify to his desire to justify what others considered his singular ways. Throughout these letters, Rousseau showed himself to be extremely sensitive to the criticisms made by his contemporaries.

145

Accordingly, he was anxious to set forth his reasons for his life of solitude in the woods of Montmorency, to insist that he experienced a unique happiness in his seclusion, and to defend the social usefulness of his withdrawal from Paris and the court. His explanations led him to describe his natural temperament in detail and to contend that no man was better than he, that he in fact had a great deal of esteem for himself.

Rousseau's high appreciation of himself was based on his judgment that the traits in his character which permitted him to cherish lonely country existence were in harmony with those which prompted him to write and publish and that they had nothing to do with vanity. It was his opinion that these activities arose from two incompatible qualities in his soul: a love of liberty or spirit of independence which manifested itself as a kind of laziness that made all the burdens of civic life unbearable to him and an ardent sensitivity which was easily aroused by the perception of injustice, regardless of whom it was directed against. Rousseau did not try to explain his writings in these letters; he referred to them only to show that despite his love of liberty or natural laziness, he had done useful things for people and had done them precisely because his fervent temperament had been stirred by the wrongs he had seen in society. Although he did not go so far as to claim that he could write well only while removed from men, he did insist that his withdrawal had not prevented him from fulfilling his basic civic duties.[5] These same themes are taken up again in the *Reveries*, but this time the earlier accounts of his happiness and social usefulness undergo important alterations and his reasons for his conviction that no man was better than he as well as his reasons for his great self-esteem are more thoroughly explored.

The major purpose of the *Letter to Christophe de Beaumont*, written less than a year after the *Four Letters to M. le Président de Malesherbes*, was to answer the charges made by Beaumont, archbishop of Paris, against the *Émile*. In August 1762, the archbishop published a public letter or mandate in which he attacked Rousseau personally and tried to argue against the religious teaching of the Savoyard vicar set forth in the *Émile*. The archbishop concluded his mandate by condemning the *Émile* for "containing an abominable doctrine such as to overturn natural law and destroy the foundations of Christian religion," a doctrine which he believed also tended "to trouble the peace of states and to make subjects revolt against the authority of their sovereign." [6]

Offended by the *ad hominem* character of the archbishop's remarks, Rousseau began his reply with a kind of autobiographical sketch to prove that he had always been the same and had always set forth the same principles in his writings. He argued that he had neither changed his character nor altered his teaching and then contended that since the very people who had previously praised his character and vaunted his writings now accused him of being a scoundrel and condemned his writings, it was necessary to explain this change by looking for causes other than purported defects in his character or reprehensible errors in his teaching. In these opening remarks, in a sort of autobiographical sketch of his personal religious beliefs given toward the middle of the letter, and in his concluding arguments, Rousseau insisted that a correct understanding of his character would prove him incapable of saying or doing the things of which he had been accused by people like the archbishop. Rousseau's letter was dominated by the theme that a necessary relationship existed between the kind of person he was and the kind of book he wrote: since he was good and gentle, his book could not have been as pernicious as the archbishop charged. In the explanation he gave of his writings, an explanation in which he explicitly stated the goals of his other writings and showed how they were meant to help his fellow man, Rousseau elucidated this point. And in the account he gave of his personal religious beliefs, he tried to show that far from deserving to be considered as one who sought to destroy religion, he should be considered as one who defended God's cause. [7]

Whereas the *Four Letters to M. le Président de Malesherbes* had centered primarily around the problem of Rousseau's voluntary withdrawal from Paris and the *Letter to Christophe de Beaumont* had been addressed principally to the defense of the *Émile,* the *Confessions* had a much broader purpose. Rousseau wrote his

Confessions because he felt that he had been wrongly understood. People considered him a faithless friend, a seeker after glory, and a dangerous thinker. To prove his badness, they frequently cited things he had done. In attempting to explain in the *Confessions* what he was really like, Rousseau admitted his most shameful deeds and even confessed to some that were not public knowledge. When it was not possible to excuse himself, he admitted his guilt. When he did try to excuse himself, he did so on the grounds that he had acted according to a particular kind of feeling. His reasoning was that even though the act may have been wrong, the feeling which prompted it had never been wrong. It was his contention that however misplaced these feelings were at times, they were basically good; on more than one occasion, they alone had kept him from truly evil deeds.

There was something more to Rousseau's insistence on the goodness of his feelings than the idea that despite the bad and unfortunate things he had done, he was a good person because he wanted to do what was right. These justifications pointed to the more fundamental question of the difference between goodness and virtue. Rousseau fully recognized that it was not enough to follow good feelings blindly, that it was also necessary to be wise enough and courageous enough to choose what was correct— whether the prompting of sentiment was present or not.[8] But he ignored that point. The reason is that in the *Confessions* he was intent upon showing why he was unique. As he saw it, his uniqueness arose from his ability to follow his feelings more than any other person and was a sign of his uncorrupted character. Whereas other people calculated every action they performed, Rousseau followed the first promptings of his heart. Thus, he protested that he alone was natural, simple, and decent. If people would only look beyond his deeds to the feelings that prompted them, they would praise him for having remained so close to original human nature and would perhaps be persuaded to try to capture something of his delight for the simple and natural pleasures of the world.

Like the *Four Letters to M. le Président de Malesherbes* and the *Letter to Christophe de Beaumont*, the *Confessions* was an inadequate autobiography. But whereas the first two were too limited, the *Confessions* was superficial. According to the argument of the *Confessions*, Rousseau's difference from others consisted in a kind of simplicity and innocence rather than in a thoughtful approach to human affairs. However, nowhere in the whole work did he make any attempt to defend the soundness of his simplicity and innocence. In part, this came about because Rousseau devoted very little attention to his other writings in the *Confessions*. He was far more concerned with explaining the events of his life in terms of the sentiments that had guided his conduct than with restating his thoughts. In this work, he wanted to present the "only portrait of a man painted exactly according to nature" and to leave an "accurate monument" to his character, not to explain his writings.[9]

The purpose of the *Dialogues*, like that of the *Confessions*, was to show that the public's image of Rousseau was mistaken. What prompted him to write the *Dialogues* was his shock at learning that he was generally considered to be a debauched person, a lecher, an assassin, and a teacher of immorality who praised virtue out of sheer hypocrisy. He was also motivated by the suspicion that the series of misfortunes which had plagued him for the twelve or so years since the condemnation of the *Émile* was the work of a group of powerful people who wanted to destroy him and his reputation. Moreover, he was convinced that these people intended to distort his teaching after his death. For these reasons, Rousseau dedicated the *Dialogues* to a much more thorough examination of his character and deeper consideration of the goal of his writings.

He placed major emphasis in the *Dialogues* on his unique goodness. Here, more than in any other writing, Rousseau tried to present himself as the natural man, as the one person who had preserved the character originally possessed by all men. Thus, he considered in detail his love for solitude, his sensitivity, and his lack of overweening pride as qualities that were his as natural man, and he attempted to prove that even though he had few virtues, his misdeeds were not due to wickedness. Once that argument was made, Rousseau turned to an explanation of his

writings. The basic premise was that his extensive criticism of
society derived from his ability to stand outside the prejudices of
his day. By stating the core of his teaching, he sought to prove
that all of his works had developed the same theme and that in
them he had striven for the good of human society, not its destruction. In sum, the *Dialogues* was the most complete defense of
his writings and sentiments he had ever presented. Whereas the
Four Letters to M. le Président de Malesherbes and the *Confessions*
had considered Rousseau's writings only to the extent that they
better explained his sentiments and the *Letter to Christophe de
Beaumont* considered his sentiments only insofar as they cast light
on his writings, the *Dialogues* explored his writings and his sentiments thoroughly. That is why Rousseau was persuaded that
anyone who read the *Dialogues* carefully and without predisposi-
tion would, like the French interlocutor of the *Dialogues,* recognize the errors in the view held about him by the public.[10]

The *Dialogues* was his last attempt to defend himself and to
justify his difference from all other human beings. When he
turned to *The Reveries of the Solitary Walker,* his last work and
thus his last autobiographical writing, he was still convinced that
the public judgment about him and his thought was erroneous.
However, unlike any of the other autobiographical writings, the
Reveries is addressed neither to a particular individual nor to a
general audience. It is marked by a profound sense of resignation.
Rousseau's explanation for the resigned tone of the work is that by
the time he sets about writing these essays, he has completely
given up the attempt to change the opinion the public might have
of him. Even though he has been wronged, it no longer matters.
His goal henceforth is to center his thoughts upon himself, to
explain and explore himself, but no longer to seek to justify
himself to others. An unwilling victim of the hatred of other men
and of their refusal to open themselves to his affection for them,
he turns toward himself in a way he has never before done.

In keeping with his lament that he has been forced to have
recourse to these writings for his only fellowship during his last
years, Rousseau invests them with stylistic features which make
them appear to be precisely the kind of companion a lonely old

person would choose. They are written in the form of musings which arise during solitary walks or of reminiscences about solitary walks taken in the past. The thread of any given musing or reminiscence is frequently broken by anecdotes or bitter reflections apparently unconnected with the larger subject of the essay. And several Walks open with an allusion to a chance event which prompted Rousseau to mull over a particular topic as he walked away his afternoons.[11] There is, nonetheless, an order underlying the *Reveries,* and each of the essays contributes to the exposition of a general theme. This theme arises from Rousseau's conscious acceptance of his enforced solitude and is developed as he attempts to identify the sense in which he is truly a solitary person or to reflect on how he has always been moving toward complete solitude. Stated in the form of a question near the end of the first paragraph of the First Walk, the theme of the *Reveries* is the exploration of self: "But I, detached from them and from everything, what am I?"

The direction the investigation of self takes here is primarily sentimental: Rousseau gives an account of his feelings, not of his ideas. Although he has spoken about his feelings or sentiments in his earlier autobiographical works, there is a different emphasis here—an emphasis arising from considerations other than his new awareness of his enforced solitude or resigned acceptance of that situation. He spoke about his sentiments in those earlier works only to show that they are good. Here he speaks of his sentiments in order to explore the possibility that the core of his being must be appreciated in terms of its sentiments, not in terms of its ideas. Moreover, as Rousseau investigates the significance of this psychological trait, he introduces a consideration which distinguishes the *Reveries* from his nonautobiographical as well as from his autobiographical writings.

His account of happiness in the Fifth Walk shows that he does not identify his own personal happiness with contemplation. And in the Seventh Walk he claims that thinking is a chore for him, a task he used to perform for the sake of others so that he could explain the world to them and show them how to live in it correctly.[12] To state this observation in a somewhat paradoxical manner, Rousseau thought and wrote about thinking to draw others away from the pernicious effects of thinking and to bring them back into closer harmony with their own feelings. He did not arrive at his awareness of the importance of feeling by thinking. All thinking did for him was show him how to make the kind of arguments that would draw people to his teaching. But this activity was in the name of service to others; it did not advance his own happiness. Here, as the declaration of the theme makes perfectly clear, the emphasis is exclusively on Rousseau. The self-knowledge he pursues in the essays of this work centers around his perception of himself as a solitary being. A central feature of this work is that in it Rousseau explicitly renounces his social conscience. The investigation of self in the *Reveries* is so directed to Rousseau's own enlightenment that the problem of why he is in this unusual condition does not arise. That is to say, it does not arise as a political problem. Rousseau does not turn his thoughts to the question of how a better organization of society might keep others from being subjected to this kind of enforced solitude or even of how it might mitigate his own solitary position. Instead, he uses what he characterizes as undesired solitude to take a final, and apparently undisciplined, look at himself.

In this respect, the *Reveries* is fundamentally distinct from all of his earlier works. Rousseau's nonautobiographical writings—the *First Discourse,* the *Second Discourse,* the *Letter to M. d'Alembert,* the *New Héloïse,* the *Social Contract,* and the *Émile*—were works intended for the common good of his fellow men. In these writings, Rousseau addressed himself to the problems that beset man in general, political society in general, particular political regimes, different human groupings within political society, and individuals as citizens. He frequently spoke of Geneva or tried to provide for the well-being of his fellow Genevans. All of these works had the same basic goal: to destroy the prejudices which gave rise to the vices and misfortunes besetting men or, differently stated, to persuade men to stop admiring the arts and sciences which enslaved them and to stop scorning the useful virtues which could bring them happiness. They were intended to turn people away from the excessive concern with appearance and reputation on which despotism thrived and to encourage them to prize instead the homely traditions and habits which fostered political freedom. And these were themes to which Rousseau returned in his other works, either to draw attention to his own basic goodness, that is, to his freedom from these prejudices and vices, or to speculate on the way his identification of these problems had caused men to turn against him. Here, however, his focus is so steadfastly on himself that he considers nothing which concerns other human beings.

The basic premise of Rousseau's entire teaching was that nature is good, that the first movements of nature tend toward the preservation and happiness of human beings. Since he thought that man is naturally good and happy but recognized that men were actually bad and miserable, his problem was to discover how that change had come about. Rousseau's analysis taught him that the source of human evil was men's tendency to make comparisons among themselves. Increased social relationships with one another, the progress of ideas, and the greater cultivation of each individual's mind led men to compare themselves with one another and to be more concerned about their conflicting interests than about the goals they held in common; they rushed to satisfy their own personal interests with almost total disregard for others. Once Rousseau recognized this problem, he understood his task to be that of discovering how to prevent his fellow men from becoming wicked or at least how to slow down the progress of human vice.[13] The *First Discourse* and the *Second Discourse* contain Rousseau's analysis of the human condition and his explanation of how human arrangements differed from what nature had intended. In each of his other works, he tried to show men how to avoid evil, how to preserve what was still good and prevent the things that would bring about misery.

After the fate of the *Émile*, Rousseau ceased to speak about the public good. Only in his defense of himself and of Geneva in the *Letters Written from the Mountain* and in his discreet attempts to give Poland and Corsica legislative advice did he come close to his former role. Otherwise, as has already been noted, his works were apologetic; they were dedicated to clearing his name. At the moment of writing the *Reveries*, however, even that goal was abandoned.

It appears, then, that *The Reveries of the Solitary Walker* is as different from Rousseau's other writings in its internal features as in its external features. His exploration of himself in terms of sentiments, like his exclusive attention to himself, gives the work a subjective and almost private character, but also gives it a more philosophic appeal. If Rousseau seriously intends to describe himself as a greater friend of feeling than of thinking and if he ultimately holds that happiness is of purely personal value, it becomes necessary to reconsider his whole philosophical teaching. A myriad of questions concerning the intelligible character of the universe, the end of human life, and individual political obligation then arises. In these essays, Rousseau not only expresses himself in such a manner as to prompt these kinds of questions, he also addresses himself to them in a very subtle way.

Part of the subtlety is in the very order of the *Reveries*. As was observed earlier, there is an order to the essays. However, to speak of the *Reveries* as having an order is not the same as to say that there is a beginning, a middle, and an end to the work. Given the incomplete nature of the text, that would be impossible. But there is a beginning, and the argument does take a certain direction. Nonetheless, contrary to what might be expected, the argument does not build toward a conclusion that is never reached. It seems instead that the peak of *The Reveries of the Solitary Walker*, the explanation of happiness which occurs in the Fifth Walk, is reached rather early in the work and that all of the essays are to be viewed in relation to this peak.

II

The First Walk serves as both preface and introduction to *The Reveries of the Solitary Walker*, but does so indirectly. Without being as explicit as either a preface or an introduction, it presents the basic theme of the work and indicates how it will be developed in the essays that follow. It also suggests what the merit of the *Reveries* is and to what kind of reader the work might appeal. However, because all of this is accomplished with very little formal explanation, the First Walk also alerts the reader to what is most characteristic of the *Reveries:* its obliqueness or subtlety. At the same time, the First Walk provides a very good example of the emotional prose so prevalent in this work. Unfortunately, both the subtlety of expression and the use of emotionally charged prose render the *Reveries* somewhat inaccessible.

Rousseau dwells at length here on the general character of his solitude and its painful history. His struggle to learn to accept this unwanted solitude is described in morose, at times even despondent, terms. In the first paragraph, for example, he portrays the pervasiveness of his solitude and testifies to his irritation that it has been forced on him. He carefully enumerates the thorough character of his isolation and plaintively contrasts his overflowing love for his fellow men with their remorseless rejection of him. Then, in tones of nearly complete despair, he raises his mournful query: "But I, detached from them and from everything, what am I?" Inclined by such prose to consider all this nothing more than an attempt by Rousseau to bewail his unhappy lot, the reader is easily turned away or at least tempted to follow the argument of the First Walk less attentively. Indeed, the whole tone of the passage is so personal and lachrymose that the reader is almost inclined to doubt the accuracy of Rousseau's perception and thus to move from an explanation of the text to an examination of the author.

However, the real intent of this passage is not to catalogue Rousseau's despondency at having been excluded from society but to indicate his intention to explain the way it has affected him. The mournful query presupposes his acceptance of this new kind of solitude and proclaims his resolve to make sense of what it means to him. It succinctly states the theme of *The Reveries of the Solitary Walker,* the exploration of self, and is basic to the development of the rest of the First Walk. In this sense, the first paragraph functions as an introduction to the Walk. An account or a history of how he has arrived at this new attitude follows.[14]

Then, in the third section of the First Walk, he relates his resolve to explore the meaning of his solitary existence to his decision to write the *Reveries* and briefly indicates what he intends to do in the following essays.[15]

Rousseau's account of how he came to accept this externally imposed solitude consists of three parts. First there is his description of the way it originally affected him.[16] According to his recollection, he was completely disoriented when he first became aware of what was happening. Although he is exceedingly vague in his references to this period of time, speaking only of the "fifteen years and more" since he was first plunged into this unique situation or the "no less than ten years" it has taken him to return to an inner calmness, he probably means to trace his troubles to the condemnation of the *Émile* by the Parliament of Paris and to the issuance of an order for his arrest. What strikes him now as he thinks about those events is how suddenly and unexpectedly they occurred. He remembers being taken so unawares by them that he could not fathom why such a strange fate had befallen him or why, as subsequent events were joined to these, he found himself in the unprecedented role of social outcast. What especially bothered him at the time and still continues to puzzle him is the way his social status had been so thoroughly transformed when he could conceive of nothing he might have done to warrant it: whereas he had changed none of his ways, the public abruptly stopped extolling him and began instead to treat him as a scoundrel and a wretch.

This is no new complaint. The account he gave in the *Confessions* of his departure from Paris, of his flight to Switzerland, and of the cruel way he was chased from one refuge there to another until he finally concluded that he could find respite only in England powerfully documents the vague allusions he makes here. Similarly, his attempts in the *Letter to Christophe de Beaumont* and in the *Dialogues* to clear his name offer abundant testimony to this expression of astonishment at the way the public changed its opinion about him almost overnight. What is novel about this complaint, however, is the setting in which it is made. Here, Rousseau is neither trying to prove to others that he is unique and that no one is better than he nor seeking to clear his name. He is purportedly interested solely in understanding himself and pursues such self-awareness only for his own sake. This book is intended, after all, for him rather than for us. Why, then, can he not get to himself without thinking about the way he is perceived by others?

One reason this most solitary of men must approach himself by first thinking about the way others think of him is that his situation is simply cruel. Try as he might, he cannot forget the hardships he has endured. He is now aware that his own errors sometimes made his sufferings harsher. He is even willing to acknowledge that his first reactions to his new situation were excessive and frequently foolish. And he recognizes that by surrendering to them, he only made his position less tolerable. But these admissions do not mitigate the misery he felt nor lead him to think that he is entirely responsible for the way he has been treated by his contemporaries. As he speaks even now of what he experienced, his description is poignant and almost overwhelming. His suffering appears to have been so deep that any recollection of those experiences leads him to speak in a tone of utter pathos.

Still, we must not forget that Rousseau could very easily not have harked back to these earlier memories. If he chose to call them forth or elected to approach himself by referring to the distorted perceptions his contemporaries had of him, he must have had a reason. Differently stated, however great the sympathy for Rousseau's plight this description of his suffering evokes, its deeper purpose must lie elsewhere. And that deeper purpose would seem to be the eloquent testimony it offers that he is no longer disturbed by his enforced solitude. Whether the *Reveries* is really written only for himself or is also intended to be read by others, there is a place for such testimony: to appreciate his current psychological state, Rousseau must explain how he acquired his present sense of calm or how he overcame his previous concern about his strange destiny.

As the second part of this account explains, something has happened which permits him to find a new sense of tranquility.[17] In fact, two things have happened. Prompted by a sense of futility, by the simple realization that it was foolish to rail against necessity, Rousseau resigned himself to his fate. That act of resignation arose from total despair: seeing no way to escape his fate, he stopped trying to fight it. By that decision he achieved tranquility, to be sure, but a very repugnant kind of tranquility. Now he discerns something that is actually encouraging. In reflecting on what has already occurred, he concludes that his enemies have exhausted all their tricks and can do nothing more to increase his misery. The significance of this conclusion derives from Rousseau's own psychological constitution. Although he had long been painfully aware of the way his imagination caused him to be overly fearful and to react excessively, he had never found a way to control it. Now, by forcing him to suffer the most terrible experiences, his enemies have solved that problem for him: they have liberated him from the torments of his imagination. As a result, he is able to temper his earlier attitude of resigned tranquility with a sense of confidence.

The third part of this account describes more fully Rousseau's new position and testifies to the difference in attitude between the *Dialogues* and the *Reveries*.[18] Above all, the *Dialogues* differs from the *Reveries* because it was addressed to others in the hope that future generations would form a better judgment of him. That hope was founded on the idea that future readers would sense the justice of his teaching and would be able to strip away all the lies that had been built up by his enemies. Rousseau considered it impossible that people in later times would believe the stories so freely told about him during his life. And he believed that the feeling for virtue and justice which he considered to be natural to all human beings would win out in time, thereby clearing his name. These hopes and beliefs strengthened him while he was writing the *Dialogues* and encouraged him to continue his efforts at self-justification.[19]

However, he claims that he lost the spirit of hope which prompted the *Dialogues* shortly before he began to compose the *Reveries*. A sad and unforeseen event, apparently the failure of his last attempt to interest fellow Parisians in the injustice of his plight, persuaded him that the plot was so extensive that he could not overcome its effects.[20] Yet sad as it was, this failure no longer causes Rousseau to despair. He maintains the tranquil confidence already alluded to and embraces the solitude that he now perceives as irrevocably forced upon him, claiming that in it he is a hundred times happier than he ever could have been while living among his fellow men. Even though he had always preferred a measure of solitude and considered himself naturally disposed to it, he had never wished to turn his back completely on society. Heretofore his penchant for solitude could be traced to his need to collect his thoughts and to muse at leisure about the kind of world in which he would have desired to live.[21] During his periods of solitude, he reflected on the problems which beset his fellow men and composed the striking analyses of these problems that first brought him fame and later seemed to be the source of the misery described here. The novelty of the *Reveries*, then, consists in Rousseau's willingness to accept his destiny as a solitary outcast and in his resolve never again to try to lighten it, because of his conviction that he can never again return to a normal life in society.

According to the final section of the First Walk, Rousseau's decision to write the *Reveries* arises from his unconditional acceptance of this total solitude.[22] A work devoted to the study of himself, to the portrayal of the different moods of his soul, it is characterized as a special kind of sequel to the *Confessions*. Apparently Rousseau considers it, rather than the *Dialogues*, to be a sequel to the *Confessions* because in it he will dwell at length on his feelings and on his natural temperament. Like the *Confessions*, the *Reveries* will explore his inner being more than it will attempt to prove that the conduct of others toward him is unjust. But whereas the *Confessions* was directed to others and was intended to explain his character in the manner of an apology or defense, the *Reveries* will be written only for himself and will have no justificatory intention. The *Reveries* will be more concerned with his inner dispositions and his feelings than with his interpersonal relationships. The way the principle is stated here, the attention to his inner dispositions is at the expense of his body: because Rousseau is no longer able to participate in society, he sees no reason to worry about his body and therefore proposes to concentrate on the life of his soul.

At the same time, his emphasis on the way these essays are directed to an exploration of his inner self seems to be intended to restrict the potential audience. He explicitly states that he intends to write these essays only for himself, that he will actually carry out the goal Montaigne only pretended to aim at in his *Essays*. Rousseau presents himself as the future reader of the *Reveries:* he will read these essays over and thereby enjoy former pleasures again. He claims to be so intent upon writing this work for himself that he is not concerned about giving any order to the way he presents the modifications of his soul in these essays. He calls them a simple diary of his thoughts and feelings. And he asserts that he is totally unconcerned about what might happen to these essays, so unconcerned that he will take no special efforts to protect them from his enemies or to pass them on to posterity.

The First Walk ends, then, in much the same way as it begins, that is, on a note of inaccessibility. The emphasis here on the personal character of the *Reveries* corresponds to the subtlety of expression and emotionally charged prose that was so striking in the opening lines of the Walk. Still, to draw attention to this characteristic of inaccessibility in the First Walk is not to suggest that the Walk is impenetrable. Simply by giving more thought to the way the theme of the work—the exploration of self—arises. from Rousseau's unique kind of solitude, it can begin to make sense. His explanation of his new willingness to accept his status as a totally solitary being is emotionally charged, because that kind of solitude is so overwhelming. Unless one feels quite capable of doing without human fellowship completely, something Rousseau declares himself no more naturally disposed to here than in any of his other works, recognition of what that solitude entails must lead to an appreciation of the pathos he evokes here. And his claims about writing the *Reveries* only for himself can likewise be understood in terms of the basic theme of the work. Precisely because he finds himself so utterly apart, his exploration of himself can be conducted without concern for others. The detailed manner in which he expresses his lack of concern only serves to show the completeness of his solitude. In this sense, those features of the First Walk that make it appear inaccessible are inextricably related to Rousseau's unique situation and ought therefore to turn no reader away from a closer look at the work nor induce any reader to think that the only way to approach the *Reveries* is by a putative examination of Rousseau's mental well-being.

Differently stated, to approach the *Reveries* intelligently, one must take note of Rousseau's rhetoric and of the effect it would normally have upon the reader. But then one must refuse to be swayed by that rhetoric and ask instead about what Rousseau is trying to achieve by his use of it. The most persuasive reply to this question is that he wishes to create a special kind of mood, to evoke all the emotions which would arise if one saw oneself condemned to utter solitude, and to ascertain why he has the ability to enjoy this solitude. He prefaces his discussion of what he will do in the following essays by a statement of all the things which keep him away from human society and by an explanation of how his new solitude is so much deeper than any solitude he has hitherto experienced. Whereas he previously used solitary withdrawal as a means of avoiding bothersome social relationships, he can no longer form any kind of social tie. He thinks he has been wronged by having this solitude forced upon him, but henceforth he will not worry about such questions. Instead, he will use his new solitude to explore his soul and will no longer seek to justify himself. Thus, just as he now finds himself in a unique position for a human being, these essays will occupy a unique position among his writings: they will testify more than any other writing to what sets him apart from other men, but they will not be addressed to other men. They are intended to capture the moods of his soul rather than to persuade others about how to discipline their own souls. And this is why the *Reveries* is both the deepest and most forthright of Rousseau's autobiographical writings, while being at the same time the most difficult to comprehend.

On the surface, the Second Walk manifests a return to the despondent resignation that preceded Rousseau's declarations of tranquil confidence toward the end of the First Walk. There is greater emphasis here on the pathetic elements of his plight than on those which can lead to happiness. This difference in mood is evident from the very beginning of the Second Walk. It is best exemplified by Rousseau's change from his earlier expression of happiness at living in solitude and thus at being able to enjoy conversing with himself to his complaint in the second paragraph of the Second Walk that his decision to write about his reveries has come too late because his imagination is now too feeble to carry him off into ecstasy as it did formerly. One consequence of his now feeble imagination, he sadly recognizes, is that he will have to be content with what he can recall of his earlier reveries. When simple candor forces him to acknowledge that it is nonetheless pleasurable to recall earlier reveries, he prepares to cite an example to illustrate the point. However, the example he gives is* of a recent reverie, not a recollection of an earlier reverie. The example becomes somewhat confused, because the reverie itself was followed by a strange and revealing accident. Forgetting completely the point he set out to illustrate, Rousseau turns first to an account of that accident and then of the various incidents which followed it and which apparently brought him back to his earlier despondency. At each new step of the account, the problem of the relationship between remembering former reveries and pleasure or happiness becomes dimmer, while the stifling effects of what Rousseau takes to be the plot against him become more visible. By the end of the Walk, the inner turmoil generated by the plot has become the dominant issue, and Rousseau seeks to explain the new significance he attaches to it. Properly understood, this explanation shows that the tension between Rousseau's earlier resigned, but slightly defiant, acceptance of his fate and the more despondent attitude toward it arising from his reflections on the incidents which followed his accident reflects a deeper tension in his view of human life.

There are three major divisions, then, in the Second Walk. The introductory section is a discussion of the way Rousseau proposes to carry out his enterprise of writing the *Reveries,* of the benefits to be derived from such a method, and of its difficulties.[23] It is followed by his example of the pleasures this method procures, as well as by the story of the accident and its numerous repercussions.[24] Then the Walk concludes with Rousseau's explanation of what these events mean to him and his indication of how this interpretation corresponds to his new resolve.[25]

The major theme in the introductory section arises from Rousseau's explanation that it makes no difference whether he writes down the reveries he has during his daily walks or the recollections he has of earlier reveries: he contends that he falls back into his reveries whenever he attempts to remember them and is thus able to circumvent the barriers imposed by his languishing imagination. This assertion is important for what it implies about the status of reveries in *The Reveries of the Solitary Walker*. Properly speaking, there is only one account of a recent reverie in this work, the one which precedes the accident recounted here. All of the other reveries described in the following essays are recollections of earlier reveries. In other words, Rousseau presents the solitary walker's recollection of former reveries here, not the reveries the solitary walker now has. Moreover, since Rousseau is persuaded that he is closest to his natural self only during these moments of reverie,[26] this assertion is crucial for his attempt to accomplish the goal proposed in the First Walk of studying his inner dispositions and keeping a diary of them. Similarly, his admission that he did not reach the highest kind of happiness in his earlier reveries because of the constant worries he then had about other matters and that he is no longer able to embark upon new reveries casts his whole enterprise into doubt. How can he be confident of achieving the happiness he hopes to attain through reverie when all that is left to him is the possibility of remembering former reveries and of sometimes falling back into them?

The only viable answer is that he must equate mulling these former reveries over during his long walks and writing about them in these pages with a new level of actual reverie. At the very least, by recalling former reveries he can attain as much happiness as by actually having reveries. Both recollection of reveries and engaging in reveries require the kind of solitude so delightful to Rousseau, and both have the characteristic of self-sufficiency he desires. And under the best circumstances, it would be possible for him to reach a deeper level of happiness by recalling former reveries: the act of remembering would serve as a filter, thus permitting him to screen out any unpleasant features which might have been present in those former reveries and to preserve only the pleasant ones. What is more, by permitting him to bring the pleasant features of those earlier reveries together in a more intense manner and to dwell on them as long as he might wish, recollection would greatly enhance his pleasure. The same line of reasoning explains how Rousseau can accomplish the goal set forth in the First Walk, even though he no longer engages in actual reveries. As he turns his former reveries over in his memory and thereby falls back into them, he experiences the same inner state or natural self as he would by engaging in actual reveries.

Nonetheless, the question of whether Rousseau can aspire to the same kind of happiness by recalling former reveries as by actually engaging in reveries is far less important than that which seeks to determine the precise character of this happiness. Above all, it seems to be an intensely private activity. According to Rousseau, the beginning of reverie is withdrawal from society. For him, the source of true happiness is within ourselves and completely independent of other human beings. In other words, as is so clearly stated in the second and third paragraphs of this Walk, the man who knows how to be happy has no need of human society. These remarks further suggest that he views happiness as a kind of psychic state which is in no way dependent on education or on the kind of institutions fostered by human society. Rousseau's lament to himself in the reverie described here about not being allowed to do good to his fellow men indirectly supports this inference: if his lament serves any purpose in this context, it is to detract from the joy of the reverie. The reverie itself is soothing and pleasant, while the momentary recollection of his past and present relations with his fellow men is disconcerting and gloomy.[27] And if the reverie itself is intended to illustrate how reverie leads to happiness, his notion of happiness very clearly does not presuppose philosophic understanding. To be sure, Rousseau strikes something of a philosophic chord in admitting that he finds the nonfamiliar more pleasant than the familiar and that he prefers the general or the whole to the particular.

However, on reflection, it becomes evident that the real source of these distinctions is the impression they make on him, not the greater knowledge either would provide.[28]

Still, as has been mentioned already, not that reverie but the accident which followed it and its repercussions are the major focus of the Second Walk. Their importance derives in part from Rousseau's lyrical account of his fall with its very strange image of his sense of a new birth: when he regained consciousness after being bowled over by the Great Dane, he felt as though he had come into the world again and had done so without a body. The whole description of the sensations he experienced in these waking moments is a perfect illustration of the lack of concern for the body that became evident in the First Walk.[29] For a short time, Rousseau was able to view natural phenomena and to converse with other human beings while free from concern for his body or for his own self. He moved among men as though he were a walking and talking body whose soul perceived everything that occurred but remained majestically unperturbed and somehow distant.

Rousseau is not the first author to express this feeling of looking at himself as though he were standing outside of his body. In his *Essays*, Montaigne speaks at some length about a somewhat similar accident and the sensations resulting from it.[30] However, unlike Rousseau, Montaigne was knocked unconscious after being thrown from his horse during a ride in the countryside. And whereas Rousseau's fall resulted from the recklessness of a wealthy man, Montaigne's was caused by the recklessness of one of his servants. Yet both authors liken the sensations they experienced during this period of unconsciousness to what they might expect at the moment of death, Montaigne explicitly and Rousseau implicitly. Montaigne, who claims—falsely, according to Rousseau—to write his *Essays* only for himself, recounts this whole incident as part of his reflections about what philosophers have said about death and thus contrasts their views with his own experience. Even so, what he deduces from this experience or recounts elsewhere in the *Essays* is hardly helpful for the philosophic task of learning how to die. He is too concerned with the body and with physical sensations to ever raise the problem of the soul's ultimate happiness. In fact, Montaigne's failure to approach this deeper issue provoked Pascal to criticize him for speaking about death in such an excessively cowardly and spiritless manner throughout the *Essays*.[31]

From the beginning of the Second Walk, Rousseau's thoughts hover around his awareness of the closeness of death. He draws attention to the way age has affected his imagination and made his body decrepit. He contrasts his present aged and somewhat sad state with the happy moments he enjoyed in earlier times. Even when he describes his reverie prior to the fall, he is especially moved by the symbolic parallel between the approach of winter and his advanced age. In sum, he sets a scene which suggests that he is comparing his perception of things around him during his return to consciousness with the way he believes the soul may perceive the world once death has occurred. If this is indeed the analogy he wishes to call forth, he differs from Montaigne by likening death to an extended reverie and thereby removing its threat. In fact, he does more. To the extent that he makes reverie or the recollection of former reveries identical to the highest happiness he can achieve and at the same time not dissimilar to what little he can claim to know about death, Rousseau comes very close to expressing supreme confidence about being able to face it with dignity. Further evidence that this is his intention may be gathered from the way his account of the events following this accident point to the question of death.

When Rousseau first begins to speak about these events, he momentarily turns away from the question of death. But toward the end of his narration, it recurs. Unfortunately, when he does return to it, he is less interested in death as something approximated through reverie than in his death as something his contemporaries apparently desire, or so it appears from the way he organizes his discussion of the events which followed the fall. Ostensibly, Rousseau recounts his interview with the secretary of M. Lenoir in order to illustrate the bizarre circumstances that occurred after his fall and reactivated his old fears. Once he draws the desired conclusion from this story, he relates another story about the unusual events following his fall and then tells still two more stories in the same vein. In other words, not counting the fall, four stories are narrated here: Rousseau's interview with M. Lenoir's secretary, the mysterious note in Mme d'Ormoy's novel, the premature rumors about his death, and his suspicion that false copies of his writings were being prepared for publication after his death. Yet, except for the fall, the formal organization of the Walk allows for only one story: the interview with M. Lenoir's secretary. The three other stories seem to be little more than afterthoughts, as though one called another to mind. However, there is more than a tenuous relationship between these stories. Each story contributes to the despondent mood Rousseau claims as his own by the end of the Second Walk. Each serves to pull him back from the euphoria induced by the thoughts about reveries and his return to consciousness after the fall. And taken together, they justify his suspicion that his contemporaries desire his death.

The unexpected concern of such a high public official as M. Lenoir does offer striking evidence that those in power were not indifferent to Rousseau's well-being. Even a passing appreciation of the difficulties he had experienced since his return to Paris in 1770 is sufficient to suggest that this concern could not be inspired by motives of Christian charity. Similarly, the attention shown Rousseau by Mme d'Ormoy, her exaggerated praise of his talents in the preface to her novel, and her clever use of a note to express controversial political opinions which could easily be imputed to him are strong indications that other people really did want to damage his reputation or otherwise cause trouble for him. What is more, Mme d'Ormoy's position as a somewhat successful author suggests that she might have been acting in collusion with Rousseau's old enemies from literary circles. Still, neither of these two stories is as poignant or alarming as that about the obituary notices appearing in the *Avignon Courier*, especially when the notices themselves are read. Thus, whether Rousseau's suspicions about his enemies preparing a series of works to be issued in his

name after his death are accurate or not, the other stories show
how correct he is to think that others wish him ill.

Apart from the evidence of these stories, especially the two
which can be independently verified, there are additional reasons
to accept Rousseau's assertions about the existence of a plot against
him. Scholarly studies have corroborated what he said in his earlier
autobiographical writings about the devious tricks directed against
him by Diderot, Grimm, d'Holbach, and d'Alembert and about the
way he was viciously attacked in pamphlets penned by Voltaire.
Similarly, the mean-spirited maneuverings of Pastor Montmollin of
Môtiers against Rousseau have been documented.[32] Here,
however, Rousseau is less interested in speaking about the way all
of this proves the existence of the plot than in speculating about the
reasons for its success. In the concluding section of the Walk, he
goes far beyond what even the most sympathetic interpretation of
these stories will permit. His exaggerated reading of their significance brings back the question of death, but brings it back in a
very problematic fashion. Now Rousseau contends that God must
be somehow sanctioning the plot, that God must have decided to
help his enemies torture him.

The problem with such a contention is that it weakens human
resolve to strive for virtue. If God has really directed all the
details of the plot, there is no reason to worry about human
affairs: whatever a man may try to do, God will dispose of him as
He wishes. As though desirous of avoiding that implication, Rousseau attempts to express his faith in God's ultimate justice. He
does so by asserting his confidence that his patience will be
rewarded in the life to come, however much God might be
willing to let him suffer now.[33] One reason for Rousseau to blunt
the implication which follows from attributing the success of the
plot to God's will is that it goes against his whole teaching.
Rousseau is nothing if he is not a teacher of virtue. All of his
public writings were designed to show men how to improve
themselves and how to reshape their institutions accordingly.
However, the corrective he offers to that implication is not very
felicitous. It is at variance with his statements elsewhere about
God, especially with his attempt to defend God's goodness and

concern for mankind against Voltaire's bitter poems *On Natural Law* and *On the Disaster at Lisbon*.[34] In his other writings, Rousseau attributed the rise of evil to man and defended God's justice in terms of what happens here-below rather than by means of a vague vision of the life to come.

The first view he expresses in this concluding section is none-theless consonant with what he says earlier in the Walk about reverie or recalling reveries and with what he intimates about the relationship of reverie to death. Because Rousseau portrays reverie as so intensely personal and asocial, it does not matter whether he can overcome the effects of the plot or not. Moreover, to the extent that the happiness found in reverie owes nothing to moral or intellectual virtue, he can embrace this conclusion without having to forsake the joy promised by reverie. The second view, that is, the modification of the implications of this outrageous contention, has the merit of allowing Rousseau to return to his former sense of resignation and to be "unperturbed like God Himself," [35] but it does so on questionable grounds. This more conventional view about the reward awaiting the just in the life to come also conflicts with what Rousseau intimates here about reverie and death. As the Walk closes, then, Rousseau seems to be wavering between a view of the world that allows him to find personal happiness only if he renounces all of the human goals he previously defended and one that offers him contentment only if he reorients his basic views about good and evil. Faced with such a dilemma, he pursues the only viable path: he devotes the next Walk to a consideration of his thoughts about God.

The opening of the Third Walk is abrupt. No attempt is made to develop the problem raised at the end of the Second Walk, nor does there seem to be any attempt to relate the subject of this Walk to what went before. However, the spirit of resignation which was revived in the Second Walk is modified here. In this Walk, the emphasis is on old age and on the greater difficulties it places upon Rousseau because of his strange situation.

A phrase attributed to Solon is set out as a kind of title for the Third Walk. It is reported that during his old age Solon frequently affirmed that he continued to learn many things as he grew older. When Rousseau attempts to apply this statement to himself, he is led to the kind of question an old man would raise. Almost as though he were railing against an impending death that will no longer be postponed, Rousseau plaintively inquires: "Is the moment when we have to die the time to learn how we should have lived?" Then, in the last paragraph of the essay, he answers his own question. Although he denies that he can imitate Solon and learn new things each day, he concedes that it is possible for him to make some intellectual progress. In other words, he seeks to emphasize the importance of identifying the kind of lessons proper to an old man in his situation. Since the concerns of old age are immediately those of how to live more virtuously and of how to improve the condition of the soul, it is not worthwhile to worry about questions of how we should have lived or of what we should have done. By this same reasoning, it is not worthwhile to worry about what we should have believed. Rousseau's reflections about Solon's phrase permit him, then, to dissociate himself from the implications of his earlier teachings about religion. These reflections also permit him to continue the theme about the afterlife which arose at the end of the Second Walk. Here, Rousseau's major query is about the kind of things he might take away with him at the moment of his death.

The Third Walk is, after all, primarily about Rousseau's religious teachings and how he reached them. It consists of three basic divisions. The introductory section investigates the merits of Solon's phrase, its applicability to Rousseau in his present situation, and the larger issue of the goodness of knowledge.[36] While we do learn as we grow older, all learning is not simply desirable. In thinking about the experiences he has endured for the previous twenty years, Rousseau concludes that he would have been better off had he remained ignorant instead of acquiring that kind of knowledge. Bitter experience has taught him the terrible cruelty of which men are capable and persuaded him that his attempts to change men, their ideas, and their institutions have been in vain.

His awareness of his old age reminds him that learning has a purpose: we seek knowledge so that we might learn how to live better. Knowledge, in other words, is not simply good; its goodness derives from its usefulness. Since so much depends on living life correctly, the most useful knowledge is that concerning the end of our life. But old age is not the time to acquire such knowledge. If anything, it is the time to put such knowledge into practice. Or, to state the same idea in approximately Rousseau's words, the only learning appropriate to an old man is that of learning how to die.[37] In the most important respect, then, old men are eminently qualified for the study of philosophy: they are the ones most likely to understand the reason why Socrates defined philosophy as learning how to die.

But even though Rousseau claims that old age and bitter experience have brought him to endorse this more traditional view about learning, he also admits that he has always been peculiarly open to the demands of the philosophic quest. He has always felt a certain estrangement from the demands of the world and tried to find his happiness in activities other than those pursued by most men. Already in his youth he was moved by strong desire to escape the bustle of society and to seek the calm of solitary contemplation. During those moments of solitude, Rousseau focused on the problem of understanding himself and on seizing the meaning of his existence. Even his early studies and experiences inclined him in this direction. In a way, everything—natural disposition, chance occurrences, and will—seemed to pull him away from the values of the larger society and to bring him into closer dependence on himself. Above all, this estrangement from the world and its demands led him to an awareness of the way action depends upon thought and thus to a concern with the grounds for his own action.[38] Whereas that concern with thinking originally led Rousseau to deep reflections about the world and about God, here his explanation of how that concern influenced him serves as a transition to the second division of the Third Walk, that is, to his account of how he came to formulate his ideas about religion.

There are three parts to this account, and they all relate to the conscious reform undertaken by Rousseau when he reached the age of forty.[39] The first part concerns the period of time leading up to the reform, a period marked by his growing sense of estrangement and by his allegiance to the principles and maxims he had accepted from childhood without ever seriously questioning them.[40] Throughout this period, Rousseau grew increasingly aware of fundamental differences between himself and his fellow men. In the beginning, he realized that whereas he sought knowledge and studied to learn, they sought fame and studied to teach—that is, to be viewed as having something to say. They desired recognition, not understanding or truth. Ultimately he found that nothing valued by his fellow men answered his needs and recognized that he would never find happiness by embracing their goals. According to the account of the *Reveries*, this was the moment in which he decided to undertake a thorough reform of his habits and opinions.

The second part of this account consists of an enumeration of the actions Rousseau took as part of the reform and an explanation of how he reached the thoughts which characterize it.[41] As he outlines this period of time here, it extends from his fortieth year until the publication of the *Émile* in 1762, that is, for about ten years. It began with his renunciation of the conventional patterns of dress by which men tried to distinguish themselves from one another and with his turning away from all career concerns in order to pursue a simple occupation that would meet his needs while leaving him completely master of his time. The purpose of these external features of the reform was to achieve greater simplicity and independence, as well as to underscore dramatically his break with his contemporaries. There was also an internal aspect to the reform, Rousseau's severe examination of himself and of his opinions or sentiments. As though recalling the thoughts he had originally expressed in the *First Discourse*, Rousseau now attributes his desire for this inner reform to his recognition of the absurdity of the judgments made by others. And in a more obvious reference to the *First Discourse* and its success, he admits that he also desired to undertake such a reform because he had already become disgusted with the falseness of literary fame.

He traces his relentless pursuit of solitude to this moment of reform and emphasizes the sincerity with which he examined himself.

But as Rousseau relates how zealously he pursued this inner reform, he suddenly breaks away from an account of the reform and turns to an indictment of his contemporaries. Whereas his reference to them in the first part of this account is primarily to censure their vainglorious pursuit of learning, the purpose of this reference is to accuse them of having tried to harass and confuse him. He identifies them as modern philosophers, atheists, and dogmatists and contrasts them with the ancient philosophers who presumably would have helped rather than have hindered him in his quest. Although he speaks at some length about these modern philosophers and about their attempts to shake his beliefs, he emphasizes that he persisted in his task and eventually settled upon the opinions he would hold. In closing this part of the account, he acknowledges the possibility of those opinions being erroneous, but absolves himself from blame on the grounds that he did his best.

There is, however, a major problem with both parts of the account. Neither here nor in the first part does Rousseau discuss the content of the opinions he developed by means of this external and internal moral reform. All he says is that the result of his "painful seeking" came close to what he expressed in the "Profession of Faith of the Savoyard Vicar." Otherwise, the whole account of the reform is limited to a discussion of *how* these thoughts were reached. There is no description of their substance nor any defense of their logical soundness. To the contrary, there is almost an argument to the effect that they lack logical soundness. The suggestion made in the Second Walk about God's basic inscrutability is taken a step further here as Rousseau effectively denies that we can have any rational certainty about what God has allowed men to know about Himself or about the divine order which permeates the universe. In keeping with the general tone of the *Reveries*, Rousseau places major emphasis on the way these thoughts accord with his own sentiments. But he also comes close to acknowledging here that it would be fruitless

to seek anything more than a sentimental defense of these
thoughts.

This becomes more evident in the third part of Rousseau's
account, which is a description of his attempts to overcome the
nagging doubts that continue to plague him about the validity of
these thoughts or beliefs.[42] Claiming that he has made these
beliefs the principles of his conduct, Rousseau offers only the
following intellectual defense of their soundness: they are based
on the harmony he discerns in the physical universe and its
congruity with what he takes to be the moral order; what is more,
these beliefs enable him to endure the misery of his present
situation. Now, as before, they console him because of their
promise of future justice. Still, such a defense does not make him
immune to the doubts raised by his contemporaries, and he
acknowledges that they sometimes appear almost insuperable.
But, content to concede that all of these questions are probably
beyond human understanding, Rousseau refuses to embark on
another investigation. Evoking his age and weakened mental
faculties, he excuses himself and thus allows his final defense of
these beliefs to rest on a reiteration of his feelings about God's
justice first stated at the end of the Second Walk. Rousseau makes
no further attempt to defend their validity here, nor does he
explain how this view of God's justice fits in with his other
arguments about God. Instead, he renews his attack upon the
sincerity of his contemporaries. His contention is that he differs
from them insofar as he takes these beliefs as his own: in addition
to teaching them publicly to others, he is consoled by them in his
private life. His contemporaries, on the other hand, pay public
homage to these beliefs, but act according to entirely different
maxims in private. Their secret doctrine is so pernicious that it
threatens the well-being of society, whereas his offers serenity,
self-contentment, hope, and consolation, as well as political
justice.[43]

Although Rousseau does not identify his contemporaries by
name, his repeated references to their insincerity, his identification of them as atheists and dogmatists, and his attack upon their
secret and cruel morality leave little doubt but that he was

thinking of the philosophers of the Enlightenment. The whole of his mature life consisted of one long battle against them and their goals: it began at the moment of the *First Discourse,* continued through the period of self-imposed exile as well as the years of troubled wandering after his flight from France, and is present even here in this last writing. The moral reform discussed here was the beginning of Rousseau's attempt to establish a new basis for the religious faith of simple people, a faith that had been shaken by the Enlightenment philosophers. He opposed them on the grounds that their liberalism was only a facade; properly understood, their arguments really tended to further the cause of enlightened despotism or absolute monarchy. Unlike Rousseau, they believed in the possibility of a nation of philosophers, that is, of fully rational men, and directed their efforts to public education. They did not concern themselves with religion, except cynically, as a tool to keep the people obedient. Until people were sufficiently learned to conduct themselves according to the principles of reason, they would be ruled by religion. Those who had some kind of philosophic understanding were free to believe in God or not, as they saw fit. In part, the contempt the Enlightenment philosophers had for religion arose from their fear of fanaticism, which they held to be far worse than atheism. While agreeing that fanaticism was a terrible passion, Rousseau argued against the notion of an atheistic society by pointing out that such a society would lead to moral degradation. He considered the merit of religious faith to be its ability to elevate the hearts of men and to inspire them with an appropriate attitude about death, whereas he criticized atheism for fostering too great a concern with self-interest and a consequent unwilling-ness to consider the common interest. For the same reason he opposed those who, apparently inspired by Hobbes, sought to replace the fear of God by fear of the ruler in order to make the people easier to rule.

In sum, Rousseau rejected the political goals of Enlightenment philosophy and espoused radical republicanism, because he considered it the only way to protect freedom and equality. Recognizing, moreover, that a republic in which all citizens were sovereign could not function properly unless they were all united by a common set of beliefs and a mutual resolve to obey the laws, he spoke ardently in favor of a religious faith free from intolerance.[44] Because the elements of that faith were set forth at greatest length in the "Profession of Faith of the Savoyard Vicar" and because it was intended as the fullest refutation of the doctrine propounded by his contemporaries, Rousseau claims here that it "may one day make a revolution among men, if good sense and good faith are ever reborn among them." [45]

Now there can be little question but what he truly deplored the deviousness of his contemporaries and abhorred the perniciousness of their secret doctrine. He attacked them too frequently and argued against them too thoroughly to permit any doubts about his fundamental disagreement with them. What is less certain, however, is whether the beliefs he proposes in order to counter their views and secure sound popular government are beliefs he accepts for himself. Despite his claims here, one might justly wonder whether the moral prescriptions Rousseau offers the simple citizens of a popular republic and his explanations of what constitutes their happiness are addressed to himself as well as to others. Does he think of himself as a simple citizen, as a teacher of simple citizens, or in entirely different terms? After all, it is quite possible for him to have vigorously opposed the errors he perceived in the political goals of the Enlightenment philosophers by means of arguments intended to persuade others rather than himself. He may have been so impressed by the usual irrationality of most people that he passionately defended the opinions in which they needed to believe if they were to function as decent citizens of a sovereign republic and yet have been fully aware that these opinions were not completely defensible. Indeed, it seems highly probable that Rousseau did propose these beliefs in order to refute then dominant views and to redirect public opinion, but deemed other beliefs to be more suitable for himself.

Admittedly, numerous objections can be made to such a conjecture. For example, what Rousseau says here about the "Profession of Faith of the Savoyard Vicar" being "approximately" his own does not differ substantially from what he says about it elsewhere. Even though he insisted on speaking of himself as the editor of the "Profession of Faith" in his *Letter to Christophe de Beaumont,* carefully distinguishing between arguments put forth in his own name and those put forth by the Savoyard vicar, he acknowledged that it contained the same maxims and the same ways of thinking as the expression of his own creed in the *Second Discourse,* the *Letter to M. d'Alembert,* and the *New Héloïse.*[46] In at least one other writing, he has pointed to the close relationship between the "Profession of Faith of the Savoyard Vicar" and the creed of the dying Héloïse and suggested that it results from their proximity to his own views.[47] Nonetheless, when one compares the original presentation of these beliefs with their presentation here, the conjecture appears more defensible. When Rousseau originally tried to present these religious beliefs, the presentations were accompanied by long and involved arguments. Although he referred to the difficulty of attaining complete certainty in such matters in those earlier writings, the overwhelming emphasis in the presentations was on the logical soundness of the position adopted. By stressing the insuperable objections to these beliefs here, he seems to suggest that he, too, has a secret doctrine. Nor are the numerous passages in which he explicitly affirms his faith in God adequate proof against such a conclusion. Many of these affirmations occur in letters to individuals, and we have already seen that Rousseau does not consider a statement in a private letter to have any kind of general significance.[48] Similarly, given the circumstances, his protestations of belief in the *Letter to Christophe de Beaumont* and the *Letters Written from the Mountain* are highly suspect.[49]

What is especially striking in the first of those two works, however, is Rousseau's argument that since man is made for society, the truest religion is the most social and most human religion. It is striking because Rousseau never taught that man was made for society. And by alluding to his old analysis of natural man—an analysis that denied man's natural sociability—at the very beginning of that work, Rousseau indicated the specious character of this argument.[50] He made this specious argument solely to buttress the major theme of his statement to the

archbishop: above all, Rousseau wanted him to understand the
extent to which his writing had been directed to the defense of
God. Rousseau saw himself as the only author who had argued
God's case consistently and had defended the usefulness of
religion. That he had frequently used specious or rhetorical
arguments did not trouble him, for such arguments permitted him
to silence his opponents.[51] Even though Rousseau did not consider
society to be man's natural end, he recognized that for the sake of
self-preservation man was now forced to live in society. And as
has already been explained, his concern with religion arose from
this recognition of man's need for society and from his conclusion
that good political life, that is, popular sovereignty, was not
possible without a religious doctrine which would help each
citizen fulfill his civic duties. That Rousseau endorsed the
practical consequences of this reasoning in his own life is proven
by his reflections on why it was correct for him to return to the
Protestant faith when he decided to take up his citizenship in
Geneva again.[52]

Still, even though Rousseau fully dedicated himself to his self-
appointed role of spokesman for democracy and religion and even
adapted the external aspects of his personal life to the demands of
his teaching, there was another side to his thinking. His familiarity with the ancient philosophers, to whom he refers earlier in
this Walk,[53] made him aware of the tension between philosophy
and society. He recognized that in the final analysis the philosopher must stand apart from society, that the philosopher is necessarily something of a solitary walker. The philosopher desires a
way of life and an understanding that are incompatible with the
demands of usual political life. Even in the closing paragraphs of
the *First Discourse*, Rousseau testified to his awareness of this
conflict between the demands of philosophy and society. One
indication that he ultimately sided more with philosophy than
with society with respect to his personal goals is the sequel he
arranged to the "Profession of Faith of the Savoyard Vicar." After
speaking in favor of religion through the mouth of another person,
Rousseau offered, in his own name, a kind of refined Epicurean
creed that was in strict accordance with nature and completely

free from duty.[54] This creed set forth moral principles highly similar to those of the Savoyard vicar, but did so without referring to revelation or to any kind of religious doctrine. Even though these principles were derived from reflections about how Rousseau could obtain the greatest personal enjoyment, they permitted him to live in harmony and justice with others. They favored a life removed from the pressing demands of civic life without promoting unsociability. The description of happiness to be presented in the Fifth Walk and the subsequent explanation of why Rousseau considers himself temperamentally unsuited for citizenship are powerful complements to that refined Epicurean creed. Still other indications of Rousseau's ultimate predilections are to be found in the accounts scattered throughout his earlier autobiographical writings of how he naturally stood apart from society and found great pleasure in giving free play to his imagination.

By dwelling on his own doubts here, then, Rousseau intimates that the beliefs he set forth in earlier works were not as sound as they might be. Without exaggeration, he can be described as suggesting that the former accounts of those beliefs are at least partially untrue. The beliefs stated in those other works are more suitable for the majority of mankind, for those who are continuously prey to passions and who judge everything in terms of future compensation for the ills of this life. They are formulated for the sake of people who live in political society and who have no desire to foresake it. They correspond to the needs of citizens like Émile or Julie (Héloïse) and help them respond to the greater needs of their fellow citizens who understand these matters less well. They do not correspond to the needs of one who lives apart from society and who ministers to men without depending on their company for his own happiness. Anyone who can identify happiness as the sweet sentiment of existence, a feeling concerned with neither past nor future but entirely involved in the present moment, will not subscribe to such beliefs, for he will be free from the worries they are designed to ease.

This interpretation derives from skepticism about Rousseau's assertion that he founds his hope for future compensation on his

belief in God's ultimate justice. How that assertion conflicts with
what he says elsewhere about his personal beliefs has already been
discussed, as have the suspicions generated by his failure to defend that assertion here or to speak about the substance of his
beliefs. The conclusion to the Third Walk contributes to this same
skepticism. Acknowledging in the last paragraph that he can
make some progress in his old age, even if it is not the kind of
intellectual progress vaunted by Solon, Rousseau speaks of the
knowledge he might still acquire about the virtues proper to his
soul. Such knowledge does not promise to make him better, for
development in that direction is never possible: he has always
insisted that all things are good by nature and that they can never
become better; they can only degenerate. But such knowledge
might make him more virtuous; i.e., it might help him to return to
his original goodness or to preserve those features of it that are
still present. As he enumerates the different virtues he might
acquire even now, it becomes evident that they depend on nothing but his own resolve. Commendable as they are, these virtues
in no way result from belief in God or in God's ultimate justice.[55]
As the Third Walk closes, then, Rousseau returns to the optimism
about his fate which he proclaimed in the First Walk. Confidence
stemming from faith in future compensation is for others. Rousseau's is rooted in his enjoyment of reverie, not in hope beyond his
control.

   This refusal to defend the notion that God's justice will bring
future compensation, even though it was a central feature of the
religious teaching attributed to the Savoyard vicar and to Julie,
suggests that those earlier statements are based on a fundamental
abstraction from the truth. Or, to be more direct, it suggests that
they contain a basic falsehood. Tacit admission of falsehood about
the argument expressed in these writings fits in well with the
theme of the *Reveries:* Rousseau's break with society and its
demands. Now that his thoughts are centered on himself, he will
no longer strive to protect the opinions of others. But it also raises
the question of what might excuse or justify lying about such
important issues. Moreover, if the teaching Rousseau set forth in
his earlier writings was intended for others and thus does not

express the beliefs he personally holds about God and the goal of political association, what does he think about such matters? To respond to the first question, Rousseau examines himself in the next Walk about lying. Once that task is completed, a task whose relationship to the subject of this Walk is signaled by a final reference to Solon's maxim, Rousseau can pursue the other question. He can explain his own views about ultimate happiness.

Rousseau begins the Fourth Walk with an anecdote about how finding a copy of a journal addressed to him by an acquaintance on the same day that he was reading Plutarch's essay on benefiting from enemies prompted him to consider the problem of lying. He concludes by alluding to the statement of Solon cited in the opening paragraph of the Third Walk. The reflections about God occurring in the Third Walk are followed, then, by reflections about lying occasioned by a chance event. On the surface, only the references to Solon tie the two Walks together. But they are clearly related in other ways. A determination of the conditions which might justify lying is of interest primarily because of the broader issues that arose in the Third Walk. Having alluded to the pious lies he told to combat his contemporaries and defend the faith of simple citizens, Rousseau now seeks to explain how he can nonetheless claim to be thoroughly dedicated to the truth.

Rousseau's choice of Plutarch as one of his favorite authors at the very beginning of the Walk shows how indirectly this subject will be approached. Given the topic of the last Walk, a reiteration of his deep appreciation of the Bible would be much more appropriate.[56] There is a similar kind of elusiveness about the lesson he draws from his reading of Plutarch, that is, that by examining himself about lying he will come closer to fulfilling the Delphic maxim. When he first mentions what he has learned from Plutarch, Rousseau seems to agree with Plutarch's contention that only the man who intends to censure must be unimpeachable.[57] However, this kind of lesson has no relevance for the *Reveries,* whose purpose is to explore Rousseau's moral character. Not until the concluding lines of the Walk does Rousseau explain that he really understands Plutarch to mean that only the man who

intends to stand apart from society can be simply truthful. Even
the lies Rousseau cites as he examines himself about lying are
unrelated to the pious lies of the Third Walk. His examples of
useful lies (the one to protect young Fazy and that about the
wound he received from Pleince) are lies concerning events, not
ideas. These, like the other two he recounts (the lie involving poor
Marion and that told to Mme Vacassin's impertinent daughter),
were prompted by some kind of passion. He makes no explicit
reference to the more intriguing kinds of lies, that is, lies about
ideas that are not prompted by passions.

The Fourth Walk, the longest of all the Walks, consists of four
parts. Rousseau's opening anecdote and his reflections about the
number of lies he has told serve as an introduction.[58] Then,
referring to a definition of lying he found in a philosophy book, he
tries to determine the conditions under which lying might be
permitted and what kind of lies might be told.[59] Once that investigation is completed, he applies the results to himself so as to
gain some understanding of why he feels no remorse for certain
kinds of lies.[60] In the concluding section, Rousseau reflects anew
on the reasons for truthfulness being valued and then, blaming
himself for not having adhered more rigorously to the truth,
reaffirms his decision to live a life apart.[61]

When Rousseau first thinks about lying, he is preoccupied by
the deep regret he still feels for a lie told during his youth. He
attributes that lie to his timidity: seeing himself in a terribly
embarrassing situation, he lied to escape further mortification.
The cause is identified simply to explain why he lied, not to
excuse himself for the lie. It was inexcusable, because it harmed
someone else. However, as he mulls over his past actions, he
realizes that he has told a number of other lies since then. And
even though he has always endeavored, to be worthy of his
motto—to consecrate his life to truth—he feels no remorse for any
of these lies. Realizing that there must be occasions when lies are
not blameworthy, when they can be justified or excused, Rousseau
decides to think more carefully about this question of lying.

He begins by turning to a definition of lying he claims to have
found in a philosophy book: hiding a truth that ought to be

declared. From this, he draws the obvious conclusion that remaining silent about the truth or even speaking falsely to someone to whom we owe nothing is not to lie. Further reflection shows that to apply the definition, even with this modification, he must determine (a) when and how we owe someone else the truth and (b) whether it is possible to deceive innocently. Rousseau approaches the first question by considering what we owe others and asserts that we owe what is important or useful to them. To make the answer more precise, he distinguishes general and abstract truth from particular and individual truth. Whereas he holds the first to be essential to man and thus necessary to tell, he thinks the latter might sometimes be indifferent or even harmful and thus not always necessary to tell. General and abstract truth, that by which "man learns to direct himself, to be what he ought to be, to do what he ought to do, to head toward his true end," is what pertains to the moral realm or justice.[62] Although Rousseau finds it more difficult to categorize particular and individual truth, he does give an example of it. For us to know whether the sand at the bottom of the sea is white or red matters not at all. Since the question is purely indifferent to us, anyone who lied to us about it would neither harm us nor deprive us of any good.[63]

Rousseau's answer to the first question, that we owe others the truth when it is useful to them, is problematic in at least three respects. In the first place it is only a partial answer: it fails to explain how we owe others the truth. Second, it is based on rather specious reasoning. To prove that we owe what is useful, Rousseau likens the useful to property, that is, what is our own and therefore our due. His contention is that the idea of property is founded on usefulness, because no one would claim as his own anything that was entirely useless. The relevant corollary is that since nothing in the moral order is useless, whatever pertains to it is, like property, our own and owed us. Therefore, general and abstract truth, that which is always owed, is part of the moral order of justice.[64] Finally, even though Rousseau insists on usefulness as the criterion for the truth we are obligated to tell, he claims that he is unable to identify those truths which are completely useless and thus not owed. Only when he momentarily sets this problem aside to turn to the question of whether we can innocently deceive does he cite the color of the sand at the bottom of the sea as an example of a useless truth. In other words, his partial answer to the first question and complete answer to the second depend upon his discovery of a rule which will permit him to distinguish the useful from the useless. To escape this dilemma, he turns to moral instinct or conscience as a guide. Even that choice is problematic. Moral instinct or conscience can only identify the intention of the speaker, and it is also necessary to be aware of the consequences of the lie. Rousseau's ultimate resolution of all these problems is to limit lying to a very narrow sphere. He selects a standard which is primarily negative: only lies which neither help nor hinder ourselves or another can be excused.[65]

However, this standard conflicts with what Rousseau has said about lying in his other writings as well as with some of the examples of excusable lies which he sets forth here. In the *Émile*, he contended that it was morally permissible to take a useful lesson from a false historical fact and disparaged his contemporaries for ignoring this possibility:

> The ancient historians are full of ideas we could use, even if the facts used to illustrate them are false. But we do not know how to obtain any true advantage from history. Critical erudition absorbs everything, as though it matters at all whether a fact is true as long as we can get some useful instruction from it. Sensible men ought to consider history as a tissue of fables whose morality is very suited to the human heart.[66]

Similarly, when he defended himself against the accusations of Archbishop Beaumont, he insisted that he had always promised to tell the truth "with respect to everything that was useful" and had kept his promise "as much as he could" and "according to his talent." [67] The obvious implication, especially given the immediate context of that declaration, is that Rousseau did not tell the truth about everything. As he explained in that work and elsewhere, he did not believe that most people could be cured of their intellectual blindness or even that they should be cured: fully in favor of changing the prejudices of the people, he did not think it necessary to try to replace their prejudices with knowledge. Sometimes other prejudices or half truths would be preferable. And in the *Confessions,* he praised Thérèse for being clever enough to lie to Mme d'Épinay about the location of his letters from Mme d'Houdetot, a strong indication that he considered lies which helped another to be excusable at times.[68] His lies on behalf of Fazy and Pleince are like Thérèse's, and later in the Walk Rousseau speaks of them as excusable lies.

In short, the negative standard presented here not only contradicts what Rousseau has said about lying in his other works, it also contradicts what he says in the fuller argument of the Fourth Walk. But ignoring such problems for the moment, Rousseau applies the standard strictly and identifies fictions as the only kind of lies which may be excused. He is especially interested in those fictions which have a moral purpose. Contending that only moral fictions, such as allegories or fables, which neither help nor harm another in any way can be excused, he condemns white lies as real lies. These cannot be excused, because they are usually told in order to give an advantage to another person or to ourselves.[69] Even fables must be condemned as real lies if they bring harm to others in any way. To illustrate his point, Rousseau cites an example of a harmful fable: Montesquieu's tale that the *Temple de Gnide* was a translation of a Greek manuscript which he had obtained from a French ambassador to the Ottoman Porte.[70] Rousseau judges the work dangerous because of its "voluptuous details and lascivious images" and contends that they destroyed any moral purpose it might have had.

The *Temple de Gnide* is a story about the pleasures and trials of love. It primarily recounts the romance between two young men living in Cnidus and two young Cnidian maidens, but is interwoven with references to Venus or Aphrodite and to the strange ways she is adored in different parts of the Greek world. Consequently, the narrative is laced with many sensual images and numerous allusions to lovemaking among gods and mortals. The story moves from the two young men telling each other about the depth of their affection for these maidens to their being mysteriously overwhelmed by jealousy and suspicion. Their moment of anguish is portrayed in great detail and with evocative prose, but they are eventually rescued from their doubts by the intercession of the god of wine. At the end, each lover is reconciled with his beloved, and there is a strong suggestion that this reconciliation ends in seduction. From Rousseau's perspective, the story and its allusions are so erotic or provocative that they can serve no moral purpose, and the lie about the manuscript is therefore "very worthy of punishment." [71]

Montesquieu's lie is very similar to the one Rousseau told about the love story he wrote, the *New Héloïse*. He presented the story as a series of letters between two young lovers of which he claimed to be the editor rather than the author. Like Montesquieu's story, Rousseau's contains erotic images and highly emotional passages. But it has, in addition, a very lofty moral teaching which is not affected by such prose. Wanting his readers to be so inspired by the depiction of morality in the novel that they would endeavor to emulate its characters, Rousseau would not admit that they were really fictitious:

> I love to think of a married couple reading this collection together, finding in it new courage to endure their common toils and perhaps new ideas about how to make them useful. How could they contemplate this portrait of a happy household without wanting to imitate such a delightful model? How could they be moved by the charm of conjugal union . . . and theirs not become closer and firmer? When they put their reading aside, they will neither be saddened about their own condition nor disheartened about their responsibilities. To the contrary, everything around them will seem to take on a more cheerful aspect; their duties will become noble in their eyes. Once again they will delight in the pleasures of nature: its true feelings will arise again in their hearts and, seeing happiness within their reach, they will learn to savor

it. They will perform the same tasks, but will perform them with another soul and will do as true Patriarchs what they used to do as peasants.[72]

When Rousseau published the novel, he defended the fiction on the grounds that it favored a moral good. To the putative criticism that it conflicted with his motto, he replied that even though he had decided not to place his motto on the title page of the novel he saw no need to relinquish it. Finding nothing inconsistent in this procedure, he insisted that he still preferred truth to glory and still considered himself to be a truthful man.

Even by the strict standard presented here, this fiction would still be justified, as would Rousseau's other fiction about having been only the editor of the "Profession of Faith of the Savoyard Vicar." But that is the limit. Although his basic purpose in this whole discussion of fictions is to prove that speech must serve justice rather than narrow self-interest, his reasoning is too restricted to achieve that goal. Condemning what is contrary to the truth and conflicts with justice as a lie, he excuses what is contrary to the truth and does not concern justice as a fiction. He thereby passes over in silence a more important kind of excusable lie: one that is contrary to the truth but serves justice nonetheless. This is the kind of lie he later calls to mind by citing Tasso when he recounts how he lied to protect young Fazy.[73] Even though this consideration is present in his own understanding of what justifies the fictions he told about the *New Héloïse* and the "Profession of Faith of the Savoyard Vicar," he does not introduce it until this reference to the lie concerning Fazy. At this point, he is willing to defend those fictions by contrasting them with Montesquieu's fiction. In doing so, he shows that even now he means to speak very circumspectly about the kinds of lies that are excusable.

Before broadening this standard so as to excuse the more interesting kind of lie, Rousseau describes the qualities he associates with the truthful man and explains why he considers his own natual temperament good even though his timidity or sense of mortification has sometimes induced him to tell lies.[74] The truthful man approaches the problem of lying from the perspective of justice. He is concerned that he do nothing against justice, because he considers justice and truth to be synonymous. Although Rousseau does not say so explicitly, his subsequent self-description and explanation of why he sometimes tells inexcusable lies suggest very strongly that he thinks of himself as being such a truthful man. And once he has shown that lies can never be excusable as long as they benefit the one who tells them, he can point to lying which is in the service of justice. As the Walk closes, then, Rousseau abandons his narrow, negative standard in favor of a standard that is primarily concerned with being just to others.

This standard excuses the kind of lie he defended in the *Émile* when he said that it was morally permissible to take a useful lesson from a false historical fact. It also excuses the kind of lie he applauded in the *Social Contract* when he praised founding fathers for "resorting to the intervention of heaven and honoring the gods with their own wisdom" to make the citizens more willing to accept their civic duties.[75] But it leaves unanswered the truly interesting question: whether Rousseau would consider a lie relating to the substance of his teaching as justified. The closest he comes to raising this question is his reference to Tasso's praise of Sofronia's lie, a lie fraught with religious overtones. And that reference would seem to indicate his answer. In the Third Walk, Rousseau admitted that it was difficult to be confident of certainty with respect to his religious teaching. Here he excuses telling a likely story if the cause of justice is thereby served and concludes by speaking of the same subject that prompted his reflections in the Third Walk. To raise the question directly, Rousseau would have to speak about problems that he has held in guarded silence for a number of years, and it is by no means clear that such candor would serve the cause of justice.[76]

In the last lines of this Walk, Rousseau resolves to lie no more. Ostensibly, this resolve is prompted by his recognition that his efforts to give others their due has caused him to slight himself: to tell useful lies, it is necessary for him to be arrogant and somewhat presumptuous. Had he followed his motto in earlier years as strictly as he sets it forth in these concluding remarks, he never would have depicted the ills of human society so severely nor refuted his predecessors and his contemporaries so forcefully. When he wrote for the public, he was more concerned about the justice that was due others and was confident that he saw more clearly than other critics. Now, his reflections on Father Rozier's irony and Solon's example awaken a greater desire to be just to himself. His reasoning is that only the solitary man who has no social concerns can be modest and true to himself, and this confirms him in his decision to pursue a life of solitude. Such a decision makes sense only if a life of solitude promises personal happiness, and it is to this subject that he turns in the next Walk.

The Fifth Walk is the most beautiful and most moving essay of the *Reveries*. From the very beginning, it is clear that this Walk is different from the rest of the essays. Its tone is more lofty. It evokes images of natural beauty and of basic harmony. Constant attention is paid to man's greatest concern, the attainment of happiness. The reasons for Rousseau's love of solitude are stated much more fully in this Walk. Moreover, the pleasantness of the narration is not marred by painful accounts of his past or present suffering. Even stylistic elements set the Fifth Walk apart from the other Walks. Paragraphs of two and three sentences intermingle with paragraphs of two and three pages. At the same time, the prose is sharp and focused, yet light and lyrical. And the argument of this Walk is more precise than the argument of any of the other Walks, especially that of the Third and Fourth Walks.

There are three major divisions to the Fifth Walk. The introduction consists of a description of St. Peter's Island, the place where Rousseau claims to have experienced his truest happiness, and a short explanation of how he came to live on it.[77] In many respects, St. Peter's Island is the focal point of the Fifth Walk, and two things stand out in Rousseau's description of the island. In the first place, he is especially charmed by its suitability for a person who prefers solitude. He notes, of course, that simply as an island it favors solitary withdrawal. But he also emphasizes that St. Peter's Island is located in a lightly populated and seldom

frequented region and is itself almost uninhabited. Second, Rousseau's description of the island makes it appear to be something of
a paradise. He creates the impression that all of nature's charms
have been brought together on this island and its neighboring
shores so as to form a splendidly peaceful setting. Special praise is
reserved for the varied terrain and the abundance of gentle kinds
of animals, both of which contribute to the overall attractiveness
of this idyllic refuge.

Rousseau's attention to his environment is an important element in his description of ultimate happiness. Even though he
tries to argue at one point that enjoyable natural settings are not
essential for the man who knows how to engage in reverie, his
whole argument is cast in terms that show how much pleasant
surroundings facilitate his meditations, and he eventually acknowledges this.[78] In addition, St. Peter's Island is so isolated that
he had little contact with human beings during his stay there and
no contact at all with people interested in serious conversation.
Besides Thérèse, Rousseau's usual companions were the custodian
of the island, his wife, and the servants of the household, "who in
truth were all very worthy people but nothing more." Rousseau
also describes these people as "gentle and sweet" and explains
that apart from limited exchanges with the custodian about the
maintenance of the household and the general care of the island,
the only kind of speech they engaged in was laughter, chatter,
and song.[79] It seems, then, that a major part of Rousseau's pleasure was to enjoy the natural beauties of the island without having
to worry about explaining their significance. Consonant with this
passive enjoyment or mental relaxation, he left his books and
papers packed up and wrote only to answer importunate letters.[80]

Rousseau's decision not to unpack his books and papers is also
indicative of what he considers the "first and principal delight" of
his sojourn on St. Peter's Island, his devotion to idleness. The
other elements of delight in his sojourn there and how they
contributed to his happiness are accounted for in the second
major division or the main body of the Fifth Walk.[81] Rousseau's
account consists of two parts, a description of the way he spent
his time and an explanation of how that kind of activity led to his

truest happiness. To a certain extent, Rousseau's description of the way he spent his time on the island is a challenge to a putative contemporary audience: forgetting momentarily that he is writing the *Reveries* only for himself, he refuses to provide a direct explanation of why he was so happy there and declares that "from the description of the life I led there, I will let all the men of this century guess at it." [82]

Rousseau arranged his days on St. Peter's Island into morning and afternoon activities. Regardless of the weather, every morning was spent in botanical excursions. He became so enchanted with his discoveries that he set about writing a book on the flora of the island, even though such an activity went against his desire to stay away from books and papers. His recollection of his reason for writing about plants and explaining their reproductive processes is that such an activity was so pleasant and amusing that it involved no mental toil. As Rousseau expresses it, bringing La Fontaine into the ranks of the Protestants, he became so excited by his observations that he "went around asking whether one had seen the horns of the self-heal plant like La Fontaine asking whether one had read Habakkuk." [83] The joy he remembers having felt in this occupation is so deep that in describing his activities here, he devotes twice as much space to botany as to any other activity. Rousseau spent the rest of his mornings visiting the workers in the company of the custodian, his wife, and Thérèse, sometimes even putting his hand to the chores of the day. Then, after a pleasant but quick lunch, he would turn to his afternoon and early evening activities.

For some reason, the weather never kept him from his botanical excursions. However, it did affect the way he spent his afternoons. If the weather was pleasant, he would go out to the middle of the lake in a boat, stretch out at length, and give himself over to reveries until he was forced by the coming on of night to return to shore. Other fair weather pastimes included gliding along the banks of the island in a boat or rowing over to the smaller island and taking short walks around it. If the weather did not permit Rousseau to engage in any of these sailing activities, he would wander around the island looking for plants or go and sit in some secluded spot to look at the beauty of the lake and its shores. Toward the end of such days, he would come down to the water's edge and sit watching the water lap against the shore. Like the days he passed stretched out at length in the boat, the evenings spent sitting beside the water would pull him into deep reveries. In both instances, he would become so absorbed in his reveries that it was often hard for him to break away at the fall of night.[84]

Varied as Rousseau's activities were on St. Peter's Island, they had a certain constancy. His morning botanical excursions seem to have set the mood for the day. The discoveries he made pricked his curiosity and inspired a feeling of joy. But the moments of real happiness, the times when he truly approached what he considers to be the sweetest ecstasy, were the moments he spent stretched out in the boat in the middle of the lake or seated by the water's edge as night was drawing on. In Rousseau's account of his activities, these two are the first and the last of the five afternoon pastimes which he enumerates. In other words, they encompass or surround all the other activities. Moreover, they are the ones to which he gives the greatest attention. And in his explanation of the state which leads to highest happiness, they are mentioned again. In keeping with the basic argument as to what constitutes his truest happiness, these two activities are characterized as being supremely solitary. Whether stretched out in the boat or sitting on the shore, Rousseau was shut off from the disturbing influence of other human beings and was able to concentrate all his thoughts and feelings on himself.

Such solitude depends, nonetheless, upon a number of other conditions being fulfilled. Because of the way this problem affects his whole account of personal happiness, Rousseau approaches it in a very gingerly fashion. The problem first arises with respect to his allusive account of the activity which occupies the central place in this enumeration, his trips to the smaller island. When Rousseau first speaks of the smaller island, he describes it as a typical victim of human injustice: that its earth was constantly taken away to repair the damage waves and storms made to the larger island, illustrated "that the substance of the weak is always used for the advantage of the powerful." His subsequent descrip-

tion of how his afternoons on the smaller island were usually
spent is followed by an account of his idea that it would be good
to found a rabbit colony there, a project he had described in the
Confessions and describes again here in terms resembling the
founding of a nation. In recounting the actual founding here,
Rousseau proudly explains that he so adeptly handled the helm of
the boat in carrying his fellow colonizers and the inhabitants of
the new colony across the water that everyone had complete
confidence in him. Curiously, he passes over the obvious parallel
between this boat and the ship of state as well as that between his
skillful piloting of the vessel and the art of ruling in order to draw
a playful analogy between himself and Jason, the pilot of the
Argonauts.[85] But Jason's skill as pilot of the Argonauts was due at
least in part to his early education by Chiron the centaur, the
original teacher of the importance of guile in political activities.
This unobtrusive political allusion seems to be of the same character as Rousseau's admission in the Fourth Walk that useful lies
can be justified and his hints in the Third Walk that his earlier
teaching about religion is open to major difficulties. That is to say,
it seems to be an allusion which points to a broader issue. In this
case, its significance arises from the light it casts on Rousseau's
attempt to portray his happiness as purely solitary happiness. The
whole tone of the Walk is that Rousseau's truest happiness is a
perfectly solitary happiness. He even argues that such happiness
is not within the grasp of most people because of their attachment
to the demands of a socially active life. Yet he admits, almost in
passing, that he depended upon others for his physical well-being
on St. Peter's Island and that fellowship with these other people
was one of the pleasures he enjoyed there. To be able to appreciate the moments of truest happiness with their supreme solitude,
Rousseau needs some kind of society, however limited it might be.
Like a clever pupil of Chiron, he states this important truth
deceptively. The activities associated with the lake and with the
larger island which led to reverie and to happiness were solitary.
The spirit of solitude and of idle reverie was broken only by the
activities associated with the smaller island, the island that first
prompts Rousseau's political reflection and that later spurs him to

a kind of political action. Although his ultimate happiness tran-
scends political society, although it is radically asocial, it depends
on the supportive presence of others. Rousseau's recognition of
their importance is indicated by these preliminary allusions. At
the same time, his desire not to give them more than their due is
fully suggested by his utter silence about them when he actually
explains what constitutes his greatest happiness.

Admittedly, this whole interpretation of the significance of
Rousseau's activity on the smaller island and of that island itself is
conjectural. The interpretation is strengthened, however, when it
is noted that the two other activities mentioned by Rousseau add
nothing whatever to his description of the happiness he found on
St. Peter's Island and seem to have been placed in the enumeration only to accentuate his account of his visits to the smaller
island. As has been already noted, the only subsequent development of this theme is his statement that the kind of happiness
described here is not within the grasp of most human beings.
When Rousseau turns to his explanation of how these activities
constitute his truest happiness, he emphasizes their contribution
to his solitary reveries and is almost silent about political considerations. That explanation consists of five paragraphs, two devoted to Rousseau's statements of what his happiness is not and
three devoted to his attempts to describe what it is.[86]

Rousseau's major criticism of what other people hold to be
happiness is that it is characterized by a feeling of intense pleasure. He contends that however delightful and moving feelings of
passion might be, they occur too rarely and last too briefly. They
bring only momentary joy, whereas he thinks happiness should be
a lasting state. Part of his rejection of intense pleasure is based as
well on his criticisms of the superficial character of most human
attachments. Aware that life is constantly changing, human beings tend to be either looking forward to the future or regretting
the past. Having no solid and lasting attachment to the present,
they chase about seeking what does not exist. In criticizing what
he sees others praise as happiness, Rousseau tries to draw the
reader's attention to what really exists and to what can endure.
Stressing the joy to be found in a feeling that is not intense in

itself, he argues that its duration will increase the pleasure to be found in it. Such a feeling is the sentiment of one's own existence. His argument is that each person can enjoy the sentiment of his own existence. It requires no striving for yet unattained goods nor any longing for things that have passed away. If anything, it depends upon the refusal to look to the end of life or to think in terms of improving one's condition. It requires that we be content with our present existence and desirous of enjoying an awareness of it. That is why most people, who are concerned solely with the kind of achievements recognized and demanded by society and who judge themselves accordingly, cannot embrace such a view of happiness.

As Rousseau defines this moment of happiness, it is purely sensual. However, it is passively sensual: we enjoy our being, but we do so in the quiet of the passions. Such a moment is by no means contemplative. Ideas, like the natural environment, contribute to this moment of sensing our own existence only to the extent that they keep us from falling asleep. Still, to be enjoyed, the moment must be a conscious moment. The imagination can contribute to the enhancement of this moment by leading us to consider what life will bring, but it does not delight in trying to foresee the end of life.[87]

Rousseau is perfectly suited for the view of happiness that he presents here. Barred now from society, he can easily turn his back on the things erroneously valued by his contemporaries. Content with himself and persuaded that his natural goodness is superior to the factitious virtues cherished in society, he is not anxious to conform to those goals. The description of his natural temperament and active imagination given in the preceding Walks also shows him to be uniquely qualified to enjoy the sentiment of his own existence. And since he has cast the question of teleology into doubt by the argument of the Third and Fourth Walks, he can enjoy the sentiment of his existence as part of the whole without worrying about whether or not it corresponds to a natural or revealed end for human beings.

However, there is a problem with this account. The happiness described in the Fifth Walk is ostensibly a recollection of the happiness Rousseau experienced almost a dozen years earlier. Yet when his earlier description of what constituted that happiness is compared with the account given here, a very different view of happiness appears. The earlier description, a lengthy account in the *Confessions* of Rousseau's sojourn on St. Peter's Island, is neither as detailed nor as well organized as the account given here. Nor is it as moving as this account. But the account given here especially differs from that given in the *Confessions* in its description of the daily activities that were the basic elements of Rousseau's happiness.

In the *Confessions,* Rousseau said that idleness characterized his sojourn on St. Peter's Island and he tried to justify his inclination for idleness by showing how it helped him to be free. Because he thought of idleness as doing pleasant things without any purpose, he cited his pursuit of botany as the primary example of his idleness. According to the account of the *Confessions,* he began each day by going out on the terrace to admire the beautiful scenery that surrounded him. Apparently this moment of admiration always ended with his joyful acknowledgment of the divine order behind such beauty. After answering a few letters after breakfast, he spent some time unpacking and arranging his books and papers, and then went off to look at plants. He usually spent his afternoons rowing around the lake in a boat, often letting the boat float about while he enjoyed countless reveries. At times, he was so moved by his musings and by the scenery that he could not keep from proclaiming aloud his reverence for nature. But since his dog did not like to be out on the water too long, Rousseau claimed that he soon returned to shore and wandered about the smaller island. After describing how he carried out the idea of founding a rabbit colony there, Rousseau mentioned that he, Thérèse, and the custodian's wife sometimes helped the workers bring in the fruit. Late in the evening, he went to sit along the shore and enjoy the calm of the lake.[88]

Clearly, there are a number of discrepancies between the two accounts. What especially sets them apart is that even though he claimed in the *Confessions* that he was happy on St. Peter's Island and wanted to remain there as long as possible, in that work he did not explain what constituted his happiness as he does here in the *Reveries*. For example, in the *Confessions* he spoke about reveries only in passing; reverie did not occupy the major role it does in this work. In keeping with his attempt to show his goodness and piety in the *Confessions*, Rousseau spoke of some activities in a way that made them seem to be acts of worship. But in the *Reveries*, his explanation of the sentiment of existence and a full account of the meaning of happiness replace the description of these acts of worship. In fact, Rousseau goes so far here as to liken the enjoyment of self in reverie to the sense of self-sufficiency God, too, must feel.[89] Another way in which he tried to portray his goodness in the *Confessions* was to claim that he sacrificed moments of ecstasy in the boat for the sake of his dog; in the *Reveries*, Rousseau never speaks of having had a dog while he was on St. Peter's Island. According to the account of the *Reveries*, the only companionship he had was that of Thérèse, the custodian, his wife, and the household servants. Moreover, whereas Rousseau mentions practical conversations with the custodian and frivolous speech with the others in the *Reveries*, he made no mention of such amusements in the *Confessions*. A final difference between the two accounts is that despite his emphasis on his idleness in the *Confessions*, his statement about the time he spent unpacking and arranging his books showed him to be less idle than he describes himself as being here in the *Reveries*.

When all of these differences are considered, it is impossible to accept the account of the Fifth Walk as simply a recollection of the happiness Rousseau enjoyed twelve years earlier on St. Peter's Island. Not only does he alter his description of the activities which constituted his happiness, he also emphasizes different facets of those activities. These differences do not arise from any changes in Rousseau's natural temperament, for it purportedly remained constant over the years. Nor can they be traced to the fundamental change between his desire to be accepted again in society when he was writing the *Confessions* and the defiant break with society that he declares in the First Walk. Indeed, the opening lines of Rousseau's story about St. Peter's Island in the *Confessions* testify to his joy on realizing that a sojourn there

would separate him physically and spiritually from other people.[90] The only way to explain these differences is to consider
Rousseau's recollection in the *Reveries* of what took place during
his earlier sojourn on St. Peter's Island as a new interpretation of
that earlier experience and of how it contributed to his ultimate
happiness.

This is not to suggest that Rousseau comes to a new understanding of ultimate happiness at the moment of writing the *Reveries*.
In other parts of the *Confessions* and in the *Four Letters to M. de
Malesherbes*, Rousseau showed an awareness of the importance of
the sentiment of existence and testified to his conviction that
solitary reverie is an essential element of true happiness.[91] Yet
because of the different goals in those works, he presented his
view of happiness differently in them. In the *Confessions*, for
example, where he was concerned with proving that despite his
strange and blameworthy actions he was really a good man, he
spoke extensively—in fact, almost exclusively—about the way his
relationship with Mme de Warens made him supremely happy.
His primary intention there was to justify that relationship as
good and moral.[92] When he recounted his sojourn on St. Peter's
Island in the *Confessions*, he was more interested in showing that
he had enjoyed his stay there, that he had wanted to remain there
and had been wronged by being forced to leave the island, than
he was in explaining what constituted his happiness there. By
describing the pleasantness of his sojourn and his sadness at being
forced to leave such an idyllic spot, he sought to portray more
graphically the misfortunes he experienced during the years immediately following the condemnation of the *Émile*. Similarly,
even though the description of his solitary happiness in the *Four
Letters to M. de Malesherbes* is highly similar to the description he
presents here in the Fifth Walk, the emphasis is different. When
Rousseau wrote to M. de Malesherbes, he was trying to show why
he enjoyed living alone outside Paris. His account of the pleasant
days spent alone in the forest of Montmorency was intended to
explain why his natural temperament allowed him to enjoy such
activities and why they were activities that any good man could
enjoy. It was not intended as an explanation of why such solitary

reveries constituted man's highest happiness. Even the explanation of his love for reverie and of his inclination to laziness in the *Dialogues*, an explanation as complete as that of the Fifth Walk, was meant for justification rather than for instruction.[93]

In *The Reveries of the Solitary Walker*, however, Rousseau is more interested in explaining what he considers true happiness to be than in trying to justify himself. From the very beginning of this work he has emphasized that he is no longer concerned about what society thinks of him. Moreover, just as he has allowed his reflections in the Third and Fourth Walks to lead him to broad suggestions that there are discrepancies between what he said in order to combat pernicious opinions or in order to defend the faith of simple citizens and what he himself believes, so here he allows his reflections about his view of ultimate happiness to point to the basic tension between his need of society and his desire to go beyond it. As has already been stated, Rousseau's description of happiness as being thoroughly immersed in the sentiment of his own existence presupposes the existence of others. He can devote himself to idleness because others provide for his basic needs. And he can pass long days in solitude because he can return to pleasant but undemanding fellowship in the evenings. Yet he does very little for the community in return. Besides obeying the basic conventions of the community, the only positive actions in which he engages—picking fruit and founding a rabbit colony—are activities of a playful nature. Rousseau assumes no onerous duties during his sojourn on St. Peter's Island. He does nothing that contributes to the well-being of the community. If anything, his pursuit of happiness threatens the community. In the first place, the state of reverie which gives rise to the sentiment of existence borders on an imitation of death. There is a constant temptation in reverie to want to slip away from everything, to say: *"I would like this instant to last forever."*[94] Reverie thrives on our ability to move away from the senses of the body and from our awareness of daily needs, civic or personal. It permits us to experience our existence more immediately by giving us some sense of what the life of our mind unimpeded by the body might be. Second, were all the citizens of a community to pursue happiness through reverie, there would be no one to tend to the practical business of the community. Now, even though Rousseau reminds us of this tension by the novel way he describes his experience of happiness here, he does not defend his pursuit of it until the next Walk. While he might be excused for having pursued his happiness along such lines during his sojourn on St. Peter's Island or for remembering those reveries with a sense of longing given his current situation, he offers no apology. By his very silence, he seems to raise the more important question of whether this vision of ultimate happiness accords in any way with his earlier presentation of himself as the citizen of Geneva.

In the Sixth Walk, Rousseau explores the political implications contained in his description of true happiness as solitary. Because the pursuit of solitary happiness is so clearly at odds with the demands the political community makes upon its citizens and thus inappropriate, it is necessary to ask how one can justly pursue such happiness. Rousseau's answer leads him to exempt himself from the critical judgment of one of his earliest maxims. Whereas he had proclaimed in his first writing that "in politics as in morality, it is a great evil to do no good" and concluded that "every useless citizen can be considered a pernicious man," here he argues that although he abstains from doing good to others as a consequence of his natural goodness and of his strange situation and is therefore useless, he is not pernicious.[95] The intricacies of that argument force Rousseau to return to a discussion of two themes he has set forth in the earlier essays—the goodness of his natural temperament and the significance of his banishment from society—and to develop them more fully.

Like the arguments of the Third and Fourth Walks, that of the Sixth Walk is difficult to unravel. There are three basic divisions to the Walk: an introduction, a long discussion of Rousseau's attempts to benefit others, and a concluding paragraph. Even the introduction is somewhat convoluted. The opening paragraph suggests that the theme of the Walk will be a discussion of how we can find the inner cause of our habitual actions. It is followed by an example of how Rousseau actually made such a discovery and by a reflection about that discovery which leads to a much narrower statement of the theme.[96] The narrower statement sets forth the real problem of the Sixth Walk: why Rousseau does not do good to others.

The Walk opens with Rousseau's admission of bewilderment about why he habitually follows one particular route when he goes out to the Bièvre River for plant excursions. After thinking about it, he realizes that he chooses this route in order to avoid a vendor and her lame son. When he had first become acquainted with the vendor and her son, he was pleased to chat with the boy and to give him some coins. Eventually, however, that feeling of pleasure was replaced by a sense of annoyance at having to participate in this little game. Rousseau recognizes that his new attitude arose primarily from the feeling that he had a duty to chat with the boy and give him money: once he felt obligated to do this, a sense of annoyance replaced his earlier feeling of pleasure. Even though Rousseau acknowledges that he was also somewhat put off by the little boy's habit of frequently calling him Monsieur Rousseau, the question of duty or obligation is the real source of his annoyance. It is this question of his response to duty or obligation which leads to the fundamental problem of the Sixth Walk, why he does not do good to others. That, of course, is simply one version of the question raised by the definition of happiness as the solitary enjoyment of the sentiment of existence, that is, why Rousseau is a useless citizen.

This problem is explored in the main body of the Walk.[97] Like the Walk itself, this second section consists of three parts: a history of Rousseau's experiences in benefiting others, an explanation of what that history signifies about Rousseau's virtue, and an interpretation of how his natural temperament has been affected by his misfortunes. In the first part, Rousseau explains that just as he had enjoyed helping the little lame boy until he felt obligated to do it, so too had he enjoyed doing a good deed for others until he felt his good deeds becoming duties in their eyes.[98] He likes to do good and feels happy doing it, as long as the decision to do good is his own and is freely taken. But when those whom he benefits cease viewing his good deeds as favors and begin to consider them as something to which they have a right, the pleasure he takes in doing good for others ceases.[99] Their demands, implicit or explicit, threaten his feeling of freedom and thus cause him to refuse or simply to avoid those who are so importunate. He refuses them or avoids them, because he sees no reason to restrict his own freedom. His indomitable desire for freedom is so strong that he deems the greatest good to consist in not having to do what he does not want to do. For him, that is even more important than doing what he wants.[100]

Now even though Rousseau would insist that he does not need to discipline himself or limit his sphere of action because he never wills anything but the good, such a position runs counter to the demands of virtuous conduct. The core of virtuous action consists in subjugating our desires and actions to the dictates of reason, not in allowing our desires to direct our action or inaction. Recognizing that he cannot claim to be virtuous, Rousseau turns, in the second part of this section, to an exploration of how his propensity for doing good only when he feels so moved is justified, even though not virtuous.[101] He acknowledges that his inclinations force him to go against the demands of virtue in two ways. First, these inclinations are so strong he cannot subjugate them so as to submit to the voice of duty. When his inclinations come into conflict with what virtue demands, it is almost impossible for him to do anything·but follow his inclinations. Although he gives no example of such a conflict, he does indicate that the only way he can conform to the requirements of justice when persons dear to him are involved is to refrain from acting. Presumably, then, Rousseau could never bring himself to tell one friend that he was being cheated by another friend, but he could resist helping the second friend cheat the first. Rousseau could not act in such a manner as to end the cheating, but he could keep from ministering to it. The second way his inclinations force him to act contrary to what virtue requires is by rendering him incapable of performing a good deed under compulsion—even if the act is something he wanted to do before the element of compulsion was introduced. While Rousseau sometimes yields in the latter case, he always does so reluctantly. The explanation for his resistance to the demands of virtue in both of these instances is the same: he does benevolent deeds only when prompted by his natural goodness combined with his excessive pity and his extreme generosity. Because he follows his feelings rather than the dictates of his reason, it is difficult for him to refrain from doing good when moved by his feelings or to compel himself to perform a good deed when there is no emotional impetus.

The basic issue is how he can be sure that he never wills anything but the good. To prove that in the present context, Rousseau explains that his benevolent deeds arise from his sense of pity and from his generosity, qualities he treats as passions rather than as virtues. They are passions, because they arise in him naturally; they do not need to be cultivated or developed. Sensitive by nature and gifted with a very vivid imagination, he is always ready to help those who are less fortunate or in any way needy. And his own sense of moral superiority allows him to be ever generous: he has no reason to fear that others will get the better of him.[102] Throughout the Sixth Walk and especially in this passage, Rousseau substitutes confidence in the soundness of his natural goodness for efforts to control his will or to strive to direct himself toward prescribed goals. By nature, all men are good. Other men have become corrupt or have turned away from their natural goodness, because they have substituted the standards of society for those of nature. They have turned to the voice of reason and thus shunned the promptings of conscience or sentiment. Rousseau simply took advantage of his naturally vivid imagination and used it to help him think his way back to a life based on sentiment and freedom. He lived primarily in a world peopled by the creatures of his own imagination, in a world where people acted according to their feelings rather than according to the maxims of society. As Rousseau thought about this world and described it in his writings, he was able to recover a sense of his own natural goodness and to follow its dictates. This does not mean that he considers virtue to be of no use in human life. Elsewhere he has argued forcefully for its cultivation and insisted on its importance for sound civic life, acknowledging that its pursuit requires an enormous amount of willpower. He was quite aware that most people could overcome their misdirected passions and learn to guide themselves according to a better standard only by virtuous conduct, and he urged them to do so.[103] But there is an alternative to virtuous conduct, namely, preserving natural goodness; and Rousseau's argument here is that he has been able to preserve his natural goodness, that for him it takes the place of virtue.

Thus his admission that he is not virtuous is not meant to imply that he is wicked. Nor is his admission that he no longer tries to benefit others intended as a suggestion that he now seeks to harm them. Rather, he wants to stress that he has done good to others for a long time and has been pleased to do it, but has ceased his good deeds because of the obligations they engendered. As he thinks about benevolence and the relationships to which it gives rise, he thinks about duty and thus about society. He wants to explain how he can follow his own inclinations and yet not be blamed for doing so. At this point his basic defense is that even though he has occasionally avoided doing what is just by following his natural inclinations, he has never on that account been induced to commit unjust acts.

However, things became more difficult for Rousseau as he became more famous. When more people began to demand favors as a right, he became less willing to grant them. More important, with the beginning of his misfortunes, it became less possible for him to be certain that the good deeds he intended to do would really help others. And as his suspicions grew, he changed from avoiding importunate persons to avoiding people in general. These are the topics discussed in the last part of this section.[104] Rousseau acknowledges that he might have overreacted as a result of his misfortunes, but he also tries to explain how difficult it is for him to have any standard for judging the true intentions of the people with whom he comes into contact. Because he is aware of a fundamental change in people he once considered to be close friends and recognizes that they have turned against him, he has become fearful that any attempt on his part to do good to another person might bring him into a dreadful trap. In sum, the suspicion that his enemies are trying to dupe him prompts a return to his natural laziness and thus to refrain from doing good deeds even when he can discern no possible dangers.[105]

Whether his perception of what was taking place around him is correct or not, Rousseau does acknowledge that his reaction has led to one very important consequence. The more concerned he has become about others trying to trick him, the more he has fed the passion of self-love. All he says here about the danger of his self-love having become more dominant is that it has led him to feel repugnance for good deeds and to resist them. However, since he has always considered self-love to be the source of human vice,[106] this admission that it has gained strength within himself contains grave implications. He explains that increased self-love has also caused him to become disgusted with men, to find them as repugnant as the good deeds he now resists. But self-love itself prevents his repugnance from turning to hatred. Rousseau considers himself too far above other men to hate them. In other words, his natural temperament is such that even harmful passions do not lead him to evil. When self-love prompts him to compare himself with other men, the result is that he decides they are not worth bothering about. Rather than stimulate him to emulate them and strive for recognition among them, self-love induces him to scorn them and therefore to avoid them, that is, to lead a life of solitary withdrawal.

Rousseau's point is that his solitude is in no way a sign that he wishes others ill. If anything, it is a way for him to escape the harm others want to do him. He argues that he is still concerned about justice and is affected by the good and evil deeds he sees people do to each other, but that he has resolved to interfere no more. As proof of his good will, he speculates about what he would do if he had the ring of Gyges.[107] However, unlike the individual whose escapades with the ring are recounted in the *Republic,* Rousseau claims he would use the ring to make every heart content. He would try to bring about public felicity. And that is really what Rousseau has tried to do with his own ring of Gyges: he has judiciously used falsehood to conceal himself while inducing people to believe things they otherwise would have rejected. But without bothering to make that obvious parallel explicit here, Rousseau drops the example of the ring of Gyges on the grounds that its powers are too likely to tempt him to commit a folly.

He does not make that obvious connection, because his intention in the *Reveries* is not to justify his present solitude by explaining that he has done good in the past and should now be allowed to live out a few years in a useless, but harmless, solitary retreat. Rather, his argument is that he is good now and has always been good, that he has done good in the past and would be willing to do good now were things different, but that nevertheless he is not now and never has been a virtuous citizen. The whole theme of the Sixth Walk is contained in Rousseau's bold proclamation in the first sentence of the last paragraph:

> The conclusion I can draw from all these reflections is that I have never been truly suited for civil society where everything is annoyance, obligation, and duty and that my independent natural temperament always made me incapable of the subjection necessary to anyone who wants to live among men.

What Rousseau is trying to say is that the former citizen of Geneva [108] is not now and never has been a citizen in the ordinary sense. He has always recognized that civil society is necessary for almost all people and that to have decent civil society, it is necessary to make it possible for most people to be good citizens. When Rousseau first began to write, he tried to show his fellow men how to live better in civil society. He differed from them primarily because his point of reference was an imaginary society of perfect beings he had created for himself. While other men wore themselves out comparing themselves with one another, Rousseau let his imaginary beings become his points of comparison. His reason led him to pursue the possibilities of this imaginary society more and more, thereby keeping him from the normal duties of daily society. In time, therefore, he came to resemble perfectly that wise man who "withdrew from the crowd as much as was possible for him and stayed patiently in the place that chance had assigned him." [109] There is room for such a man in society, and sometimes it is even necessary to look to him for guidance. While it is obvious that dedicated citizens are a fundamental requirement for good civil society, it is also obvious that political society frequently needs to heed the counsels of those who see beyond its immediate horizons. But the one who sees beyond in this manner is thus aware of the limits of society and may betray that awareness in his daily conduct. Rousseau argues here for such a person in his own name, thereby returning to the age-old question of the tension between the political philosopher and the city. According to the terms of the argument, he is right to claim that he has never been a pernicious member of society, but wrong to contend that he has always been a useless one. His dedication to the recovery of his own natural goodness was, for a long while, beneficial to his fellow men. However, this resolution of the question is entirely too limited. The more interesting question is whether Rousseau's substitution of sentiment for reason and of solitary happiness as described in the Fifth Walk for ultimate happiness as contemplation is defensible.

In the Seventh Walk, the problem investigated in the Sixth Walk is approached from another perspective. Although Rousseau argued in the Sixth Walk that his uselessness as a citizen does not make him pernicious, he made no attempt to argue that his uselessness has any merit. If anything, he wrongly conceded its lack of merit. Returning to the same issue here, he tries to show that even if his uselessness is not beneficial to society, it is good in itself. The presumption is that only a person with an unusually good natural temperament can relish Rousseau's way of life. Presented as a series of reflections about the significance of his renewed interest in botany, the argument leads to a deeper understanding of the view of solitary happiness first elaborated in the Fifth Walk.

The introduction states the problem from the perspective of Rousseau's renewed interest in botany being a clear indication of his goodness.[110] Even though his absorption in botany threatens to take him away from writing these essays, his inclination to it is so strong that there is no way for him to resist. What is more, even though he finds himself faced by a number of handicaps when he turns back to the study of botany, he overcomes them all and pursues his interest.

There are three separate statements about the things which ought to prevent him from engaging in botanical studies. Each list is somewhat repetitive of the preceding list or lists, but each adds something new. At first, Rousseau cites his interest in botany, despite the following impediments, as proof of his extravagant infatuation with it: his old age, his sedentary state in Paris, his lack of strength, his preoccupation with copying music, his lack of a herbarium, and his lack of books. Then, calling the study of botany a folly, he notes that even though he is old, forgetful, weak, and without a guide, books, garden, or herbarium, he has given himself up to botany again and has done so more ardently than when he first took it up. Finally, noting that the study of botany brings him no gain or progress and leads him to exert himself like a young man as well as to learn the lessons of a schoolboy, in spite of his old age, weakness, and lack of aptitude or memory for this study, he concludes that he should try to understand the reason for his interest in it. Each list testifies to Rousseau's concern about his age. Because of the demands it makes on the body, botany is a pursuit for a young person. It is also a study that demands mental agility and memory, qualities that older people seem to lack. And two of the lists show that he feels hampered in his present desire to pursue botany by his lack of equipment: he no longer has the books which one needs to pursue the study carefully.

Clearly, there are numerous reasons for him to stay away from the study of botany and there is no good reason for him to take it up again. The only argument favoring his continued pursuit of it is psychological: for him to become distracted by anything is a way to avoid thinking about the injustice of his situation and thus to keep from hating other men. And as the rest of the argument tries to demonstrate, he has not only become interested in something other than his situation, but has also become interested in a very fine and praiseworthy activity. That he pursues this interest despite the numerous obstacles he has listed is presumably an even greater indication of his natural goodness.

Rousseau's explanation of the reasons for his pursuit of botany constitutes the major part of the Seventh Walk.[111] It consists of three basic arguments. He first tries to show that his pursuit of botany is really little more than another way for him to continue his reveries.[112] As part of this argument, Rousseau comments on the significance of reverie as an alternative to thinking. Subsequently, he contrasts botany as a way to study nature with the study of minerals and with the study of animals in order to show that botany is more cheerful and more inspiring than either of the others.[113] Finally, he argues that because botany or the study of plants is private and allows him to go off into secluded areas, it helps him avoid his fellow men and thus resist any blameworthy feelings toward them.[114] However, because each of these arguments is flawed in an important respect, a rather unexpected conclusion must be drawn.

Rousseau describes himself here as someone who has thought with difficulty and as someone who has taken no pleasure in thinking. According to the way he presents it here, there is something about thinking and writing which has made him toil excessively. Even though he enjoys letting his mind function and takes pleasure in the play of his imagination, he does not at all enjoy applying his mind to problems and derives no pleasure from trying to think about the larger questions of human existence.[115] Now, an immediate implication of this admission is that all of his writing has been unpleasant and has been done for the sake of others rather than for his own enjoyment. That poses a problem, because Rousseau has insisted that he must enjoy writing in order to write well and has asserted that it is impossible for him to continue doing anything that he does not do with pleasure.[116] But what he really seems to be suggesting by this admission is that things have changed for him. Even though he found it difficult to think, he was happy to do it and even happy to write as long as he thought his toil was of some value to his fellow men. He took pleasure in doing good deeds for them. Now that he has been cut off from human society, he finds that the solitary withdrawal he once enjoyed as a means of getting a better understanding of the world around him can be enjoyed much more deeply. He finds that it allows him to enjoy the richest of human pleasures: it allows him to experience the sentiment of his own existence. Thus, although he used to do good for others because he felt a desire to do so, he now realizes that these activities never gave him true enjoyment.

However, his admission of his distaste for thinking is above all significant for what it says about Rousseau's idea of man's being. It constitutes a clear denial of Aristotle's view that reason is essential to man and that man must develop his reason to achieve ultimate happiness. This same issue seems to be at the root of Rousseau's explanation of his attraction to botany. Ostensibly, grief and anxiety have driven him to the study of botany. As he walks through the woods, a particularly pleasing object will catch his attention, then another, and yet another until his imagination is stirred up by the harmony of all these objects and he is carried away in rapturous enjoyment of the harmonious beauty of the whole of nature.[117] He insists that all human beings can experience the same kind of rapture when they perceive these kinds of objects and he suggests that the failure of some individuals to have such an experience can be attributed to three different causes. Some people are naturally insensitive. Others are too preoccupied with different kinds of ideas. Although Rousseau says nothing more about either of these two groups of people, his earlier remark in the Fifth Walk about how the preoccupation of most people with the concerns of society prevents them from enjoying his view of solitary happiness evokes the same kind of image as the way he categorizes the second group of people here. The final thing that keeps people, especially "people of taste," from appreciating the rapturous beauty of nature is their tendency to reduce everything to their material interest—to ask continually what a plant is good for.[118] To illustrate this explanation, Rousseau cites Theophrastus and Linnaeus as examples to follow when approaching the study of botany and contrasts them with Dioscorides as an example to avoid. Dioscorides apparently studied plants only in order to discover their pharmacological uses, whereas Theophrastus and Linnaeus studied plants in order to appreciate them as part of the whole of nature.

According to Rousseau, we should consider Theophrastus "as the only botanist of antiquity." However, that judgment excludes a very famous botanist of antiquity, one who happens to have been the teacher of Theophrastus: Aristotle. While it cannot be said that Aristotle looked for remedies in his study of plants, he did ask about ends in his study of all natural phenomena, including plants. Rousseau's real criticism here, then, is directed against those who ask about the end of nature. If a person is naturally sensitive, if he is not preoccupied with other ideas, and if he is a person of taste, then he will appreciate natural things as he observes them and will not be concerned with why they exist. Rousseau's interest in botany, as well as his interest in reverie, seem therefore to derive from an antiteleological bias. Because he does not think it possible to explain the whole, he insists that all one can hope to do is to enjoy being a part of the whole.

However, as he explains here, that is a personal notion related only to his individual happiness.[119] The happiness suitable for most men is not solitary happiness. It has nothing to do with ecstasies or with forgetting the demands of the body in order to become "one with the whole of nature." Instead, the happiness suitable for most men is earthbound and is centered in the concerns of the political community. As a result of Rousseau's concern with the needs of his fellow men in all of his previous writing, he never stated fully the grounds of his solitary happiness. Only now, when he perceives that his solitude is insurmountable, does he give a full account.

Still, however solitary Rousseau's happiness is, however remote from the concerns of other men, it presumably arises from beautiful and cheerful surroundings. By contrasting the study of botany with the study of minerals and animals, he tries to show why it is preferable to approach nature by means of plants and trees.[120] The premise here, as earlier, is that Rousseau has been so overwhelmed by his misfortunes that in order to ascend to the rapturous ecstasy in which he feels himself one with nature, he has to begin by observing particular natural objects. He denies that the

study of minerals will help him in this task. Above all, there is
nothing attractive or pleasant about the mineral realm. To get to
the sources, harsh toil and danger are involved. Exploring the
bowels of the earth is a dark and unhealthy occupation that most
people pursue only out of desire for immoderate gain. Moreover,
the apparatus needed for bringing minerals back up to the surface
is dirty, smoky, and noisy. The study of minerals presupposes
other kinds of learning; it demands time, money, and equipment.
And it is a deceptive kind of study that frequently allows people
to believe they have made great discoveries when in fact they
have made very insignificant ones. The study of animals is somewhat more appealing, but Rousseau denies that he has the means
necessary to pursue it diligently. It is hardly possible for a solitary
person, especially a weak old man, to go chasing after animals in
order to observe them. Moreover, the proper study of animals
requires carefully observing their habits over long periods of time
and eventually studying their anatomy. That entails depriving
these creatures of their natural freedom and subjecting them to
unnatural constraint only later to engage in all the distateful
operations of killing them and cutting them open. So Rousseau
turns instead to the prettiness, pleasantness, and cheerfulness of
the plant world. Claiming to be no longer interested in instruction, he vaunts botany as an amusement he can engage in without
expense or trouble, as a pastime that requires few instruments and
no learning.[121] It is the perfect pastime for a person who loves
idleness, provided that no motive of interest or pride ever troubles this pastime.

This caveat shows the basic flaw in Rousseau's comparison.
When he discusses the study of minerals, he enumerates the
problems which arise from a misplaced motive of interest—for
example, the excesses arising from the profit motive and the
foolish confidence that one has made a great discovery—as an
integral part of that pursuit. Similarly, his discussion of the difficulties besetting the study of animals is unduly harsh and is not
balanced by any consideration of the pleasures involved in that
activity. He entirely neglects, for example, the possibility of
studying domestic animals in order to circumvent the problem

supposedly engendered by his old age and insufficient means. In short, Rousseau's argument wrongly exaggerates the shortcomings of the study of minerals and of animals in order to favor the study of botany. This seems to be willful and to be done in order to make botany's goodness—and thus Rousseau's own goodness— much more apparent.

The last explanation Rousseau offers for his renewed interest in botany is that it allows him to escape from other men.[122] However, his description here of how the pursuit of botany permits him such an escape is a description characteristic of his earlier interest in botany. While living in Paris, Rousseau cannot "clamber up rocks and mountains" nor "go deep into vales and woods in order to slip away, as much as possible, from the memory of men and from the attacks of the wicked." Even the three anecdotes he recounts here are from that earlier period of interest. As Rousseau later explains, his reason for speaking about the privacy of earlier botanical excursions to illustrate the privacy he claims to continue to find in botany is that he remembers those earlier moments when he sees again the plants he has previously collected.[123] His renewed interest in botany depends, then, as much on his memory as on new activities.

Given the context, these anecdotes about his earlier plant excursions should illustrate the way botany allows Rousseau to escape his persecutors. However, they do nothing of the sort. The first, a story about a botanical excursion that led Rousseau to what he considered to be the outer limits of wilderness, proves that it is never possible to escape the influence of human society: just a few feet beyond the point he had judged to be utterly uncivilized, Rousseau discovered a stocking mill.[124] As he reflected upon his discovery, it became apparent to him that people dedicated to hurting him were probably working in that mill, that even in that remote spot it was not possible for him to escape his enemies. By free association, this thought led him to consider the way Switzerland is laid out and to the realization that it is more like a big city than anything else. For example, on another plant excursion to a mountaintop, Rousseau and some friends discovered that the only house on the mountain belonged to a book dealer who did a very lively business despite his solitary location.[125] Then, modifying his original theme yet again, Rousseau recounts a third anecdote to illustrate the character of people from Dauphiné. Once when he was in Grenoble on a visit and walking along the Isère with his host, he saw some wild, but poisonous, berries which he began to eat. Rather than dare to warn Rousseau of the danger, his host stood by in a respectful silence ever obedient to the requirements of Dauphinois humility.[126]

There is clearly something wrong with these anecdotes. The first, rather than illustrating the way botany has allowed Rousseau to escape from his enemies, only shows that his enemies have always been a few feet away. At the most, the second explains why in Switzerland it is never possible to be very far from the traces of civilization. And the third contributes in no way to the general theme. All it does is illustrate the physical dangers connected even with the study of botany.

So the third explanation of Rousseau's renewed interest in botany, like the second explanation, is insufficient. The pursuit of botany cannot be justified on the grounds that it helps Rousseau avoid his enemies. There is yet another problem with the third explanation. Cast in terms of previous botanical excursions, its relevance for Rousseau's renewed interest in botany is based on his ability to remember the earlier excursions as he thumbs through his herbarium at this later period. But in the very beginning of this Walk, Rousseau complains about having sold his herbarium before he became interested again in botany and bitterly bemoans his lack of memory.[127]

It appears, then, that the only viable explanation for Rousseau's renewed interest in botany is the first. And as has already been noted, the first explanation is really a statement about Rousseau's nonteleological view of the universe. According to this interpretation, the Seventh Walk is an elaborate and often misleading account of what is at the core of Rousseau's solitary happiness. The argument in favor of his goodness now, despite his present uselessness to society, rests on the juxtaposition between the happiness he pursued for the sake of others and the happiness he holds to be truly his own. Only by understanding the deeper significance of his account of his renewed interest in botany does the relationship between the two become clear. And that is precisely the purpose of the Seventh Walk. There is something else that must be said: for Rousseau to appreciate botany as he does, he has to be intimately familiar with many of the subjects that he rejects as useless. That Rousseau knows about the kinds of investigation he rejects is a clear indication that he is neither a plain and simple citizen nor a primitive and savage natural man. Far from either of these character types, he is in reality a very complex and civilized person who worked very hard at understanding why natural simplicity is praiseworthy.

The Eighth Walk is a continuation of the theme considered in the two preceding Walks. Whereas the argument of the Sixth Walk was an attempt to prove that Rousseau's uselessness was not a sign of his perniciousness and the ostensible argument of the Seventh Walk was that his return to the study of botany was a sign of his goodness, here there is an attempt to prove his goodness by means of an explicit investigation of his soul. By showing that he truly has to struggle to be natural or simple, this investigation also confirms one of the conclusions reached at the end of the Seventh Walk. Moreover, to the extent that the argument here proves the necessity of solitary life for achieving that natural state, it strengthens Rousseau's contention that ultimate happiness is solitary and points to the fundamental problem of civil society, that is, the tension between what is required of the citizen so that the regime and all other citizens may survive and what is necessary so that the individual may enjoy complete happiness without regard for the demands of the regime.

As with most of the arguments set forth in the *Reveries*, these are not stated explicitly. Formally, the Eighth Walk is a plaintive attempt by Rousseau to solve a personal paradox. In thinking back over the events of his life, he observes that his memories of the feelings which affected him during the periods of his deepest misfortunes are happier than his memories of those which affected him during his periods of prosperity.[128] Then, turning to a rambling and often bitter description of his unfortunate situation,

Rousseau gradually explains how he has succeeded in finding happiness in the midst of personal miseries. His explanation turns out to contain an important moral lesson, but at many points his complaints and pathetic characterizations of his misfortunes threaten to derail the argument completely.

Heretofore, Rousseau has spoken of his earlier years as being years of happiness. Now he tries to argue that even though he enjoyed numerous pleasures during those years, he was never truly happy. The problem as he sees it is that the very things which constitute what most people think of as happiness are things that draw us outside ourselves. Happiness is usually thought to consist in pleasant contact with other people and numerous, varied activities; it is characterized by constant motion. Consequently we are deprived of any time to be with ourselves. Even when moments for solitary reflection can be found, we usually try to avoid them in order to rush back to boisterous involvement with others.[129] As Rousseau reflects on those earlier years of cheerfulness and exuberance, he recognizes the extent to which they were filled with such consuming activities. More important, he now perceives that those kinds of activity are inadequate in an important respect. Claiming to be unable to identify what was inadequate about them even though he has just explained what it was, Rousseau simply concludes that ordinary joy or the usual idea of happiness does not make him happy.[130]

By way of contrast, he notes that since he has been forced to be with himself and to draw upon his own soul for his spiritual needs, he has found that he enjoys a greater kind of happiness. Stated in these terms, that assertion seems to repeat the basic theme of the First and Second Walks. There, it will be remembered, Rousseau defiantly proclaimed that he would accept the solitude that had been forced upon him and be happy in it. Moreover, his description here of all of his mental and emotional reactions to his first discovery of the plot is very similar to what he said in those two Walks. Frequently the language and the images recall the tone and general character of those Walks. Yet despite this apparently deliberate allusion to those earlier statements, he makes no explicit acknowledgment of the different approach he now adopts as he explains how he has come to accept his solitary situation. In keeping with the method sketched out in the First Walk, Rousseau allows himself to set forth his ideas just as they come to him "and with as little connection as the ideas of the day before ordinarily have with those of the following day." [131]

Rousseau's explanation consists of two distinct parts. Characterizing the basic problem as one of learning to accept necessity and to view it as impersonal, he states why he had first to undertake an intellectual reform and then a moral reform in order to learn that lesson.[132] The intellectual reform preceded the moral reform, because it was essential for him to arrive at an appreciation of his fellow human beings and their opinions before he could determine how to conduct himself with respect to them. He contends that a long and careful examination of their actions and of the reasons they give for them has convinced him that the real principles behind those actions are different from the ones they proclaim and that these principles are not sound. Although that conclusion has general as well as particular consequences, Rousseau stresses only the latter here: since he can find no reasonable principle to justify their conduct toward him, he has decided to turn his attention away from them.

Yet, granted that there is no sound reason for men to be so hostile toward him, the problem of how they have managed to succeed in their plot still remains unsolved. Even though Rousseau has determined how to structure his relationships with respect to other human beings, he has made no progress toward answering this question. He still has no idea as to why he has been singled out as the person to be so sorely persecuted. In contrast to the allegations he made at the end of the Second Walk, Rousseau refuses here to attribute his fate to God or to explain it as anything but the result of blind necessity. In keeping with this resolve, he does not once mention God in this Walk. Instead, he likens himself to a wise man and claims to be hurt only by the physical consequences of the plot. He uses that simile to indicate that he has learned to stop considering the attacks upon him as personal affronts.

However, Rousseau has not really *learned* to accept necessity as blind. This phase of his reform is moral rather than intellectual. The real source of his earlier incorrect judgment about the role God may or may not play in his fate was his passion of self-love *(amour-propre)*. His reason shows him the folly of that explanation, but his self-love pushes reason aside.

According to Rousseau, the source of all human passions is the love of self *(amour de soi)*. We must have some kind of love for ourselves if we are to strive for self-preservation, and it is love of self which provides that impetus. It is a good passion in that it pushes us only to meet our real needs and does not compel us to endless striving. Moreover, it can be guided by the voice of reason. When love of self comes under the tutelage of reason, it gives rise to the various human virtues. Self-love, however, is neither natural nor beneficial. It arises from the importance we attach to our own selves when we compare ourselves with other human beings. Thus, as long as we can avoid invidious comparisons, we can avoid self-love. But given the character of human society, neither can be avoided for very long. Self-love is a completely factitious passion in that it feeds on false needs and drives us to endless striving, without meeting any of our real needs. Moreover, it is recalcitrant to the voice of reason and thus gives rise to all the human vices. Without going into the larger problem of the merits of this analysis of the human soul, it should be noted here that Rousseau's description of the love of self is a basic element of his argument that man is naturally good. Similarly, his description of self-love and explanation that it is engendered by human society is an important part of his argument that society tends to corrupt human beings. Now since self-love feeds on false needs, one way to bring it back under control is to limit our needs. Similarly, since it is characterized by ceaseless striving, we can stifle it by devoting ourselves to a sweet and unambitious laziness. Some indication that this is the way to control self-love can be gained from reflecting about the habits of primitive natural man, the only human being apart from the wise man who is free of this passion. Primitive natural man is indolent, concerned only with his immediate needs, and completely independent. Far from seeking contact with others, he flees his fellow men.[133]

Obviously profiting from these kinds of reflections, Rousseau claims here that he has been able to bring his self-love back under control by breaking off the external relations which nourish it and by learning to accept his goodness without making comparisons. In this respect, he differs fundamentally from most of his fellow human beings. According to his analysis, most men are so enslaved by self-love—that is, so corrupted—that they can never hope to master it. They are so enslaved by it primarily because they are unable to break away from the opinions that dominate human society. As Rousseau goes on to describe in detail the benefits he receives from bringing self-love back under control, it becomes apparent that freedom from self-love is primarily confident tranquility. It consists in living with the knowledge that he can be harmed, but choosing to enjoy the present moment of life rather than worry about the harm that might arise. More specifically, it consists in enjoying his reveries or the memories of his reveries and all the flights of imagination connected with them. However, the deeper significance of Rousseau's having been able to bring his self-love back under control is that it explains the earlier paradox: it is the reason for his happy memories of the sentiments which affected him during his moments of misfortune. As a result of those hardships, he was able to succeed in controlling his self-love. Thereafter, despite the misery that has surrounded him, he has come to enjoy the "happy and sweet life for which [he] was born." [134]

Once Rousseau becomes aware of what allows him to be happy in the midst of his misfortunes, he also observes that by controlling his self-love he has been able to return to the cheerful tranquility of his natural temperament. This is one of the factors permitting him to describe ultimate happiness as he does in the Fifth Walk. The freedom from self-love that allows him to delight in the fanciful life of his mind contributes to that happiness, because his fancies can so easily take the place of normal human fellowship for him. And this solitary pleasure is perfectly compatible with his natural lethargy, with his desire for simplicity and idleness. The only thing that threatens this new tranquility is contact with his fellow human beings. His basic problem is that

The Reveries of the Solitary Walker

association with other human beings always leads him to discern an insult and thus to lose control over his self-love.[135] Although he speaks of these insults as real, it does not matter whether they are real or imagined: the passion of self-love can be as quickly aroused over an imagined insult as over a real one. However, because Rousseau differs from other men to the extent that he is prey to these emotions only when he is in the presence of people who threaten or seem to threaten him, he can therefore escape these emotions by avoiding people. In other words, the life of the solitary walker is not the way for most human beings to solve the problems created by the passion of self-love. Solitude is a viable solution only for those who, like Rousseau, are able to bring this passion back under control. Other human beings must be content to see themselves in Rousseau's description of himself as someone completely subjugated by the passions of society: he had allowed himself to become so overwhelmed by "the fumes of self-love and the tumult of the world" that he could no longer enjoy those solitary walks which had been so delightful to him when his self-love was under control. Largely because most human beings are still attached to social passions, they resemble Rousseau during these bitter moments of his fame and prosperity.

There is more. Aware that no matter how hard he tries he cannot control his reaction to the way others affect him, Rousseau abandons the attempt. He adheres to no morality of self-control or of the mean. He can discern no end proper for man and thus does not think that he should try to discipline himself to conform to a particular way of life. As became clear in the Seventh Walk, Rousseau rejects any teleological view of the universe or of human development. Instead, he permits his senses to have their full play. He can afford this luxury, he contends, because his natural temperament is so good. However, his natural temperament is good because he has purified his soul, so to speak, not because he has been created differently from other human beings. Once subject to the same passions as his fellow men, Rousseau has escaped the tyranny of his passions by his victory over self-love. That victory has allowed him to embrace indolence and solitude, as well as to respond impetuously to his environment. In turn, his enjoyment of indolence and solitude helps him to preserve his victory over self-love. It is in this sense that Rousseau can be confident that his praise of solitary happiness will be enjoyable to a person with a good natural temperament. And because his pursuit of that happiness fosters such a temperament, he can claim that it is good for him to pursue it even though it means that he thereby neglects his civic duties.

The Ninth Walk is a discussion of contentment. It is prompted by Rousseau's claim at the end of the last Walk that, except for the rare moments when he falls prey to the assaults of other men, he enjoys a permanent state of solitary happiness. Clearly an exaggeration, that claim needs to be modified. For one thing, as Rousseau implicitly admitted in the Fifth Walk, the moments in which ultimate happiness can be enjoyed are few and require extraordinary preparations. For another, not all of his contacts with other human beings were painful and oppressive. Precisely because his natural temperament is good, he can enjoy communicating with others and is sensitive to the simple pleasures of human relationships. By exploring what it is that he shares with others in these more pleasant moments, Rousseau tries to explain what pleases him when he is not caught up in the ecstasies of supreme happiness.

Because of the subject, this Walk is more concerned with other people and the effect they have on Rousseau than any other Walk. The basic premise is that his feeling of contentment or satisfaction, the pleasure he enjoys in his association with other people, depends on his being able to perceive their contentment or satisfaction with him. He then tries to argue that this kind of shared or mutual contentment is the only sound foundation for any kind of human fellowship and advances his argument by means of a series of anecdotes and comments about them.

There are nine anecdotes in this Walk, two more than in any other Walk. The first one (d'Alembert's satiric eulogy of Mme Geoffrin), the fifth one (throwing gingerbread to the peasants at la Chevrette), and the last three (Rousseau's morning walks among the laborers, his unpleasant experience with the veterans at the

Invalides, and his pleasant trip to the Île aux Cygnes with the newly arrived veteran) center around adults.[136] Of the four other anecdotes, two concern children (Rousseau's enjoyable afternoon with the du Soussoi children and his touching encounter with the little waif near Clignancourt) and two are about adolescents (the lighthearted games with the little girls and the waferman and Rousseau's generosity to the young Savoyards).[137] All of the anecdotes, except the one about his generosity to the young Savoyards, concern events occurring during the period of Rousseau's present sojourn in Paris. In two instances, Rousseau played a political role: with the little girls and the waferman he acted as an arbiter, while to the Savoyard boys and the girl selling apples he appeared as something of a modern Heracles. And in recounting yet another anecdote, the one about the veterans at the Invalides, he is reminded of a verse from Plutarch's life of the great Spartan lawgiver Lycurgus.

As these last remarks indicate, there is a political theme underlying the larger discussion. Rousseau is able to describe the way in which a whole people show contentment or satisfaction and what form contentment or satisfaction would take either among a few persons or in the soul of a single person.[138] He is also aware of what prevents the wealthy from recognizing the basis of true contentment and from enjoying it.[139] Moreover, by speaking of the differences between nations and regimes with respect to the contentment of the people in general, Rousseau seems to be thinking of a broader question, namely, what political institutions have to do with rendering a people contented. If contentment is a criterion for political well-being, Rousseau implies, one can easily judge the political soundness of a people. After all, "contentment is read in the eyes, in the bearing, in the lilt of the voice, in the manner of walking, and seems to be transmitted to the one who perceives it." [140] But Rousseau never develops that issue any further. He is satisfied to allude to it here and to indicate that public contentment is the highest goal toward which a legislator or statesman can aim, since it will never be possible to render a whole people happy. True happiness is more intense and lasts longer than contentment or satisfaction. It is also harder to obtain because it depends on a particular development of the soul, rather than upon pleasant interchanges with others. But instead of pursuing these differences here, Rousseau decides instead to reflect upon the extent to which contentment presupposes a basic egalitarianism. His contention is that contentment has to be shared to be enjoyed.

Rousseau's procedure here is to explain how he came to enjoy contentment with others in a variety of situations. However, before he embarks upon that explanation he finds himself obliged to answer a possible objection. It might be objected that he is a misanthrope, a man who has an evil natural temperament and who cannot get along with his fellow human beings, a man who cannot even enjoy the company of children. The grounds for such an objection would arise from the fact that he has placed his children in a foundling home rather than raise them himself. Rousseau's account of the way d'Alembert's eulogy of Mme Geoffrin was brought to his attention is intended to show that some people do consider him in this light. His reply is cast in terms of the anecdotes about the du Soussoi children and the encounter with the child near Clignancourt.

Rousseau claims that he loves children and that he placed his own children in the foundling home only because he had been concerned about the way they would otherwise have been raised. His contention is that since he could not have brought them up himself, they would have been left to the care of Thérèse or her family and would have been raised in a wretched manner. However, the reason Rousseau was unable to raise his own children is that he was more concerned about the children of his mind, his writings, than about those of his body. Consequently, his assertion here that "it would assuredly be the most unbelievable thing in the world that the *Héloïse* and the *Émile* were the work of a man who did not love children" focuses the problem more sharply, but it does not remove the objection.[141] The most that can be said in Rousseau's favor is that he turned away from a hard, but pleasant, duty in order to devote himself to an even harder, and perhaps less pleasant, task.

Still, Rousseau's major concern here is with showing that he does enjoy children and with explaining why he does not play with them more frequently. He maintains that his slowness of speech and inability to find the right expression quickly, as well as his concern about his aged appearance, keep him from forcing himself upon children. Rousseau's point is that he wants to bring joy and contentment to children, not simply to please himself at their expense. That is why in the case of the du Soussoi children, as well as in that of the child near Clignancourt, Rousseau's reserve had to be broken down by the advances of the children. For the same reason, when he noticed the animosity of the old veterans at the Invalides toward him, he tried to avoid them. He does like to interact with others, to converse with them or simply to enjoy plain fellowship. And he greatly enjoys the spontaneity and the affection shown by children in their play. But just as his indomitable desire for freedom keeps him from frequenting others or doing good deeds for them when he thinks it would thereby be threatened, so too does his respect for the freedom of others keep him from reaching out to them when he fears he might thereby threaten theirs. Rousseau does good deeds to others only because he gains pleasure from doing them, and he studies children—not to mention adults—because that is the only pleasure now remaining to him. Since he cannot enjoy their company directly, he enjoys it indirectly through the play of his imagination. The pleasure he might have found in society he seeks instead in standing aside and watching others.[142]

Now, when the reasoning behind his respect for the feelings of others is generalized, it explains another aspect of Rousseau's general inclination toward solitude. Such an argument is characteristic of a very sensitive person, which is precisely the way Rousseau has always described himself, but it also suggests that mutual contentment is the basis of true contentment. Mutual contentment was present in the instances of the little girls and the waferman, the Savoyard boys and the girl selling apples, and the old veteran who sailed over to the Île aux Cygnes with Rousseau. It was present because in each of these instances a good deed was done. In each example, Rousseau became involved with others because of a desire to bring them joy. Although he maintained his customary reserve in each instance and even acted as a sort of political leader in two instances, he never considered the people involved as contemptible. Conversely, those who started the gingerbread war among the peasants acted from a feeling of contempt. Proof that the gingerbread war was symptomatic of a deeper social and human problem is that the people who were normally the objects of this contempt could rise to contentment no more than those who scorned them so: as Rousseau sees it, the French people cannot enjoy themselves, even when they try, because their joy so often arises from hurting one another or from trying to maintain a sense of superiority to others. But the Genevans and the Swiss in general, people disposed to treat each other on equal terms in politics and in fellowship, can find contentment in their festivities.[143] Even though Rousseau has not been able to function as a citizen of Geneva or of any other Swiss republic, he can enjoy the egalitarian outlook that serves as a base for the pleasures of the Genevans and the Swiss.

These principles of egalitarianism and mutual contentment add another dimension to the discussion of beneficence in the Sixth Walk. When Rousseau helped the little girls obtain wafers, solved the apple dilemma for the young Savoyards, and showed kindness to the old veteran, he maintained the rule of freedom introduced in the earlier discussion. Because none of these activities can occur again, there is no possibility that his acts of generosity can lead to demands for continued assistance. But because of the interplay here between egalitarianism and mutual contentment, bonds of fellowship were created. They arose from the joy that all participants sensed to be shared or desired to be shared and they allowed human beings to enjoy each other's company for a brief moment.

Ironically, the very conditions that allowed Rousseau to engage so readily in each of these activities are also a cause of some sadness. Since these pleasant moments of contentment were not onerous and could not be lasting, he was first attracted to them. But since they could not be prolonged, even the opportunities for contentment must be fleeting. In this respect, the very dispositions that have permitted Rousseau to maintain his independence

have also prevented him from appreciating continued social relationships. As a result, he has been obliged to forgo the pleasures of
fellowship for those of solitude. Only to the extent that the pleasures of solitude are deeper, richer, and more enduring than those
of fellowship can such an irony be considered a blessing. But it
cannot be turned to good account except by someone who is able
to find the full happiness present uniquely in solitary withdrawal.

As is evident from the most cursory glance, the Tenth Walk is
not completed. It appears that had Rousseau lived to complete
the essay, he would have discussed the studies he pursued during
the time that he and Mme de Warens were living at Les Charmettes.[144] However, even more interesting is what he does say
here about the time they spent together. Because Rousseau describes it as a period in which he "enjoyed a century of life and a
pure and full happiness," the question arises as to whether or not
he intends thereby to modify his earlier statement about happiness. When it is recalled that Rousseau once described his days in
Montmorency with equal fervor, the question becomes all the
more pressing.[145]

Yet when Rousseau's description of his happiness here is compared with the description in the Fifth Walk or with that set forth
in the *Four Letters to M. de Malesherbes*, it becomes apparent that
all of his accounts are consistent. Although he does not mention
the sentiment of existence in this account of his happiness at Les
Charmettes, he does indicate that the basic conditions for achieving supreme happiness were present then. He explains that he
acquired a taste for solitude and contemplation when he was
there, that he enjoyed peace and calm, and that he felt free from
subjection. He emphasizes the rural aspect of their existence. The
only difference in this account is Rousseau's claim that "I needed
a friend suited to my heart." Apparently, then, he does consider
human fellowship important and even to be an important element
of happiness. So how can he reconcile this admission with the
praises of solitude that have appeared throughout the preceding
Walks?

To a certain extent, the answer is circumstantial. Rousseau had no such friend when he was at Montmorency or on St. Peter's Island. That is why he had recourse to his imagination. He used it to re-create a society of lovely creatures whose company he could enjoy.[146] In this way, the taste for solitude and contemplation that he had acquired at Les Charmettes during the period of his great happiness with Mme de Warens became the source of a deeper happiness when he was no longer able to enjoy her company. This explanation, like all of the explanations he has offered for his solitude in every Walk since the Fifth Walk, makes his taste for solitude depend on a negative condition. And his ability to over-come even this obstacle is a sign both of his uniqueness and of the quality of his happiness. Unlike all other men, Rousseau is able to turn unpleasant circumstances to good account. His kind of hap-piness is not suitable for most people, because he has been able to master conditions that would have overwhelmed them. Moreover, the happiness he claims as his own is of exceptional merit because it depends so little on favorable external circumstances. It is primarily a result of a disposition of the soul, and Rousseau now understands much better why his soul permits him to find happi-ness even in his enforced solitary condition.

III

Ostensibly, Rousseau seeks in the *Reveries* to answer the ques-tion raised in the very first paragraph of the work: "But I, de-tached from them and from everything, what am I?" It is a question that seems to arise out of the despair he feels at finding himself excluded from the society of men. After having explored what he sets forth in these essays, a thoughtful reader might easily conclude that the only sensible answer to Rousseau's original question is: a man of paradoxes. Throughout this work, he has poignantly demonstrated how torn he is between desire for soli-tude and longing for the company of men, between repugnance for thinking or writing and enjoyment of studying children or his fellow men so as to write about them, and between a sense of being naturally disposed to embrace simplicity and a feeling that his uniqueness consists in his ability to find his way back to man's origins. Moreover, despite the stark title of the work, there is reason to wonder just how serious Rousseau is when he declares that he is no longer interested in acting as a citizen. For someone who insists that he has turned his back on society, his is surely a very political diary. And there is a basic contradiction in some of the Walks about this very point: in the First, Second, and Eighth Walks, he speaks of himself as a man who is made to live in society and who has left it only after having been forced to do so, whereas in the Third and Sixth Walks, he speaks of himself as someone who should have remained isolated and claims that isolation accords more with his natural temperament.

Even though these paradoxes and contradictions can be explained in terms of the larger argument of the work, their existence cannot be ignored. When what Rousseau says here is compared to what he has said in his other works, the nonautobiographical as well as the autobiographical, it is possible to discern their deeper significance. What is far less easy to explain is the question of the addressee of the work. Despite his claims in the First Walk that these essays are intended only for himself, that they will be his companion in his old age,[147] he makes a number of statements in the other Walks that seem to be intended for a reader. In the Second Walk, he declares, as though to a reader: "That, very faithfully, is the story of my accident." [148] He does something quite similar in the Fifth Walk, when he summarizes his account of his activities on St. Peter's Island by saying: "Leaving aside unexpected and importunate visits, this is the way I spent my time on this island during my sojourn there." [149] Moreover, in one place he speaks as though he were referring his reader to an earlier passage: "I have described this condition in one of my reveries." [150] And in two other instances, he speaks, as though to a reader, of what he has written elsewhere.[151] Above all, there is a general tone of second-party address throughout the *Reveries*. He explains things he need not have explained and recounts in detail events to which he need only have alluded were he writing for himself.

If Rousseau does intend this work for readers, he must intend them to understand that he seeks a personal happiness which differs from what he has advocated in his other writings. He taught Émile to live according to precepts of moral virtue, to follow the dictates of reason, and to seek his happiness through participation in human society. He praised the charming inhabitants of Clarens for their ability to seek happiness by spreading joy and contentment to others. Julie, Claire, Wolmar, and even St. Preux are depicted as sweet and gentle people who delight in the simple pleasures of human fellowship and ask for nothing more than to see those pleasures prolonged. Rousseau lauded such associations and painted in the most alluring colors the moral traits one must have to enjoy living in them so as to encourage his fellow men to seek such associations and fellowship, but he desires for himself a happiness which has nothing to do with political association or intimate human fellowship. He seeks such a happiness because he is fully aware of the limitations in either of those kinds of association. Yet in making such an admission, he threatens his earlier teaching. That is one reason for him to attempt to make this work purely personal. He does not want it to be considered in the same manner as his other works, because it is not addressed to the same public as they were.

In the *Reveries*, Rousseau describes the happiness suitable for someone who has seen clearly the problems of political life. This happiness is closely related to the end of life and does seem to be best described as the sum of the goods one might take away at the time of death. As such, he can show that death is not to be feared, that in many respects it differs little from prolonged reverie. After all, it is only in the reverie of death that he or anyone else can truly claim to be unperturbed and self-sufficient like God.[152] As he aptly demonstrates in this work, such claims are accurate only in the most limited manner during this life: throughout these essays, Rousseau gives little evidence of being unperturbed or of being even remotely self-sufficient. Yet such a view of happiness suggests, in the clearest possible manner, that there is no meaningful end to human life, that all is somehow in constant flux. Because such an opinion must be understood in all its nuances if simple citizens are to be preserved from feelings of utter despair, Rousseau does little more than allude to his agreement with it here. Yet this or something very much like it seems to offer the most likely explanation of the larger teaching of *The Reveries of the Solitary Walker*.

NOTES

1. See First Walk, p. 7.
2. Ibid., pp. 5-6 and 7.
3. In the *Confessions,* Book XI, *OC* 1, p. 569, Rousseau explained why he wrote these letters of January 4, 12, 26, and 28, 1762, to M. de Malesherbes: "When they [the philosophic clique in Paris] saw that I was persevering [in staying at the Hermitage], they said it was due to obstinacy, pride, and shame at backing down, but that I was bored to death there and was leading a very unhappy life. M. de Malesherbes believed it and wrote me. Troubled by this error in a man whom I esteemed so much, I wrote him four consecutive letters in which I explained the true reasons for my conduct and faithfully described my tastes, my inclinations, my character, and all that occurred in my heart. These four letters, written without a draft, rapidly, at a stroke of the pen, and without even being read over, are perhaps the only thing I have written with ease in my whole life. And that is truly remarkable given my physical suffering and extreme depression at that time." These last words refer to Rousseau's sickness during the fall of 1761, aggravated by a catheter which had broken off in his urethra. Moreover, during this whole period of time, he was especially fearful that the real reason behind the slowness in printing the *Émile* was that his enemies were trying to change the book against his will.

The rest of the passage is very important, for it shows that Rousseau did intend these letters to be read by more than one addressee, that they were in a way intended for the public: "Feeling my strength decline, I shuddered to think that I would leave such an inaccurate opinion of myself in the mind of decent people and by the hastily drawn sketch of these four letters, I tried to give some kind of a substitute for the memoirs I had already planned. These letters, which pleased M. de Malesherbes and which he showed around Paris, are something like a summary of what I am setting forth here in greater detail and therefore deserve to be preserved. Among my papers will be found the copy he had made at my request and sent me some years later."

4. On a band of paper he wrapped around the letters, Rousseau wrote: "Containing the true painting of my character and the true reasons for my conduct."

5. See *Four Letters to M. le Président de Malesherbes,* 1, 2, and 4, *OC* 1, pp. 1132-1136 and 1142-1144.

6. *Mandement de Monseigneur l'Archevêque de Paris* in *Oeuvres Complètes de J. J. Rousseau* (Paris: P. DuPont, 1823), vol. 6, p. 21.

7. See *Beaumont, OC* 4, pp. 959-86, esp. p. 961: "Penetrated with gratitude for the worthy pastor who, resisting the torrential example and judging according to truth, did not exclude a defender of God's cause from the Church, I will preserve a tender memory of his truly Christian charity for my whole life."

8. Cf. *Émile, OC* 4, p. 340 and note; pp. 522-23 and note; pp. 817-18 (see also in this section, n. 103); and p. 820.

9. *Confessions, OC* 1, p. 3. At the beginning of Book I, he was even more explicit about the unique character of this work: "I am embarking on an enterprise that is without precedent and which, once complete, will never be imitated. I want to hold up to my fellow men a man in the whole truth of nature; and I will be this man.

"I alone. I feel my heart and I know men. I am made like none I have seen; I dare believe that I am made like none who exist. If I am no better, I am at least different. Whether it was good or evil for nature to break the mold in which she cast me is something that can be judged only after having read me." Ibid., p. 5.

10. See *Dialogues, OC* 1, p. 936: "If you had not depicted your Jean-Jacques to me, I would have thought that the natural man no longer existed; but the striking similarity between the one you have depicted to me and the author whose books I have read would not let me doubt that they are the same, even if I had no other reason to think so." (The Frenchman is speaking.)

11. See the beginnings of the Fourth, Sixth, Ninth, and Tenth Walks.

12. See Fifth Walk, p. 69 and Seventh Walk, p. 91.

13. For Rousseau's own account of his basic thinking and of what he tried to do in his different works, cf. *Letter to Christophe de Beaumont, OC* 4, pp. 935-37, 945, 951-53, and 979, with *Émile, OC* 4, pp. 323-24; also *Dialogues, OC* 1, pp. 668-72, 727-31, 802-3, 806, 828-29, 932-33, and 935-37.

14. First Walk, pp. 1-5.

15. Ibid., pp. 5-8.

16. Ibid., pp. 1-2.

17. Ibid., pp. 2-3, and cf. *Dialogues, OC* 1, pp. 858 and 826.

18. First Walk, pp. 3-5.

19. Cf. *Dialogues, OC* 1, pp. 913-14, 951-56, and 969-74. This does not mean that the *Dialogues* is a positive or lighthearted work. It is not. Rousseau acknowledged the pervasiveness of the plot in the *Dialogues* and alluded to the numerous difficulties involved in attempting to escape its effects. However, he did not acknowledge these difficulties in his own name: all of the pessimistic speeches in the *Dialogues* are entrusted to the character identified as "the Frenchman" (cf. ibid., pp. 939-46, 948-49,

956-59, 960-61, 961-66, and 966-69). While it is surely important to think about the way each character develops in the course of the dialectical exchange, the fact remains that the character identified as "Rousseau" in the *Dialogues* is assigned a hopeful and almost encouraging role. The only despondent cry uttered in Rousseau's own name occurred in the appendix to the *Dialogues*, the *Histoire du Précédent Écrit;* and this was written after Rousseau's many futile efforts to pass the *Dialogues* on to posterity (see *Dialogues, OC* 1, pp. 986-87).

20. See First Walk, pp. 3-4 and n. 3.

21. Cf. *Dialogues, OC* 1, pp. 812, 813-17, 819-20, 823-24, and 853-54 with 794; also *Four Letters to M. le Président de Malesherbes* 1, *OC* 1, pp. 1131-1132, and Tenth Walk, p. 141.

22. First Walk, pp. 5-8. Cf. Second Walk, p. 13; also *Confessions,* Book X, *OC* 1, p. 494, and *Dialogues, OC* 1, p. 909 and note.

23. Second Walk, pp. 12-13.

24. Ibid., pp. 13-20.

25. Ibid., pp. 20-21.

26. Ibid., p. 12.

27. Ibid., pp. 14-15.

28. Cf. ibid., pp. 13-14 with ṗp. 14-15, especially the sentence: "Finally, after having looked thoroughly at several other plants I saw still in bloom and which I was always pleased to see even though I was familiar with their aspect and name, I gradually turned away from these minute observations so as to give myself up to the no less charming, but more moving, impression which the whole scene made on me."

29. Cf. ibid., pp. 15-16 and First Walk, pp. 6-7.

30. Montaigne *Essais* II. 6, "De l'Exercitation."

31. Pascal *Pensées,* para. 63.

32. For Rousseau's account of these incidents, see *Confessions,* Books IX-XII, *OC* 1, pp. 454-55, 472, 491, 575-78, 586-87, and 623-34; see also *Dialogues, OC* 1, pp. 881-82 and 886-91. The amount of secondary literature devoted to the historical documentation of these incidents is overwhelming; in addition to the works cited in the notes to these passages from the *Confessions* and *Dialogues,* see L.-A. Boiteux, "Le rôle de d'Alembert dans la querelle Rousseau-Hume," *Annales de la Société Jean-Jacques Rousseau,* 32 (1950-52), pp. 143-54; see also Gilbert Py, "Jean-Jacques Rousseau et la Congrégation des Prêtres de l'Oratoire de Jésus," *Annales de la Société Jean-Jacques Rousseau,* 38 (1969-71), pp. 127-53, esp. pp. 152-53.

33. Cf. Second Walk, p. 21 with pp. 20-21; also *Confessions,* Book II, *OC* I, p. 53, and *Dialogues, OC* 1, pp. 979-80 with pp. 980-81.

34. Cf. *Letter from J.-J. Rousseau to M. de Voltaire,* August 18, 1756, *OC* 4, pp. 1060-1061, 1061-1062, 1067, 1069, 1070, 1072-1073, and esp. pp. 1068-1069 with pp. 1074-1075. This letter was, however, addressed

only to Voltaire. In a subsequent letter to Voltaire, Rousseau stated that he had never given his permission for the first letter to be printed and explained that "what one man writes to another, he does not write to the public." See Letter of June 17, 1760, in *Confessions*, Book X, *OC* 1, p. 541.

35. Cf. First Walk, p. 5; also *Letter to M. de Voltaire*, *OC* 4, pp. 1061-1062 and 1069.

36. See Third Walk, pp. 27-28. Although Rousseau does not say much about Solon, there are several features of Solon's life that merit our attention. He was known for his poetry as well as for his legislation and once feigned madness to get a law repealed (cf. Plutarch *Solon* 8.1-4 and 18.4; also Plato *Timaeus* 21b-d). Plutarch especially applauded Solon's attempt to structure the laws in such a way that it would be to the advantage of the citizens to be law-abiding (cf. *Solon* 5.3 and *Social Contract*, Book I, beginning). In the same vein, he praised Solon for seeking to establish equality among the citizens because he considered it the only safeguard of freedom (cf. *Comparison of Publicola with Solon* 3.1 with *Solon* 13.1-16.3 and 18.3-5; cf. also *Social Contract*, Book I, chaps. 4, 6, 8, and Book II, chap. 4, with *Second Discourse*, *OC* 3, pp. 131-32, 187, 191, and 193-94). In Plutarch's judgment it was fitting to contrast Solon's life with that of Publicola, for it would be instructive to contrast the life of the wisest man with that of the happiest man (see *Comparison of Publicola with Solon* 1.5).

37. Third Walk, p. 28: "If there is any study still appropriate for an old man, it is solely to learn to die." See also Plato *Phaedo* 63e-64b.

38. Third Walk, pp. 28-29.

39. Ibid., pp. 28-39. The last paragraph of the Third Walk is the conclusion. Concerning the problem of Rousseau's claim that this reform took place when he was forty years old, see ibid., n. 7.

40. Ibid., pp. 28-30.

41. Ibid., pp. 30-34.

42. Ibid., pp. 34-39.

43. Cf. ibid., pp. 37-39, with *Dialogues*, *OC* 1, pp. 695, 782-83, esp. pp. 971-72 and note; *Confessions*, Book IX, *OC* 1, p. 468; and *Reply to Stanislas*, *OC* 3, p. 46, note.

44. Cf. *First Discourse*, *OC* 3, pp. 6-7 and note; *Letter to M. de Voltaire*, *OC* 4, pp. 1062 and 1072; *Letter to Christophe de Beaumont*, *OC* 4, pp. 1004-1005 and pp. 948-52 with *Émile*, *OC* 4, p. 555, esp. p. 632, note; and *Dialogues*, *OC* 1, pp. 728-29, 804-5, 879, 968-69, and 970-74. Cf. also Peter Gay, *The Party of Humanity* (New York: Alfred A. Knopf, 1964), pp. 232-33; Leo Strauss, "On the Intention of Rousseau," *Social Research*, 14 (1947), pp. 456-59 and 466-67, note 38; and Karl Barth, *From Rousseau to Ritschl* (London: SCM Press Ltd., 1959), pp. 100-104, 107-9, and 115-16.

45. Third Walk, p. 34.

46. Cf. *Letter to Christophe de Beaumont, OC* 4, pp. 933-34, 935, 957, 994, 997, and 998-99.

47. Cf. *Letters Written from the Mountain* I, *OC* 3, p. 694: "In the *Émile* the creed of a Catholic priest is to be found and in the *Héloïse* that of a devout woman. These two writings are in close enough agreement that one can be explained by the other and, from this agreement, it can be pretty well presumed that if the author who published the books they are contained in does not adopt both of them entirely, he at least inclines a great deal toward them." Cf. also *Confessions,* Book IX, *OC* 1, p. 407: " . . . the creed of . . . [the] dying Héloïse is exactly the same as that of the Savoyard Vicar."

48. Cf. *Letter to M. de Voltaire, OC* 4, pp. 1070-1071, and in this section, n. 34.

49. Cf. *Letter to Christophe de Beaumont, OC* 4, pp. 952-53, 955-57, 960-62, and 963-64; also *Letters Written from the Mountain* IV, OC 3, p. 768.

50. Cf. *Letter to Christophe de Beaumont, OC* 4, p. 969 with p. 945; also pp. 973, 975-76, 983, 990, 996-97, and 1006; and *Second Discourse, OC* 3, pp. 125-26, 144, 162, and 170-71.

51. See *Letter to Christophe de Beaumont, OC* 4, pp. 931 and 1003.

52. Cf. *Second Discourse,* note i; *Social Contract,* Book IV, chap. 8; and *Confessions,* Book VIII, *OC* 1, pp. 392-93.

53. See Third Walk, p. 32: "I was living then among modern philosophers who hardly resembled the ancient ones."

54. Cf. *Émile, OC* 4, pp. 678-91, and *Dialogues, OC* 1, p. 689. In introducing this Epicurean creed (p. 673), Rousseau explained how important it was for an author to understand the principles of good taste: "Knowledge of what can be pleasing or displeasing to men is necessary not only for the person who needs them, but also for the one who wants to be useful to them. It is important to please them even to serve them, and the art of writing is nothing less than an idle pursuit when it is not used to make the truth heard." Cf. also *Letter to Christophe de Beaumont, OC* 4, pp. 950-51; *Letter to M. de Voltaire, OC* 4, pp. 1071-1072; and Strauss, "On the Intention of Rousseau," p. 466 and note 36.

55. It is of no help to recall Rousseau's statement in the *Letter to M. d'Alembert* that: "I do not mean . . . that one can be virtuous without religion; I held this erroneous opinion for a long time but am now only too disabused of it." (See Bloom, trans., *Letter to M. d'Alembert* [Ithaca: Cornell University Press, 1960], p. 97, note.) In the preface to that work, Rousseau explained its basic purpose and identified the audience to which it was addressed: ". . . I am not dealing here with vain philosophical chatter but with a practical truth important to a whole people. I do not speak here to the few but to the public, nor do I attempt to

make others think but rather to explain my thought more clearly." Ibid., p. 6.

56. See *Confessions*, Book XI, *OC* 1, p. 580: "My usual evening reading was the Bible, and I read it through five or six times in this way." See also Strauss, "On the Intention of Rousseau," pp. 460-61, with note 22 and pp. 469-71.

57. See Plutarch *Moralia*: "How to Profit from One's Enemies," 89a-b; cf. also 86f and 89c with *First Discourse*, *OC* 3, p. 17 and note.

58. See Fourth Walk, pp. 43-45.

59. Ibid., pp. 45-51.

60. Ibid., pp. 51-57.

61. Ibid., pp. 57-59.

62. Ibid., p. 45.

63. Ibid., p. 46.

64. Ibid., p. 46. See also *Social Contract*, Book II, chap. 4: ". . . under the law of reason nothing happens without a cause, any more than under the law of nature."

65. Fourth Walk, p. 48.

66. See *Émile*, *OC* 4, p. 415, note.

67. See *Letter to Christophe de Beaumont*, *OC* 4, p. 967. To illustrate how he thought someone who respected truth should handle popular prejudices, he explained: "I have always held that public instruction had two essential defects it was impossible to remove. One is the bad faith of those who give it, the other the blindness of those who receive it. If men without passions instructed men without prejudices, our knowledge would be more limited but more certain and reason would always reign. Now, regardless of what we do, politicians will always have the same interest; but the prejudices of the people, having no fixed foundation, are more variable; they can be altered, changed, increased, or diminished. Thus, it is only from this direction that education can have any hold, and that is what the friend of truth ought to aim at. He can hope to make the people more reasonable, but not to make those who lead them more honest." Ibid., p. 968. Somewhat later, Rousseau made the same point even more directly: "To speak with frankness and firmness to the public is a right common to all men; with respect to everything that is useful, it is even a duty." Ibid., p. 994, note.

68. See *Confessions*, Book IX, *OC* 1, pp. 448-49.

69. Fourth Walk, pp. 48-50.

70. See Montesquieu *Le Temple de Gnide* in *Oeuvres Complètes* ("Bibliothèque de la Pléiade"; Paris: Gallimard, 1949), vol. 1, p. 387.

71. See Fourth Walk, pp. 48-51, esp. p. 51. Rousseau was clearly not persuaded by the explanation offered in the preface to the second edition of *Le Temple de Gnide*: "The point of the poem is to show that the sentiments of the heart make us happy, not the pleasures of the senses;

but that our happiness is never pure enough not to be troubled by chance events." See Montesquieu *Le Temple de Gnide*, p. 1063.

72. See the *New Héloïse*, second preface, *OC* 2, p. 23. Shortly after this passage, Rousseau explained how this lie could be understood in broader terms (p. 28). "R" is for Rousseau and "N" for an anonymous man of letters:

> N.   You refuse, then, to tell the truth?
> R.   To declare that one wants to remain silent
>   about it is still to honor it.

In the first preface to this work, Rousseau declared: "Although I bear only the title of editor here, I did work on this book and I do not hide that. Did I do the whole thing, and is the whole correspondence only a fiction? Worldly people, what does it matter to you? For you, it is surely a fiction." Ibid., p. 5.

73. See Fourth Walk, p. 56, n. 17.

74. Ibid., pp. 50-51 and 51-55.

75. *Social Contract*, Book II, chap. 7, end. See also Book II, chap. 6, end, and Plato *Republic* 414c-415c.

76. Cf. *Letter to Christophe de Beaumont*, *OC* 4, pp. 955-56, 963-64, and 995-96; also pp. 958-59 and 996-97 with *Émile*, *OC* 4, pp. 593-94, 607, and 630. See also Plato *Timaeus* 29c and 48d-e.

In speaking of the philosopher in general, Leo Strauss makes an observation that is most appropriate to the way Rousseau handled the problem of lying in his other writings: "For philosophic readers he would do almost more than enough by drawing their attention to the fact that he did not object to telling lies which were noble, or tales which were merely similar to the truth." *Persecution and the Art of Writing* (Glencoe: The Free Press, 1952), p. 35; cf. also p. 33 and Leo Strauss, *Natural Right and History* (Chicago: University of Chicago Press, 1953), pp. 260-61 and note 20. Even though the *Reveries* seems to be intended for no reader other than Rousseau, it is appropriate for him to be as guarded about the extent of his lying in this work as he was in his other writings. After all, his purpose here is to understand what justifies lying, not to confess to all the lies he may have told.

77. See Fifth Walk, pp. 62-64.

78. Cf. ibid., pp. 69-70 with pp. 63-64 and 70-71.

79. Ibid., pp. 64, 66, 67, and 70.

80. Ibid., pp. 64-65.

81. Ibid., pp. 64-70. The long concluding paragraph (pp. 70-71) constitutes the third major division.

82. Ibid., p. 64.

83. Ibid., p. 65 and n. 9. As was explained in that note, La Fontaine had been very impressed by the Book of Baruch. However, Baruch is

considered to be apocryphal in the Protestant tradition and is not counted among the minor prophets; Habakkuk is counted among them. When Rousseau spoke of his sojourn on St. Peter's Island in the *Confessions*, he did not mention this incident, but he cited a verse from La Fontaine's *Diable de Papefiguière;* see *Confessions,* Book XII, *OC* 1, p. 640, and Appendix B of this work.

The Book of Baruch is a letter from the Jews exiled in Babylon to the Jews in Jerusalem, whereas the Book of Habakkuk is a testimony of this prophet's complaint against the children of Israel and of the Lord's promise to punish their sins by raising up the Chaldeans against them. Rousseau, the beleaguered exile, replaces Baruch's prayer for exiles and promise of the Lord's help with Habakkuk's harsh words of blame and threat of divine vengeance. In other words, Rousseau is less in need of consolation or promise of eventual compensation for the evils he has suffered than he is desirous of speaking against evildoers.

84. See Fifth Walk, pp. 65-67 and 67-68.

85. See ibid., pp. 63, 66-67 and n. 11; see also *Confessions,* Book XII, *OC* 1, pp. 643-44 and Appendix B of this work. Cf. also Niccolò Machiavelli *The Prince,* chap. 18, and *Émile, OC* 4, pp. 393 and 869.

86. See Fifth Walk, pp. 68-70.

87. Ibid., pp. 69-70. Cf. *Émile, OC* 4, pp. 418-19; also *Second Discourse, OC* 3, p. 142 and note i, with *Emile,* pp. 247-48, 305-6, 407-8, and esp. p. 281.

88. See *Confessions,* Book XII, *OC* 1, pp. 637-45 and Appendix B of this work; also *Four Letters to M. de Malesherbes* 3, *OC* 1, p. 1141.

89. See Fifth Walk, p. 69.

90. See *Confessions,* Book XII, *OC* 1, p. 638 and Appendix B of this work.

91. See ibid., Books VI and X, *OC* 1, pp. 236 and 521; see also *Four Letters to M. de Malesherbes* 3, *OC* 1, pp. 1139-1140 and 1141-1142. In his profession of faith, the Savoyard vicar based our knowledge of our existence on our ability to sense or feel that we exist and considered thinking and feeling to be very similar; see *Émile, OC* 4, pp. 570-71, 587, and 600, esp. variant (a). Rousseau's other references to the sentiment of existence, for example, in the *Letter to M. de Voltaire (OC* 4, p. 1063) and in the *Second Discourse (OC* 3, pp. 144 and 193), were intended to illustrate his criticism of men living in society: men living in society had an awareness of themselves only through the opinion of others; they had never really experienced the sentiment of their own existence.

92. Cf. *Confessions,* Books III-VI, *OC* 1, pp. 104, 106-9, 150-51, 225-26, and 243-45, with pp. 253-54.

93. See *Dialogues, OC* 1, pp. 816-17 and 845; see also pp. 813-14 for a discussion of why he alone can find pleasure in solitude.

94. Fifth Walk, p. 68; Rousseau's emphasis. Rousseau's whole idea of

happiness as silent reverie should be compared with Aristotle's view that it is a certain kind of action; see *Poetics* 1450a18-20 and *Nicomachean Ethics* 1098a6-20.

95. See Sixth Walk, pp. 79-80 and 83-84; see also *First Discourse, OC* 3, p. 18.

96. See Sixth Walk, pp. 74-75 and n. 1.

97. Ibid., pp. 75-83.

98. Ibid., pp. 75-76.

99. In the sequel to the *Émile*, which Rousseau never published, the adult Émile aptly described the way most people view good deeds: "To ask for a favor is to acquire a kind of right to it; to grant it is almost a duty . . . ." See *Émile et Sophie, OC* 4, p. 914.

100. See *Four Letters to M. de Malesherbes* 1, *OC* 1, p. 1132.

101. See Sixth Walk, pp. 76-78, esp. pp. 76-77; see also *Confessions,* Book X, *OC* 1, pp. 497 and 503; and *Dialogues, OC* 1, pp. 823, 828, and 910-11.

102. Cf. *Émile, OC* 4, pp. 395 and 503-10; *Confessions,* Book I, *OC* 1, p. 5; *Reply to Stanislas, OC* 3, p. 42; Letter to M. de Saint-Germain of February 26, 1770 in *Correspondance Générale de J.-J. Rousseau,* ed. Théophile Dufour (Paris: Armand Colin, 1933), vol. 19, pp. 245-47; and René Descartes *Les Passions de l'Âme,* articles 54, 152-156, 161, and 187.

103. See *Émile, OC* 4, pp. 817-18. After Émile had fallen in love with Sophie, Rousseau lectured him about virtue and duty in the following terms: "My child, there is no happiness without courage nor any virtue without struggle. The word *virtue* comes from a word meaning *strength;* strength is the foundation of all virtue. Virtue belongs only to a being who is weak by nature and strong by will; that is what the merit of the virtuous man consists in. Even though we call God good, we do not call Him virtuous because He does not need to strive to do good. As long as it costs nothing to be virtuous, there is little need to know it. The need arises when the passions awake; it has arisen for you.

"By bringing you up in accordance with all the simplicity of nature, instead of preaching to you about painful duties, I have kept you from the vices which make these duties painful. It is not that I have made falsehood odious to you, but that I have made it useless. I have taught you less to return to each what belongs to him than to concern yourself only about what is your own. I have made you good rather than virtuous. But he who is only good remains good only as long as it pleases him; goodness is broken and destroyed under the hammering of human passions; the man who is only good is good only for himself.

"What is a virtuous man? He is someone who knows how to conquer his affections. For he then follows his reason, his conscience; he does his duty; he stays in the right path and nothing can turn him aside. Heretofore you were free only in appearance. You had only the precarious freedom of a slave who has not been ordered to do anything. Now, be free in fact; learn to become your own master. Rule your own heart, Émile, and you will be virtuous." The emphasis is Rousseau's.

104. See Sixth Walk, pp. 78-83.

105. See ibid., pp. 78-80; see also *Four Letters to M. de Malesherbes* 4, *OC* 1, pp. 1143-1144; and *Dialogues, OC* 1, pp. 906-7 and 962-64.

106. Cf. *Émile, OC* 4, pp. 490-94; and *Second Discourse, OC* 3, pp. 153-56 and note o, and pp. 169-70 and 174-75.

107. See Sixth Walk, pp. 81-82 and n. 13.

108. In a letter of May 12, 1763, addressed to the first magistrate of the Genevan council, Rousseau renounced his Genevan citizenship; see *Confessions,* Book XII, *OC* 1, pp. 609-10.

109. See *Dialogues, OC* 1, pp. 668-69; see also *Narcissus, Preface, OC* 2, pp. 962-63, 965-66, 967, 969 and note, and 973-74; and Strauss, "On the Intention of Rousseau," pp. 459 and 476-78.

110. See Seventh Walk, pp. 89-91.

111. Ibid., pp. 91-102.

112. Ibid., pp. 91-96.

113. Ibid., pp. 96-99.

114. Ibid., pp. 99-102.

115. See ibid., p. 91; see also *Confessions,* Book IX, *OC* 1, pp. 407-8; and *Dialogues, OC* 1, pp. 808-9, 816-18, 822, 845, 855-56, 865-66, esp. pp. 838 and 839-40.

116. See *Émile, OC* 4, p. 385, and Sixth Walk, p. 77; see also *Second Discourse, OC* 3, pp. 142-43.

117. See Seventh Walk, pp. 92-96. For his reference on p. 92 to preserving "the remainder of warmth that was about to evaporate and be extinguished by the despondency" to which he was succumbing, cf. *Dialogues, OC* 1, p. 861, and René Descartes *Discours de la Méthode,* pt. V (Paris: J. Vrin, 1964), pp. 115-18.

118. See Seventh Walk, pp. 92-95, and also Fifth Walk, p. 69.

119. Seventh Walk, p. 95.

120. Ibid., pp. 96-99.

121. Cf. ibid. p. 98, with Third and Fourth Walks, pp. 27, 39-40, and 58-59; also *Dialogues, OC* 1, p. 833.

122. See Seventh Walk, pp. 99-102.

123. Ibid., pp. 102-3.

124. Ibid., pp. 100-101.

125. Ibid., p. 101.

126. Ibid., pp. 101-2.

127. Cf. ibid., pp. 102-3, with pp. 89 and 90; also Second Walk, pp. 12-13 and Fifth Walk, pp. 70-71. In the *Dialogues,* Rousseau explained that he had sold his herbarium and all his books of botany to the Reverend Daniel Malthus; *OC* 1, p. 832 and note 5.

128. See Eighth Walk, p. 110.

129. Ibid., p. 119.

130. Ibid., pp. 110-11.

131. See First Walk, p. 6. Cf. also pp. 112-13 and 114 with p. 4; and Diogenes Laertius *Lives of Eminent Philosophers* 6. 41.

132. Cf. Eighth Walk, pp. 112-13 with pp. 113-15 and 115-17. Rousseau's statement here that he has "learned to bear the yoke of necessity without murmur" is only an apparent contradiction of his earlier statement (see Sixth Walk, p. 83) that "as soon as I feel the yoke either of necessity or of men, I become rebellious, or rather, recalcitrant." In the earlier instance, he was referring to his reaction to being forced to act in particular ways. Then he resisted. That is why he was not a good citizen. Here, he is speaking only of the need to recognize that there is no way to avoid his present situation. Cf. also *Dialogues, OC* 1, pp. 792 and 864-65; and First Walk, p. 1.

133. See n. 106 and also *Dialogues, OC* 1, pp. 805-6, 846-47, 851-52, 861-62, 863, 901, and esp. pp. 863-64.

134. See Eighth Walk, p. 117.

135. Ibid., pp. 117-20.

136. See Ninth Walk, pp. 122-23, 129-30, 132, 133, and 133-34.

137. Ibid., pp. 123-24, 126-27, and pp. 127-29, 129-30.

138. Ibid., pp. 130-31, 127-29, and 133-34.

139. Ibid., p. 130.

140. Ibid., p. 122.

141. Ibid., p. 125.

142. Cf. ibid., pp. 125-26, with pp. 133-34, 130-31, and 132. See also *Confessions*, Book III, *OC* 1, pp. 113-17; and *Four Letters to M. de Malesherbes* 1, *OC* 1, p. 1131.

143. Cf. Ninth Walk, pp. 129-30 with pp. 130 and 130-31.

144. See Tenth Walk, p. 142; see also *Confessions*, Book VI, *OC* 1, pp. 231-48.

145. See Tenth Walk, n. 7.

146. Cf. *Confessions*, Book IX, *OC* 1, pp. 426-28, with p. 425; also *Four Letters to M. de Malesherbes* 3, *OC* 1, p. 1140.

147. See First Walk, pp. 5-6 and 7.

148. Second Walk, p. 17.

149. Fifth Walk, p. 67; see also his remark earlier in this Walk (p. 64): "Now what was this happiness and in what did its enjoyment consist? From the description of the life I led there, I will let all the men of this century guess at it."

150. See Eighth Walk, p. 120.

151. See Third Walk, p. 34 and Sixth Walk, p. 76.

152. See First Walk, p. 5 and Fifth Walk, p. 69; see also *Confessions*, Book IX, *OC* 1, p. 409 and *Second Discourse, OC* 3, p. 138.

DESCRIPTION OF THE NOTEBOOKS CONTAINING *THE REVERIES OF THE SOLITARY WALKER*

These notebooks are held by the Bibliothèque de Neuchâtel, Switzerland, under the call numbers 7882 (new number: Ms R 78) and 7883 (new number: Ms R 79). The first notebook (Ms R 78) contains the first seven Walks which are written in ink in a small, but clear and usually legible, hand. The second notebook (Ms R 79) contains the remaining three Walks. In this notebook, the writing is very small and often scratched out or written over. Although it, too, is written in ink, the numerous instances in which a passage is crossed out or in which Rousseau has referred the reader to another page for an added sentence, the way words are crammed between already narrow lines, and the numerous loose sentences that seem to belong to no part of the text make it very hard to establish the sense of some passages with complete certainty. Moreover, Rousseau's handwriting in this notebook is so small that use of a magnifying glass is absolutely essential. It is quite apparent that it represents a first draft of the Eighth, Ninth, and Tenth Walks, whereas the first notebook represents a nearly final copy of the first seven Walks.

There are seventy-two sheets of paper in the first notebook, forming three signatures of twenty-four sheets bound together without a cover. The paper is good-quality linen from the mills of Cusson (Auvergne), watermarked with what appears to be a griffin. Each sheet of paper measures 10.8 cm by 16.7 cm.

Both sides of the first page of the notebook are blank. In the upper-left-hand corner of the recto side of the second page is written: "no. 15." The title of the work is centered on the upper part of the same page: *"Les reveries/du Promeneur Solitaire."* This is all written in the same ink as the rest of the notebook. The verso side of the second page is blank. On the recto side of the third page, the text of the *Reveries* begins. It continues to the recto side of the penultimate page. Each of the first three Walks is separated by at least one blank page.

Numbering begins on the recto side of the third page and continues, on both sides of each page, to the verso side of the last page which is numbered page 140. The numbering is sometimes on the upper-right-hand corner and sometimes on the upper-left-hand corner of the pages. From the beginning to page 83, the numbers are in ink and probably in Rousseau's hand. From page 84 to the end, the numbers are in pencil and in another hand.

The second notebook has a hard parchment cover with an overflap to which a string is attached so that the notebook can be fastened shut. There is worn, illegible writing in ink running the length of the cover, and "no. 16" is written in large characters. A later hand has added "7883 = Ms R 79" in pencil. Like the first, this notebook is made of good-quality linen paper, but the paper in this notebook comes from the mills of P. Daubes (or perhaps P. Daures) of Limousin and is watermarked with what seems to be a coat of arms. Smaller than the first, this notebook contains one signature of fifty-six sheets of paper each of which measures 10.5 cm by 15.5 cm.

On the inside of the cover "Made La Duchesse d'Olonne Rue des/Lions St. Paul" is written in ink. The notebook is numbered,

in this direction, on the lower-right-hand corner of the recto side
of each page. This numbering runs to the middle of the notebook,
where it ends at page 25. Written in bright red ink, it appears to
be from a hand other than Rousseau's.

Both sides of the first three pages contain draft passages of the
Premier Dialogue in pencil and ink. On both sides of the fourth
page and on the recto side of the fifth page, there is a letter to an
unknown person also written in pencil and ink. The ink passages
are sometimes crossed out, while the pencil passages are sometimes crossed out and sometimes written over in ink. The Eighth
Walk begins on the verso side of page 5 and finishes on the recto
side of page 17. Except for minor corrections or additions, writing
appears only on the recto side of pages 6-16. The Ninth Walk and
the Tenth Walk run from page 17, verso, to page 25, recto; thus,
these essays are written on both sides of the pages.

This second notebook apparently served a multitude of purposes, for by turning it over and opening it from the other direction, one encounters another set of writings. From this direction,
the pages are numbered in pencil in the lower-right-hand corner
of the recto side up to page 32, and the numbering appears to be
in Rousseau's hand. On the recto side of the first page is a numbered list of grains with their Latin names; even though the verso
side is blank except for an obscure note, there are outlines of some
of these grains appearing at the top of the recto side of pages 4, 6,
and 8. It seems, therefore, that Rousseau's original intention was
to use the notebook in his botanical excursions in order to write
down observations about these particular plants. The project was
obviously abandoned, however. Now, both sides of pages 2 and 3
contain pencil draft passages of the *Premier Dialogue* that have
been crossed out, and a draft version of the appendix to the
Dialogues—the *Histoire du Précédent Écrit*—appears in ink on
page 4, recto, to page 13, verso. The notebook is blank from page
13, verso, to page 18, recto. Page 18, verso, contains a short note
written in ink, and a passage from the *Premier Dialogue* written in
pencil occurs on page 19, recto. The remaining pages are blank
until the end of the Tenth Walk, written from the other direction,

appears on what would be page 32, verso. However, it is numbered as page 25, recto, from the other direction.

Strange pencil marks in red and black lead appear on certain
pages of the first notebook, that is, the notebook containing the
partially revised version of the first seven Walks. These marks fall
into four different categories:

(a) square brackets in red pencil enclosing certain words or
passages, for example, "a poisoner, an assassin" and "that the only
greeting . . . on me" (see First Walk, p. 2); "When all of . . .
appeased than they" (ibid., p. 5); and "If it involves . . . of facts"
(see Fourth Walk, p. 50).

(b) a large cross in red pencil through two passages which,
without making the passages illegible, clearly indicates that somebody desired that they be eliminated, that is, "Thus it is . . .
regard to me" and "Thus it is . . . white to black" (see Sixth Walk,
p. 79).

(c) certain words underlined in black pencil as though some
question existed about how they should be read—each word presenting some minor problem, for example, "depression" (see First
Walk, p. 3), "it overturns" (see Third Walk, p. 36), "All things"
(see Fifth Walk, p. 64), "pod of the" (ibid., p. 65).

(d) a large cross in black pencil through the second passage
cited in (b) which, without making the passage illegible, clearly
indicates that somebody intended it to be eliminated.

There can be little doubt that the black pencil marks are from a
hand other than Rousseau's. He would certainly have had little
difficulty reading the words which are underlined, and his manner
of crossing out passages he intended to eliminate was either to
draw a horizontal line through each line of handwriting or to
draw a vertical line through the middle of the passage. This was
always done with a pen. The same line of reasoning suggests that
the red pencil marks are probably not Rousseau's. It is quite
unlikely that the square brackets in red pencil indicate passages
needing further consideration, for no passage which is now
crossed out in ink has square brackets around it.

All of the evidence suggests that the pencil marks are proposed

emendations made by one of the early editors. A brief consideration of the crossed-out and bracketed passages easily indicates
what prompted one of the earlier editors to suggest their excision:
conventional discretion. Obviously, an editor who did not feel as
strongly as Rousseau about these matters would have wished to
silence the criticisms contained in those passages. Although it is
highly tempting to suppose that Rousseau might have wished to
temper some of his harsh statements about men in general or in
particular and even though some secondary accounts buttress that
conjecture, the actual condition of the manuscript does not confirm such an explanation. All things considered, it was decided to
translate the manuscript as it appears and not to set such passages
off by asterisks, footnotes, brackets, or other printer's signs.

APPENDIX B

TRANSLATION OF
CONFESSIONS,
BOOK XII, *OC* 1, PP. 637-46

St. Peter's Island, called Hillock Island in Neuchâtel, is in the middle of Lake Bienne and is about one and a half leagues in circumference.[1] But within such a small space it contains all the major products necessary for life. It has fields, meadows, orchards, woods, vineyards. And thanks to a varied and mountainous terrain, the different parts of the island are not seen all at once and they thus complement one another, making the whole layout all the more pleasant and appear to be even bigger than it is. Its western side, which looks toward Gleresse and Bonneville, consists of a very lofty terrace. This terrace has been planted with trees to form a long alley in the middle of which there is a large hall. At harvest time, the people from the neighboring shores come on Sundays to dance and enjoy themselves. There is only one house on the island, a vast and commodious one in which the tax collector lives and which is situated in a hollow sheltered from the winds.

On the southern side, five or six hundred feet away from the island, there is a smaller island which is uncultivated and deserted and which appears to have been separated from the larger island some time ago by storms. Only willows and willow weed grow among its pebbles, but it does have a raised knoll which is covered with grass and is very pleasant. The lake is almost perfectly oval-shaped. Its shores, not as rich as those of Lake Geneva or Lake Neuchâtel, are nonetheless quite beautiful—especially in the western part, which is very populated and which is bordered by vineyards at the foot of a mountain chain somewhat like Côte-Rôtie.[2] But the wine is not as good. Going from south to north, you find the bailliage of St. Jean, Bonneville, Bienne, and Nidau at the very. end of the lake. All these are interspersed with very pleasant villages.

This was the shelter I had arranged for myself and where I resolved to go set myself up when I left the Val-de-Travers.° This choice fit in so well with my peaceful desire and with my solitary and lazy mood, that I count it among the sweet reveries which I have most thoroughly enjoyed. It seemed to me that on this island I would be more distant from men, more sheltered from their outrages, more forgotten by them, in a word given over more to the sweetness of doing nothing and of the contemplative life: I wanted to be confined to this island in such a way that I would have no more dealings with mortals and I certainly took all the steps imaginable to remove myself from having to keep up any dealings with them.

The big problem was the cost of living. As much because of the lack of foodstuffs as because of the difficulty of bringing them in, the cost of living on this island is high. Besides, you are at the discretion of the tax collector. This difficulty was solved by an agreement Du Peyrou [4] was quite willing to enter into with me; he substituted himself for the company which had undertaken

---

° It is perhaps not useless to mention that I left a special enemy there in the person of M. du Terreaux,[3] mayor of Les Verrières. Although he had a very mediocre reputation in the area, he has a brother, who is said to be a decent man, working in M. de St. Florentin's offices. The mayor had gone to see him a short while before my incident. Small comments like this, which in themselves are nothing, can eventually lead to uncovering a number of underground tunnels.

and then abandoned a general edition of my works. I handed over to him all the material for this edition. I compiled and arranged the material. I added to that my promise to give him the memoirs of my life and I made him the general guardian for all of my papers—with the express condition that he would make no use of them until after my death, for I wanted to end my course peacefully without giving the public any new reason to remember me. In return, the annual pension he committed himself to pay me was enough for my needs. Milord Maréchal [5] had recovered all his property and offered me an annual pension of 1,200 francs, but I accepted it only after reducing it to half that amount. He wanted to send me the capital but I refused it, for I didn't know where to place it. He passed the capital on to Du Peyrou, in whose hands it has remained and who pays me the annual income according to the terms agreed upon with Milord Maréchal. Combining in this way my agreement with Du Peyrou, the pension Milord Maréchal had given me—two-thirds of which was to pass on to Thérèse after my death—and the income of 300 francs which I had from Duchesne,[6] I could count on a decent livelihood for myself and, after my death, for Thérèse, to whom I left 700 francs income from the Rey pension [7] and from that of Milord Maréchal. Thus I no longer had to fear that either she or I would go hungry. But it was decreed that honor would force me to refuse all the resources that good fortune and my work might place within my reach and that I would die as poor as I have lived. It will be seen whether, unless I was an utter scoundrel, I could have kept the agreements they were always so careful to make ignominious for me while carefully taking every other resource away from me so as to force me to consent to my own disgrace. How could they have doubted which course I would take given that alternative? They have always judged my heart by their own.

At ease with respect to the question of livelihood, I was without any other worry. Although I left the field free to my enemies in the outside world, I left behind, in the noble enthusiasm which had dictated my writings and in the constant uniformity of my principles, a testimony about my soul which corresponded to the one my conduct gave of my natural character. I needed no other

defense against my detractors. They could depict another man
and attribute my name to him, but they could deceive only those
who wanted to be deceived. I could let them comment on my life
from beginning to end; I was positive that despite my faults and
weaknesses, despite my inability to endure any yoke, people
would always find a man who was just, good, without rancor,
without hatred, without jealousy, prompt to admit his own
wrongs, even more prompt to forget those of others; a man who
sought his whole felicity in loving and sweet passions and who in
everything pushed sincerity to the point of imprudence, to the
point of the most unbelievable lack of self-interest.

Thus, I sort of took leave of my century and of my contemporaries and I bade farewell to the world by confining myself on this
island for the rest of my days. That was indeed my resolve, and it
was there that I counted on finally carrying out the great project
of this idle life to which until then I had devoted to no avail all
the meager energy Heaven had accorded me. This island was
going to become Papimania for me, that blessed country where
people sleep.

Where they do more, Where they do nothing.[8]

This more was everything for me, for I have always missed
sleep very little. Idleness is enough for me. Provided I do nothing,
I even prefer to dream while awake than while asleep. The age of
fanciful projects having passed and the whiff of vainglory having
made me dizzy rather than having flattered me, the only hope left
for me was that of living without disturbance in eternal leisure.
That is the life of the blessed in the next world, and henceforth I
was going to make it my supreme happiness in this one.

Those who criticize me for so many contradictions will not fail
to criticize me for another one here. I have said that the idleness
of social gatherings made them unbearable for me and here I am
seeking solitude solely to give myself up to idleness. However,
that is the way I am; if there is contradiction in that, it is due to
nature and not to me. But there is so little contradiction in it that

it is precisely by this attitude that I am always myself. The idleness of social gatherings is deadly, because it arises from necessity. The idleness of solitude is charming, because it is free and voluntary. In company, it is hard for me to do nothing, because I am forced to do nothing. I must remain there either nailed to a chair or standing like a picket planted in the ground, moving neither hand nor foot; not daring to run, jump, sing, yell, or gesticulate when I want to; not even daring to dream; suffering at one and the same time from all the boredom of idleness and all the torment of constraint; obliged to be attentive to all the foolish things which are said, to all the compliments which are given, and to work my Minerva constantly so as not to miss throwing in my pun and my lie when my turn comes. And you call that idleness? Why, that's forced labor.

The idleness I like is not that of a do-nothing who stands there arms folded totally inactive and thinks no more than he acts. Mine is both the idleness of a child who is in perpetual movement, but does nothing, and that of a dotard who combs the countryside while his arms are at rest. I love to busy myself with nothings, begin a hundred things and complete none, go and come as the spirit moves me, change projects every moment, follow a fly in all its buzzing around, try to uproot a rock to see what is underneath, undertake a ten-year task with ardor and let it drop ten minutes later without regret, in sum, to muse all day long without order or coherence and follow in everything only the caprice of the moment.

Botany, such as I have always thought of it and such as it began to interest me passionately, was precisely the kind of idle study suitable for filling the whole void of my leisure time without leaving any room for the delirium of imagination or for the boredom of total inaction. To wander at random through the woods and the countryside; to pluck at times a flower, at other times a branch, here and there, mechanically; to graze at whim; to observe the same things thousands and thousands of times and always with the same degree of interest, because I constantly forgot them—all that provided me with enough for eternity without being bored for an instant. However elegant, admirable, or

diverse the structure of plants may be, it does not hold an ignorant eye long enough to interest it. The constant similarity, and
yet prodigious variety, which reigns in their makeup carries away
only those who already have some idea of plants. Others experience only a stupid and monotonous admiration at the sight of all
those treasures of nature. They see nothing in detail, because they
do not even know what they should look at; nor do they see the
whole, because they have no idea of the chain of relationships and
combinations whose marvels overwhelm the mind of the observer.
I was, and my lack of memory was bound to always keep me, at
that happy point of knowing little enough about it that everything was new for me and yet enough that everything was meaningful to me. The diverse soils which divided the island, despite
its smallness, offered me a sufficient variety of plants to study and
to enjoy for my whole life. I didn't want to leave a blade of grass
unanalyzed, and I was already getting set to do a *Flora petrinsularis* with an immense collection of interesting observations.

I had Thérèse come with my books and belongings. We
boarded with the island's tax collector. His wife had sisters in
Nidau who came to see her in turns and who offered Thérèse
some company. I had a sampling there of the sweetness of life in
which I would have liked to spend my own and the desire for it
which I acquired there only served to make me feel more deeply
the bitterness of the one which was to come so quickly afterward.

I have always loved the water passionately, and the sight of it
throws me into a delicious reverie, yet one which often has no
fixed object. When the weather was nice, I never failed to run
onto the terrace as soon as I got up to breathe in the salubrious
and fresh morning air and to let my eyes roam over the horizon of
this beautiful lake whose bordering shores and mountains delighted me. I find no worthier homage to the Divinity than this
silent admiration prompted by the contemplation of His works
and which is in no way expressed by explicit acts. I understand
why city dwellers—who see only walls, streets, and crimes—have
little faith, but I do not understand how rural folk—and especially
solitary individuals—can have none. How could their souls not
soar up with ecstasy hundreds of times a day to the Author of the

marvels which strike them? With me, it is above all when I arise, worn out from my sleeplessness, that I am moved by an old habit to these heartfelt exaltations which require none of the toil of thinking. But for that to happen, the ravishing sight of nature must strike my eyes. In my room, I pray more rarely and more dryly. But at the sight of a beautiful countryside, I feel myself moved without being able to say what it is that moves me. I have read that a wise bishop, when visiting his diocese, came across an old woman who knew how to say only one prayer: "Ohh." He said to her: "Good mother, continue to pray this way forever; your prayer is worth more than all of ours." That worthier prayer is mine as well.

After breakfast, I quickly answered some wretched letters, but did so reluctantly, ardently desiring the moment when I would no longer have to write any at all. For a few moments, I bustled around my books and papers, more to unpack and arrange them than to read them. And this arranging, which became a kind of Penelope's labor for me, gave me the pleasure of musing for a few moments, after which I became bored and left it to spend the three or four remaining hours of the morning studying botany and especially Linnaeus' system, in which I became so passionately interested that even after having become aware of its emptiness I have not been able to drop it. In my opinion, this great observer, along with Ludwig, is the only one to have considered botany as a student of nature and as a philosopher.[9] But he spent far too much time studying it in herbariums and in gardens and not enough in nature itself. Because I considered the whole island as a garden, whenever I needed to make or to verify some observation, I would run into the woods or meadows with my book under my arm and lie down on the ground next to the plant in question to examine it as it was, completely at my ease. This method greatly helped me become acquainted with plants in their natural condition before they had been cultivated and denatured by the hand of man. It is said that Fagon, the first physician of Louis XIV,[10] who could name and recognize all the plants in the royal garden without a mistake, was so ignorant when he was in the countryside that he no longer recognized anything. I am exactly the opposite. I know something about the work of nature, but nothing about the gardener's.

I devoted the time after dinner entirely to my idle and nonchalant mood and to following the impulse of each instant without any order. Often, when the wind was calm, I would immediately upon leaving the table go throw myself alone into a little boat the tax collector had taught me to row with a single oar. I would go out into the middle of the lake. The moment I left the shore, I felt a joy that almost made me tremble and whose cause I can neither name nor quite understand, unless it was perhaps a secret happiness at thus being safe from the attacks of the wicked. I would then row around the lake alone, sometimes coming in close to the shore, but never touching it. Often, letting my boat drift with the wind and the water, I would give myself up to pointless reveries which were no less sweet for being stupid. Sometimes I would cry out with tender emotion: "Oh nature, Oh mother, here I am under your sole keeping; there is no crafty and deceptive man here to come between you and me." I would go as far as half a league away from the shore in this way; I would have liked the lake to be the ocean. However, to please my poor dog, who did not like such long jaunts on the water as much as I did, I would ordinarily set out with a walk in mind; this consisted in landing on the small island, walking around for an hour or two or stretching myself out on the grass on the summit of the knoll in order to gorge myself on the pleasure of admiring this lake and the surrounding countryside, to examine and dissect all the plants which were within my reach, and—like another Robinson Crusoe—to build myself an imaginary dwelling on this little island. I became very attached to that hill. When I was able to take Thérèse, along with the tax collector's wife and her sisters, to walk there, how proud I was to be their pilot and guide! We ceremoniously brought rabbits there to populate it. Another celebration for Jean-Jacques.[11] This act of populating the little island made it even more interesting to me. Afterward, I went there more often and with more pleasure in order to see the signs of progress of the new inhabitants.

To these pastimes I joined another which reminded me of the delightful life at Les Charmettes, one to which the season especially called me. It pertained to the rustic tasks associated with the vegetable and fruit harvest which Thérèse and I were pleased to engage in along with the tax collector and his family. I remember that a man from Bern named M. Kirkebergher,[12] having come to see me, found me perched in a big tree with a sack around my waist so full of apples that I could no longer move. I was not disturbed by this encounter or other similar ones. I hoped that the people of Bern, witnessing the way I used my leisure time, would no longer think of troubling its serenity and would leave me alone in my solitude. I would have far more preferred being confined there by their will than by my own: I would have been more assured that my restfulness would not be troubled.

Here is another one of those confessions which I can be sure ahead of time my readers will not believe, so set are they upon judging me according to themselves even though they have been compelled to see in the whole course of my life a thousand internal affections which in no way resemble theirs. What is stranger is that in denying that I have any of the good or indifferent feelings which they do not have, they are always ready to impute to me those which are so bad that they could not even enter a man's heart. They find it quite easy, then, to make me contradict nature and to make me a kind of monster such as could not even exist. Nothing absurd seems unbelievable to them as soon as it tends to sully my character; nothing extraordinary seems possible to them as soon as it tends to honor me.

But whatever they might believe or say, I will not continue any the less to expose faithfully what Jean-Jacques Rousseau was, did, and thought, without explaining or justifying the uniqueness of his sentiments and ideas, nor looking to see whether others have thought as he. I liked St. Peter's Island so much and staying there was so suitable to me, that by dint of centering all of my desires on this island I began to desire not to leave it at all. The visits I had to make in the neighboring area; the errands I would have to do in Neuchâtel, Bienne, Yverdon, Nidau, already began to strain my imagination. A day spent off the island struck me as a day of happiness lost, and to leave the enclosure of this lake was the same for me as to leave my element. Besides, past experience had made me fearful. All I needed was to have something good delight my heart for me to expect to lose it, and my ardent desire to end my days on this island was inseparable from my fear of being forced to leave it. I had formed the habit of going to sit on the beach in the evenings, especially when the lake was stirred up. I experienced an uncommon pleasure in seeing the waves break at my feet. I used it to make for myself an image of the tumult of the world and the peace of my habitat, and sometimes I would be so moved by this idea as to feel tears fall from my eyes. This restfulness, which I passionately enjoyed, was troubled only by my worry that I might lose it, but my worry went so far as to alter its sweetness. I felt my situation to be so precarious that I dared not count on it. "Ah," I would say to myself, "how willingly would I surrender the freedom to leave here—something I in no way care about—for the assurance of being able to stay here forever. Instead of being accorded the favor of staying here, why am I not detained here forcefully? Those who only allow me to stay here can chase me away at any moment and can I hope that my persecutors, seeing me happy here, will leave me here to continue to be happy? Ah, it's a slight thing that they let me live here; I would like them to condemn me to live here and I would like to be compelled to stay here so as not to be compelled to leave." I cast an envious eye on the fortunate Micheli du Crêt who, serene in the Château of Aarberg,[13] had only to want to be happy in order to be happy. In sum, by dint of giving myself up to these reflections and to the troublesome premonitions of the new storms ever ready to burst upon me, I came to the point of desiring with an unbelievable ardor that instead of only tolerating my living on this island they would make it a perpetual prison for me. And I can swear that had it only been up to me to condemn myself to it, I would have done so with the greatest joy; for I preferred a thousandfold the necessity of spending the rest of my life there to the danger of being expelled from it.

This fear did not remain unfounded for long. At the moment I least expected it, I received a letter from the bailiff of Nidau in whose jurisdiction St. Peter's Island fell. By this letter he informed me of the order of Their Excellencies [14] that I leave the island and their territory.

NOTES

1. Or about three and three-quarters miles; see Second Walk, n. 10.

2. This is the name of a vineyard located on the right bank of the Rhône River in the commune of Ampuis, about twenty-two miles south of Lyon.

3. Charles-Auguste du Terreau had a large house in Môtiers just across the road from Rousseau's.

4. See Seventh Walk, n. 19.

5. George Lord Keith (1686-1778), tenth earl Marischall of Scotland, was governor of the principality of Neuchâtel from 1754 to 1768 and granted Rousseau permission to live in Môtiers. They became very close friends. See *Confessions*, Book XII, *OC* 1, pp. 596-601; and Fifth Walk, n. 2.

6. Nicolas-Bonaventure Duchesne (1712-65) published the *Émile* for Rousseau using a printer in Holland named Neaulme; see *Confessions*, Book XI, *OC* 1, pp. 562-73. See also *OC* 4, pp. 1856-1862. In 1765, Duchesne established an annual pension of 300 francs for Rousseau in return for the manuscript of the *Dictionary of Music*; see *OC* 1, p. 1601.

7. Marc-Michel Rey (1720-80) published most of Rousseau's works: the *Second Discourse, Letter to M. D'Alembert, Nouvelle Héloïse, Social Contract,* and *Letters Written from the Mountain.* In the *Confessions,* Rousseau admitted that he had often made unreasonable demands of Rey and praised him for his honesty. He was especially moved by Rey's generous gesture of establishing an annual pension for Thérèse. See *Confessions*, Book XI, *OC* 1, p. 561; see also First Walk, n. 11.

8. See Interpretative Essay, n. 83.

9. See Seventh Walk, p. 93. Christian-Gottlieb Ludwig (1709-73) was a physician and a botanist. In botany, he is especially known for having devised a system of classifying plants according to the type and number of their petals.

10. Guy-Crescent Fagon (1638-1718) was a professor of botany at the Jardin des Plantes and then its director, as well as personal physician to Louis XIV. In 1665, he and Antoine Vallot (1594-1671) published the *Hortus regius,* a huge volume describing about 4,000 plants.

11. The text has J.J.

12. Nicolas-Antoine de Kirchberger (1739-1807), baron de Libiestorf, was a member of the Sovereign Council of Bern and very interested in

philosophy. He had visited Rousseau in Môtiers as early as 1762, and he eventually accompanied Rousseau to Bienne when he was forced to leave St. Peter's Island. See *Confessions,* Book XII, *OC* 1, pp. 652-54.

13. Jacques-Barthélémy Micheli du Crest (1690-1766) first distinguished himself as a Swiss military officer in the service of France. When he returned to Geneva, he became involved in a hotly contested question concerning the city's fortifications and published a tract in Strasbourg to set forth his nonmajority opinions. Censored for this act and compelled to admit his errors, he chose exile in Paris instead and was condemned to death in his absence. Eventually the sentence was commuted to imprisonment in the fortress of Aarberg, where he spent seventeen years. The fortress is located on the river Aare about five miles east of St. Peter's Island.

14. That is, the senators of Bern. See Fifth Walk, n. 4.

INDEX

This index refers to authors, works, and persons cited, as well as to groups and institutions mentioned in the preceding work. The entries cover Rousseau's text of the *Reveries* and the excerpt from the *Confessions,* as well as the translator's Preface, Interpretative Essay, Appendices, and annotations. For those instances in which Rousseau used a variant spelling of a name in the text, the person has been correctly identified in the index and Rousseau's variant placed in square brackets immediately afterwards. Parentheses have been used to provide additional information about an entry, as when Molière is identified by his full given name, or to distinguish one entry from another with the same name, as with Antoine Fazy and his son.